STAGING A SPANISH CLASSIC:
THE HOUSE OF FOOLS

By

HUGH A. HARTER and JOHN D. MITCHELL

A Spanish-English Edition with Stage Directions of

José de Valdivielso's

EL HOSPITAL DE LOS LOCOS

Cover Illustration by Caissa Douwes, based on *THE HOUSE OF FOOLS* production by Miguel Narros and featured in the film *EL GRECO*, an MGM pictures release.

Costume Drawings by Andrea D'Ororico

STAGING A SPANISH CLASSIC:
THE HOUSE OF FOOLS

Program Note From An Earlier Staging Of A Spanish Classic:

We should be more cognizant and appreciative of our Spanish past. It constitutes a significant part of our American heritage.

—JOHN DAVIS LODGE*
March 6, 1965

*Former American Ambassador to Spain

STAGING A SPANISH CLASSIC:
THE HOUSE OF FOOLS

(EL HOSPITAL DE LOS LOCOS)

A Spanish Sacramental Drama

by

Master José de Valdivielso

A Bilingual Edition with Introduction,
Stage Directions, and a New Verse Translation

by

Hugh A. Harter, B.A.; M.A.; PhD.

President

Horizons for Learning, Inc.
&
Cursos Americanos e Internacionales, S.L.

and

John D. Mitchell, Ed.D; H.H.D. (H.C.)

President

Institute for Advanced Studies
in the Theatre Arts

NORTHWOOD INSTITUTE PRESS
Midland, Michigan 48640

DEDICATION

For Mimi and for Fran, wonderful wives whose intelligence and encouragement are a challenge to continuing creativity.

TABLE OF CONTENTS

ACKNOWLEDGMENTS

As Ambassador John Davis Lodge points out, the classics of Spain are part of our heritage. I have been greatly puzzled that American urban, regional, and university theatres' repertories, year after year, have made the great comedies and dramas of both Calderón de la Barca and Lope de Vega conspicuous by their absence.

Is not the western world of theatre and music indebted to the theatre of the Golden Age of Spain for the character of Don Juan alone? Did not Molière, Shaw, and Mozart find in that character created by a Spanish writer provocative stimulation?

It has been the National Theatre of London, England, as well as the Institute for Advanced Studies in the Theatre Arts (IASTA), which have brought to the stage Spanish masterpieces; the National Theatre produced Calderón's *THE MAYOR OF ZALAMEA* (as did the Theatre National Populaire under Jean Vidal in the 1960's), recently Calderón's *SCHISM IN ENGLAND*, and Lope de Vega's *FUENTE OVEJUNA*. IASTA produced Calderón's *THE PHANTOM LADY* and Lope de Vega's *THE KNIGHT FROM OLMEDO*.

Roger Lobb, of the National Theatre of London, over the years has been most helpful in making these sterling stagings of Spanish classic masterpieces accessible to me. Heartfelt thanks are due him and his staff.

Miguel Narros, director of the auspicious Teatro Español of Madrid, Spain, sparked the idea of IASTA's producing an *auto sacramental*, and gave to the Institute for its Library a collection of *autos* compiled by the Real Academia Española. He urged for consideration Master Joseph de Valdivielso's *EL HOSPITAL DE LOS LOCOS*, with which he was well acquainted since he had directed a production in Toledo in front of the cathedral for the American film *EL GRECO*.

Time passed, for Narros' commitments to his duties as artistic director for his theatre in Madrid left very little time for an extended stay in the United States staging a Spanish classic.

Acknowledgment and much thanks are due to C. George Willard who, as Business Manager of the Institute, proposed and then negotiated a producing association with the Greenwich Mews Spanish Theatre (G.M.S.T.). Thanks are due to Gilberto Zaldivar of that theatre for his enthusiasm for a collaboration with IASTA.

Both Jose Luis Alonso and Jose Tamayo, directors of Madrid who had earlier directed for the Institute, encouraged Miguel Narros to accept the invitation to direct in New York. Andrea D'Odorico, designer, accompanied Narros, bringing with him costume designs he had created for the New York production; he supervised the cutting, draping and fitting of the challenging costumes. We wish to express appreciation for the inclusion of plates of his costume designs in this book.

Time had passed since the last performance of *THE HOUSE OF FOOLS* and, as is wont, the professional actors had dispersed for other engagements.

The Greenwich Theatre had ceased to exist as an off-Broadway theatre.

An awareness that this had been the first staging of *THE HOUSE OF FOOLS/EL HOSPITAL DE LOS LOCOS* in America, that this was at long last a translation in English, a viable acting version thanks to the actors refining of it in the crucible of rehearsal, prompted us to embark upon "Staging a Spanish Classic."

Recovering what had passed between director and actors did have, we found, the excitement and frustrations of an archeological dig, requiring on both our parts expertise in the disciplines of theatre and Romance languages and a great deal of imagination. How had their early 17th century text (which may have seemed at first old and dusty as it lay on a stage manager's table) been brought to life in performance by actors? The magnanimous cooperation of the actors interviewed

provided the 'picks and shovels,' as it were. Conversations with the bilingual actress Elise de la Roche were invaluable, for she had performed in each of the two casts and had remarkable recall.

Fulsome praise and thanks are due to Robert Main, now of Doubleday's Fireside Theatre, and to Tamara Daniel who prompted Robert Main to send me his prompt script. Robert's having preserved his stage manager's prompt script proved essential. His sharing it enabled us to proceed, and it became the rock on which this work rests. Taped interviews with Miguel Narros, the actor's script with their notes hastily jotted down during rehearsals, conversations with Miguel Narros at rehearsals and in Madrid, all added to the re-capitulation of the *mise-en-scène*. Further research and imaginative recall and my own skills and years of experience as a stage director filled in where chinks remained.

To the actors of the two casts who made each of the productions memorable, we bestow accolades and thanks: Richard Abel; Sadel Alamo; Roberto Antonio; Reinaldo Arana; Peter Blaxill; Jean Cacheral; Estaban Chalbaud; Tyrus Cheney; Harold Cherry; Tamara Daniel; Irene Di Bari; Shelly Desai; Maria Dolores; Elisavietta [Elise de la Roche]; Antonio Flores; Judy Greenway; Connie Keyse; Charles Lara; Elektrah Lobel; Anthony Madigan; Davida Manning; Ketti Melonas; Danny Metelitz; Miriam Mitchell; Con Roche; Jose Rodriguez; Marco Santiago; Isabel Segovia; Irma Soledad; Jean Sullivan; Conchita Vargas, and Julio Weber. Passionately, the actors entered into valuable and harmonious collaboration with Aida Alvarez and myself as translators. Hugh Harter, coauthor and an authority for Spanish language and theatre, added his inestimable polish to the English version. Aida functioned as Production Supervisor in both languages as well.

We wish to acknowledge certain friends and colleagues who have contributed generously of their insights. Among them are Robert Epstein, Tony DiBenedetto, George Drew, Professor Benito Ortolani, Mary W. John, and Caissa Douwes. The Mitchell children and their spouses proved especially understanding of time taken away from them while working on the book in Maine.

Friends in Spain had prompted correspondence with Professor Bruce W. Wardropper, a friend of Miguel Narros (they said) and a scholarly admirer of Narros and *EL HOSPITAL DE LOS LOCOS*. Letters sent to him went unanswered.

Since plans for *THE HOUSE OF FOOLS* began, Gilbert Forman, my personal assistant and IASTA staff member, has been central to the evolution of the book. His enthusiasm and computer skills have made my life easier and have added greatly to this endeavor.

Thanks and acknowledgment, as well, to those who have seen the book through to publication; Francine Douwes, Virginia Morrison, Melodie Greer, Michael Guerette, Thomas Orr and Irene Shawtell. Deep appreciation is extended to David E. Fry, Arthur E. Turner, and R. Gary Stauffer for their support and encouragement.

Last but not least, thanks are to be expressed to the theatre professionals who worked hard and long making the production a reality; as well as the Trustees and the Advisory Council of IASTA and G.M.S.T. We add an expression of gratitude for the cooperation of the Spanish Consulate General in New York, The Spanish Institute, and both the Village Presbyterian Church and the Brotherhood Synagogue where the Greenwich Theatre once was located.

FOREWORD

by

Mrinalini Sarabhai [1]

The Institute for Advanced Studies in the Theatre Arts is an organization committed to international theatre understanding. Each production has often focused on an ancient form, bringing a new knowledge of Eastern and Western techniques to actors who need to expand their perspectives of interpretation with creative methodology. From all over the world, outstanding directors have been invited for workshops, culminating in productions that specialize in the techniques of their particular disciplines as varied as the Japanese Noh, the Indian Nataka, and the Greek Theatre.

This interdisciplinary international dialogue realizes and releases a limitless horizon of new ideas, drawn from the depths of older and ancient cultures.

Interaction between the director and the actors is a process that both identifies the differences of cultural norms and simultaneously recognizes the familiarity of similar processes of theatrical art.

This search for style - an almost anthropological, yet practical research, is the Institute for Advanced Studies in the Theatre Arts' great contribution to modern American theatre.

My own experience in directing a Sanskrit play, THE VISION OF VASAVADATTA, in the ancient Natya Shastra technique, was a wonderful journey of discovery into a basic cultural identity that all of us share in the vast world of theatre.

Imagine the actors of Broadway, moving each separate finger, learning to use their eyes as distinct from expression, to bend their bodies in unfamiliar attitudes and to evoke mantric dialogue to the sound of the music of India. Yet they did and it became a part of their 'being' and the space between their background and mine disappeared. The final performances generated the quality of a culture thousands of years old.

Particularly interesting was the revitalization of these techniques in later popular productions. Not a revalidation but a rethinking of values. There was no longer any isolation of theatrical norms of Western usage from the Eastern universality of presentation where dance, drama and speech belong together.

The training in my own workshop at the Institute for Advanced Studies in the Theatre Arts that lasted nine weeks released emotions of a basic togetherness in the exploration of theatrical truths that were shared by all of us. It was an intense relationship that, while trying to comprehend a strange form, also penetrated deep into the psyche of each actor.

The technique of Indian drama is a spiritual strengthening of the individual. It is learning to participate and yet be an onlooker in the landscape

---

1 *In the world of dance-drama, Mrinalini Sarabhai holds a universally recognized position today. She founded Darpana, an academy of dance, drama, and music in Ahmedabad, India. Her troupe has toured world-wide.*

of life, a totality of vision which is aware of the body and the soul. As Rabindranath Tagore wrote 'I am the sky and I am the nest as well. For as on the stage we play a role for a few hours, totally involved, yet with the knowledge that it is only for a while, so, too, does philosophy teach us that we are but sojourners in this vast universe. That is drama.'

THE HISTORICAL BACKDROP

by

Hugh A. Harter

The year 1492 was a landmark year for Spain, less for the discovery of the New World by Christopher Columbus, the importance of which was not recognized until much later, than for the impressive accomplishments of Isabella and Ferdinand, the Catholic Monarchs of, respectively, two separate kingdoms, Castille-Leon and Aragon. The last Moorish stronghold on Spanish soil, the Kingdom of Granada, finally fell to the Christian forces. After almost 800 years, the centuries-old struggle of reconquest was over. The Muslims had ruled all or some of Spain since the invasions from Morocco in 711. Those centuries during which Muslims, Jews, and Christians lived side by side were to leave an indelible stamp on Spanish life and Spanish culture down to our times, but with the end of any formal rule by "alien forces" on what we now see as Spanish territory, the geographical unity of what is present-day Spain was a reality. Spain became **geographically** the first European nation in the modern sense, but that, as both Ferdinand and Isabella astutely saw, was only the first step towards a veritable unification which they vigorously sought to attain in the areas of language, culture, and, above all, religion.

Once Isabella was firmly on the throne and her hegemony established, it was clear that the heir, or heiress, to the thrones of the kingdoms of Ferdinand and Isabella would reign over a landmass stretching from the Pyrenees to the Mediterranean. It was their grandson, the child of their daughter Juana, known as Joan the Mad, and of the Hapsburg, Philip the Fair, Spain's Charles the First. He was better known to history as the Emperor Charles the Fifth, who was to be the monarch of two kingdoms, but one country. His reign, or at least part of it, was marked by the spirit of the Renaissance. His open-mindedness to new ideas and new concepts, his exuberant creativity and intrepidity, and his strength blended with sensitivity was epitomized in the courtier-warrior-lover-poet Garcilaso de la Vega who came to be known as the conqueror of Mexico, Hernan Cortez.

The task of unification had only begun, however. The deep medieval divisions of Spain continued (and continue) to exist. Different regions spoke different languages: Basque, Galician, Catalan, and Castilian, and a number of sub-languages and local dialects incomprehensible to the outsider. Language was divisive. Ethnic and religious groups were divisive. Under the Muslims, Spain had been essentially tri-religious. The Arabic regimes were tolerant, for the most part. As the dominant political group, the Muslims imposed rule, laws, and taxes, but with the exception of certain periods, Christians, Jews, and Mohammedans worshipped in peace and lived and worked side by side and even inter-married. Many families of the nobility, including that of Ferdinand of Aragon, had Jewish blood in their veins. Jews or *conversos* (converts to Roman Catholicism either voluntarily or through force) held high positions of great responsibility and trust, and some major figures in the Church, in the government, and in the arts and literature were partially or fully of Jewish blood. The multicultural life of the Middle Ages was at a close, but its enrichment of Spanish life made the Golden Age of the sixteenth and seventeenth centuries, with its great flowering of the theatre possible. Paradoxically, the Middle Ages in a cultural and theological sense was to persist in Spain, a fact important to the understanding of the unique phenomenon of the creation and continued popularity of the *auto sacramental* in Spain well into the Age of the Enlightenment in the eighteenth century.

Medieval Spain was polylingual. The language which we now call Spanish, the basic idiom spoken throughout the so-called Hispanic world, came from the heartland of the vast plateau that forms the core of modern Spain, the kingdom of Castille. That language was a relative late-comer. The language of Galicia in the north-western corner, had been the initiator of lyrical verse; Catalan, the language now militantly strong in Catalonia, whose capital is Barcelona, was well developed and established long before Castilian Spanish's prominence; the Basque language goes back into the mists of time so far that scholars have been unable to identify its origins to this very day. Language was, therefore, and continues to be, a serious political problem for Spain where linguistic identity of ethnic groups can arouse intense passions and conflicts.

Queen Isabella saw, however, that language could also be a singularly important medium **for** unification: a national language and a national culture were needed to establish a sense of nationhood. Linguistic unity was essential for communications, but it was also important for the development of a national culture, and a national identity.

Even more dear to the Queen's heart, however, was the question of religion. In an age when religious belief and practice permeated every phase of life and thought, either directly or indirectly, this constituted a major problem. In the face of the vigorous efforts to dissuade her by prominent Jewish advisers Abraham Senior and Isaac Abrabanel, she decided on the expulsion of all Jews and Muslims that did not convert to Roman Catholicism. The decision was to have a marked and continuous impact on Spanish society, at home and abroad. The New World was subjugated in the name of the monarchs of Spain and of the Roman Catholic religion. The Spaniard armed with sword and cross, of the same shape as subsequent historians have pointed out, brought the countless populations of the great pre-Columbian empires to heel and to baptism. Rapaciousness and fanaticism were to become associated with the conquistadors abroad and the Inquisitors inside Spain. By coercion or by fervor, all subjects of the Crown were to be conformists in all matters religious and social. Any appearance of relapse into Judaic ways carried with it the threat of death and total destruction for one's self and one's family. The impact of this on Spanish society and particularly on the development of Spanish culture in the sixteenth and even seventeenth century was still to be carefully studied and will surely change our perceptions of many areas of Spanish life, not least of them the theatre's development. Two major figures of the early development of drama, Fernando de Rojas, the author of the *Celestina*, and Juan del Encina, called the "father of Spanish theatre," were of *converso* families.

The instabilities of medieval language had to be diminished. A *converso* of Isabella's court, Antonio de Nebrija, wrote a grammar of Castilian, the first such codification of a Romance tongue in Europe. Language, of course, is fundamental to theatre, as language is fundamental to human life, and by the sixteenth century, Castilian Spanish had developed into a highly flexible and substantial idiom, capable of great subtlety and the exuberant genius of writers like Lope de Vega, Calderón, Gongora, Quevedo or Cervantes. Spaniards of all social and economic levels became passionate theatre-goers, those who could not read as well as the relatively few who could; they formed a cruelly exacting and demanding audience insistent on action and movement, spectacle and entertainment.

The visual arts were also highly communicative and developed by painters of genius such as El Greco, Velazquez, Murillo, and Zurbaran. And there was extraordinary creativity in the areas of religious art, the prodigiously sensitive carvings of polychromatic saint's statues, the intricate altars, and the like, which have been unjustly neglected by non-Hispanic art lovers and critics.

Religion as unifying agent, we must insist, became all- pervasive. The portion of the population that did not live in constant fear of being denounced to the Inquisition was just as imbued with Catholicism. The streets, the squares, the parishes and neighborhoods all had, as they still do for the most part, names of saints or religious figures. Social life revolved around baptisms, weddings and funerals, all in the hands of the Church. Saint's days were celebrated and every town and village had its special fiesta, usually with elaborate processions involving costumes, symbolic figures, what we would call floats, singing, instrumental accompaniment, dancing, and the like. Activities sometimes began in the church and then proceeded to the street, or on other occasions, began in the street and ended up in the church. The Church, directly or indirectly was a part of the fabric and activities of every day of Spaniard's life.

Many a writer and scholar has attested the fact that the Spanish people, the ordinary people of Spain, were fervent believers and deeply and often fanatically devout. In the first half of the sixteenth century under the reign of Charles IV, there was a relative openness to foreign ideas and cultures, to the beginnings of scientific and objective reasoning, and to a new wakening to the world of man's surroundings. The reign of Philip II, changed things drastically. Spain turned in on itself; students were forbidden to study abroad; the control of thought and deed became more stringent. It is the period of the great religious figures, the mystics Saint Teresa of Avila, Fray Luis de Leon (both of Jewish blood), Saint John of the Cross, and the predominantly religious painter El Greco. The *auto-da-fe* (in Spanish an *auto de fe*, literally an "act of faith," and actually a public confession of faith) became massive rallies for the faithful, and/or those forced to attend, with intricate preparations and stagings that became increasingly elaborate and costly. And they were fairly frequent. They were, in essence, the enactment of a religious **drama**, a **dramatic** reality for the spectators **and** the participants, each with his or her carefully defined role that had to be coordinated and planned, sometimes by the very playwright-producers of the *corral* of regular theatre.

Spain's defenders assert that the *autos da fe* were unjustly utilized by Spain's enemies to propagate the Black Legend of Spanish cruelty and fanaticism, but whatever the truth of the matter, they have come to epitomize an aspect of Spain's past that extended, astonishingly enough, into the nineteenth century. The other *autos*, those with which our study is dealing, the *auto sacramental* or "sacramental play" as the translation inadequately calls them, might be considered the **positive** form of the *auto*, but one no less related to the religious outlook and the religious atmosphere of the periods of their subsistence. Both spectacles were attended by everyone from the monarchs and highest prelates on down to the simplest worker. No theatre audience today would match the Spanish one of the period in mass fervor and zealotry.

WHAT IS AN *AUTO SACRAMENTAL?*

by

Hugh A. Harter

The Spanish, and Portuguese, word *auto* comes from the Latin *acto*, from which our word *act* is derived. It is also found spelled *aucto* in the titles of early sixteenth century plays. Its sense is clear in the expression *auto da fe* or *auto de fe*, a public *act* of expression *of faith*, as we have pointed out earlier. In fact, the earliest Spanish theatrical work extant is a fragment of a Nativity play entitled *El auto de los Reyes Magos*, (*The Play of the Magi*), which dates from the middle of the twelfth century. For our purposes, however, the word *auto* is the equivalent of a short or one-act play on Biblical themes, and in the *auto sacramental, sacramental one-act play*, the word *sacramental* itself gives us a key to the fundamental orientation of the genre, that of the seven sacraments of Baptism, Confirmation, the Eucharist, Extreme Unction, Matrimony, Orders, and Penance. This is the genre to which *El Hospital de los Locos* belongs, a short drama related to the Eucharist, i.e. the taking of Holy Communion as the sacrament of the Last Supper. The work was to be performed in conjunction with the celebration of Corpus Christi on the Thursday after Trinity Sunday, in commemoration of the institution of the Eucharist.

Although the *auto sacramental* is uniquely Spanish, it forms part of the liturgical drama and "pageants" that were performed in western Europe, such as the Wakefield "Townley" plays of Corpus Christi processions in England, and related to mystery and miracle plays, but the Spanish "version" has singular differences, most notably the emphasis and reliance on allegorical figures rather than "historical" Biblical figures as fundamental in the casting of the dramas.

The establishment of this particular observation, Corpus Christi, came about relatively late in the history of the Catholic Church. A nun belonging to the Cistercian monastery of Mont-Cornillon in Liege, Belgium, one Sister Juliana or Julienne, acted as a spokesman for a group of co-religionists who petitioned the bishop to initiate the feast of the Eucharist, and this was duly ordered and locally observed in the year 1246. In 1264, Pope Urban IV extended the celebration to the entire Church, but the result was of limited success. Half a century later, however, the Council of Vienna of 1311-1312 made the feast obligatory, and in 1317, Pope John XXII added a proviso that the Blessed Sacrament was to be carried in solemn procession through the streets to be worshipped by the populace, an addition which was to be of significance in the development of the overall presentation of the sacramental play itself.

By the time of the Council of Trent in the mid-sixteenth century, with the Protestant Reformation under way, the earlier Papal decrees were reconfirmed, and the Corpus Christi celebration took on new importance as an instrument for countering the spread of heretical ideas and the propagation of the Verities of Catholic Christianity. As a part of the great upsurge of religious devotion, and the emphasis on piety and orthodoxy, liturgical drama, and the *auto sacramental* in particular, was given significant impetus. Major playwrights, including Lope de Vega and Calderón de la Barca, cultivated the genre, and it is generally conceded that, while Calderón brought the form to its ultimate elaboration, Valdivielso is the other master of the *auto sacramental*.

Lope de Vega himself gave us a kind of definition of the *auto*, calling it a *comedia a honor y gloria del pan*, i.e. a play to the honor and glory of the Communion bread that would counter heresy and glorify *our* faith through stories of divine thematic material. Calderón also wrote of the *auto*, calling them *sermons put into verse* that represent questions of Sacred Theology. The definition is particularly incisive in pointing out that the dramatization made possible the communication of abstract concepts of considerable complexity to a public, with the possible exception of nobility and clergy, that had little formal education, and certainly very little in literature and theology. In the space of a single act, the *auto* was to express the significance of man's past, present, and future, from the Fall in the Garden of Eden to Christ's Redemption as embodied in the act of taking communion, the mystery of the miracle of transubstantiation. In addition to this, we must remember that these performances were considered a part of the liturgy itself and constituted a sermon with a moral lesson.

The plays were not only performed on the day of Corpus Christi itself, but also for several days before and after the celebration, and for different audiences. We know that the Corpus Christi spectacle was created first and foremost for the common people whose very credulity, when coupled with the skills of the actors and the elaborate stagings, resulted in a singular impact on the audience. The performances were not exclusively for the common folk, however, as the king, all of the court, including high officials both lay and ecclesiastical, would participate in the main procession and were a part of the audience; lesser officials participated on other days.

The use of allegorical figures as the cast of characters of the *auto* was, as we have pointed out, fundamental to its form and conception. Allegory offered certain singular advantages for communicating with an audience of wide range in tastes, education, and background. The use of poetry provided the playwright with various possibilities for erudite and intellectually appealing expression and which, like allegory, offered the writer a highly malleable form capable of subtlety of expression that was also eminently comprehensible for even the least erudite of those present at the performance. Interpretation was and is, in the case of this form of drama, proportionate to the capacity for comprehension of the observer.

Chandler Post in his study of medieval allegory defined the *auto sacramental* as a type of literature which could crystallize an abstract idea by presenting it in the concrete from of a personage or of an object or a fictional happening. Consequently, allegory makes use of a system of parallels or equivalents similar to symbol and metaphor; allegory presents abstraction as something concrete and identifiable: Faith, Reason, Fortune, Ambition, Greed, Gluttony, Lust, Youth, Age, Illusion, Disillusion, Pleasure, Wealth, Truth, Falsehood, Man, World, Death, Soul, to name some of the most frequently utilized. Valdivielso also includes such figures from the Old Testament as the Prodigal Son, the Traveler of the parable of the Good Samaritan, or from the New Testament, John the Baptist and even Christ himself who appears in such clearly identifiable guises as the Pastor, the Good Shepherd, and the Spouse. Obviously Evil also must be portrayed and consequently the Devil plays an important role in these dramatic struggles for the soul. He sometimes appears as himself, but more often in various guises and disguises with the purpose of confusing and confounding the other characters in his struggle to possess them for his nefarious ends. He also has numerous henchmen who try to lure the virtuous and unsuspecting into the realms of the Prince of Darkness, of heresy within and without Spain's borders, and error that can lead to perdition.

A happy ending is essential. Faith must, and does, win out. The Church and virtue triumph through Christ whose second coming may be represented in the *auto*, just as the Eucharist is the prophetic sign of that coming and of its ultimate fulfillment.

THE STAGING OF THE *AUTO*

by

Hugh A. Harter

The staging of an *auto sacramental* is of particular interest in the light of what it shows of the Spanish society of the sixteenth to the mid-eighteenth centuries and its affinities with secular Spanish drama, the *comedia*, with which, not unimportant, the form has significant parallels in plot and situation development, and in overall production. We must also keep in mind that the Spanish *comedia* - the word means simply play, and not comedy in the contemporary sense, i.e. a drama that could include both comic and tragic elements - was a much later development than liturgical and religious theatre, religion and drama being, as we know, closely related since very ancient times. The fact that the *autos* were considered an extension of the liturgy intensified rather than diminished the desire for luxurious productions. Various documents concerning costs for materials, costuming, scenery, painting of the carts and backdrops, plus designs for them, have come down to us. The Spaniard of the Golden Age's taste for opulent dress and finery which reached such extremes that special laws were passed - unavailingly - to curb the expenditures, finds its counterpart in the *auto*'s staging.

The procession that by Papal decree was made a part of the celebration, as mentioned earlier, was an integral component of the spectacle whose culmination was the *auto* itself. These processions were of great pomp and ceremony as the highest national and/or local figures of Church and State, accompanied by various members of the religious orders, civic groups and guilds, walked behind the Host as it was carried through the streets. Each parish was to have its own procession for the adoration and contemplation of the Host, usually accompanied by music and dance, as the Corpus Christi feast was one of rejoicing and thanksgiving for the blessings the Sacrament accorded to the faithful. This sort of carnival spirit with its melding of solemnity, song, dance, and music, still typical in processions in Spain today, is something which has caused consternation and surprise in foreign visitors over the centuries.

An example of this juxtaposition of opposites can be noted in the figure of the *Tarrasca*, a kind of gigantic dragon, half serpent and half woman, drawings of which have survived. Various authors of the period have left descriptions of the figure and of the special interest which it held for the public. Other giant figures, of a kind still to be seen on religious holidays in provincial cities and towns, were a part of the procession, as were also acrobats, dancers, musicians, and singers.

The streets were specially prepared for the passage of the procession. Bright banners emblazoned with coats of arms were hung in front of the mansions of the nobility, richly designed rugs and tapestries were spread over the balconies along the route, and canvas awnings, kept cool by sprinklings with water, protected the passersby from the sun. The streets themselves were covered with sand over which was strewn a veritable carpet of fresh flowers.

The Renaissance had seen the development of elaborate triumphal carts or wagons usually bearing an allegorical scene or tableau, not unlike the floats utilized in parades today, with their varying structures, their costumed participants from fantasy and fable, preceded by marching bands and majorettes. Some of these same carts may have doubled for the *auto sacramental* productions, but two of them were always used, called *medio carros*, half-carts, for moving the scenery, in addition to a third wagon which served as a platform stage. The carts usually were drawn through the streets by teams of bullocks whose horns had been gilded. The outside of the carts were painted with scenes suggestive of the *auto* to be performed, the superstructures being made of wood over which canvas was stretched. Bright colors were used both to attract attention and to reinforce the joyousness of the celebration. These carts were two-storied, and action took place on both levels of them as well as on the platform stage. Instances of the use of the two carts for contrasting scenes, suggestive or symbolic of good and evil, a garden of Eden or a mouth of Hell, in the stagings of Valdivielso's works, for example, have come down to us in detail, as have documents and billings discussing costs, often excessive, for the various materials required for a presentation, and the protestations of the guild or municipal officials making the objections.

Costumes, as we have mentioned, were elaborate and costly. In two productions of 1592, God the Father wore a tunic of satin or taffeta decorated with purple and gold, with a white taffeta cloak, angels had their "usual" costumes, devils wore black outfits embroidered with red hell-mouths, and the figure of Christ appeared with a costume whose symbolic embroidery identified him for the spectators.

Costly and elaborate stage machinery was also a necessity. Angels swept down onto the stage, the innocent were swooped up off the stage to safety from heresy and sin below, trap doors opened and closed, dragons with seven heads belched fire and smoke, clouds floated by, and even the pillars of fire and the opening of the Red Sea were staged. There were working fountains in garden scenes, hills that moved from place to place, rocks and globes that opened up to reveal devils or saints, sinners or the blessed. The towers shivered and shook in earthquakes, there was thunder and lightning, and Noah floated by in the Ark.

The spectators were seated on bleachers or on special platforms, or, as in the case of the special performance before King Philip IV in honor of the visiting Charles, Prince of Wales, and the Duke of Buckingham in 1623, on balconies at the palace windows. Sizes of the seating areas varied, but had to be increased with the years as the presentations became ever more popular and greater comfort was required.

Additional Note

"Theatres were originally the yards of houses. At the back was the stage and persons of quality viewed the play from the windows of the houses built round the yard. In the yard stood the populous. Raised benches surrounded it for those who could afford to pay for seats, and the women sat in a gallery, called the *cazuela* or stew-pan, which had a separate entrance and into which men were not admitted. Nevertheless, it was hard to keep them out, and I've read that Bernardo de Soto, having got in, raised the petticoats and touched the legs of the women who were watching the play, by which great scandal was occasioned. So keen was the demand for seats that sometimes windows and benches were left as heirlooms.

The public that stood in the pit, students, artisans and ruffians, were most disorderly. As many of them as could got in without paying and there were frequent brawls at the door as they tried to force their way past the doorkeeper who took the entrance money. Once in they waited noisily. Itinerant vendors walked about crying their wares (as they still do at bull fights), selling fruit and candy; someone would throw down money in a handkerchief and the vendor, wrapping up in it what was wanted, would throw it back. Now and then a spectator would be tapped on the shoulder and asked if he would pay for a dozen oranges for a woman he had ogled in the stew-pan.

Performances began at 2:00 in winter and at 3:00 in the summer. They were given by the light of day and at first under the open sky so that a downpour of rain cut the play short and the money was returned. At the appointed hour, more or less, the musicians appeared, with guitars and harps, and sang a ballad. After this a member of the company came on the stage and recited a monologue, called a *loa*, which was designed to put the spectators in good humor.

Then the first act of the play was given. It proceeded in so great an uproar that the words would often not be heard. When the public were displeased they broke into shrill whistles, cat calls, and scurrilous abuse. The women in the stew-pan were as vociferous as the men in the pit. But when they were moved by a noble sentiment or charmed by an adroit piece of versification, they shouted, 'Victor, Victor!'

To prevent the audience from being bored a short, often topical farce followed the first act. This was called an *entremes*. It was accompanied by music and ended with a dance. Then came the second act, another *entremes* and the last act. But the public had a passion for short pieces called *jacaras*, which were roistering ballads and thieves' slang, and the mob clamored for them at every interval. A final dance brought the proceedings to a close. The audience surely got their money's worth." [1]

---

[1] Maugham, W. Somerset. Don Fernando: Or Variations on Some Spanish Themes (p. 161-162). Garden City, New York: Doubleday & Company, Inc., 1935.

VALDIVIELSO
AND
EL HOSPITAL DE LOS LOCOS

by

Hugh A. Harter

The currently accepted form of Valdivielso's name, José de Valdivielso, is not the only form used when writing of him. His contemporaries spelled his first name in different ways: Joseph, Josep, Ioseph, and the surname: Baldiuieso. Fluctuations of this kind in the spelling of proper names was not unusual, as it was not until the eighteenth century that systematic codification of phonetics and spelling took place for the Spanish language.

Surprisingly little is known of the early life, and for that matter, the adult life of Valdivielso, especially when we consider his prominence as a writer and as an ecclesiastical figure. No record of his birth has been found, but it was undoubtedly sometime between the years 1560 to 1565 as the first document known that specifically refers to him is in a book published in Toledo in 1585 that contains a sonnet written by him in praise of the author. No specific document names Toledo as his place of birth either. Contemporaries do, however, make literary references to him as a native of Toledo. Consequently, scholars generally concede that Valdivielso first saw the light of day in the city in which he grew up and came to literary and ecclesiastical prominence. By his time, Toledo had been superceded as capital of Spain by nearby Madrid, but it still was home to a number of prominent men of letters and the arts in the reign of Philip II, not least of whom was the painter El Greco whose house across from the Synagogue of El Transito can be visited today. Valdivielso certainly knew the artist and may even be one of the unidentified figures portrayed in the famed "Burial of Count Orgaz."

It was not unusual for men of the cloth to be prominent men of letters in the period of Spain's Golden Age. Among the most prominent are Valdivielso himself, Tirso de Molina (Fray Gabriel Téllez) who wrote the first play clearly delineating the figure of Don Juan, that "monster of nature" who took religious orders late in life, the extraordinarily prolific Lope de Vega Carpio, and, in the next generation, Calderón de la Barca. Ironically, there seems to have been no sense of incompatibility in this participation in what would now seem eminently worldly to us, writing for the theatre and producing plays, while serving as a priest or prelate. Of course, in the case of Valdivielso, who wrote only works of a religious nature, whether *autos sacramentales* or poetry, there is no ambiguity, real or apparent.

Valdivielso's literary career began with non-dramatic works. In 1597, Valdivielso published his *Vida, excelencias y muerte del gloriosísimo Patriarca San José* or *Life, Excellences, and Death of the Most Glorious Patriarch Saint Joseph*, written "for His Majesty and Other Princes" at the urging of Friar Gabriel de

Talavera, the prior of the prestigious sanctuary of Nuestra Señora de Guadalupe in Estremadura to celebrate the transferal to the shrine of certain important relics. By then, it is supposed that the author had obtained his *licenciatura* at the University of Toledo, and he was already a respected participant in the literary societies of Toledo, a membership attesting his prominence by that time.

By 1603, Valdivielso had probably already entered his life as priest in the Cathedral of Toledo where he held the title of *Capellán Mozárabe*, i.e. the chaplain or priest of the Gothic Mozarabic (used for Christians living under Muslim rule before the reconquest of Granada) rite, and then, by 1607, as the Chaplain of the Cardinal Bernardo de Sandoval y Rojas, member of a family of great power and influence under Philip III. By 1608, however, the poet must have moved to Madrid, as certain documents concerning important literary events in Toledo make no mention of his participation. On the other hand, a legal document of 1609 of Madrid includes Valdivielso in it. He was to reside in Madrid the rest of his life.

Although Valdivielso had been well known in literary circles of Toledo before his move to Madrid, his fame was just to begin. In 1612, his *Romancero espiritual* or *Spiritual Ballads* was published. Clearly within the medieval traditions in form and thematic development,the poetry of the work was of a sensitive beauty that partook of both popular and erudite expression. In 1622 in Toledo, Valdivielso published his *Doze autos sacramentales, dos comedias divinas* or *Twelve Sacramental Plays and Two Religious Dramas*, to which we shall return later on. In 1623, Valdivielso's fourth book appeared: *Exposicion Perifrastica del Psalterio y de los Cantos del Breviario* or *Periphrastic Exposition of the Book of Psalms and of the Songs of the Breviary*. A fifth book followed in 1630, the *Elogios al Santíssimo Sacramento, a la Cruz Santíssima, y a la Puríssima Virgen María Señora Nuestra* or *Eulogies to the Most Holy Sacrament, to the Most Holy Cross, and to the Most Holy Virgin Mary Our Lady*, which was a kind of manual for prayer, conversation or solitary contemplation. In it is some of Valdivielso's finest poetic expression in the "culto" traditions of Spanish baroque writing. By the time of Valdivielso's death in 1638 in Madrid, thirty-six editions of his works had been published, clear evidence, together with the praise of well-known contemporaries, of his wide-spread prominence in his own times.

In addition to the twelve sacramental plays published in the volume of 1622, scholars speculate that some of the anonymous *autos* that have come down to us may also be Valdivielso's. They were the object of great praise in their time, and they and the other works he wrote brought him the friendship and close association with the major writers of the capital. These included not only Lope de Vega, who was a very close friend, but also Cervantes, Quevedo, and Góngora, to name only a few of the best known today. As censor, Valdivielso approved works by major writers, including Cervantes' *Viaje del Parnaso*, the second part of the *Quijote*, the *Ocho comedias y ocho entremeses*, and the *Persiles*. He also was a collaborator in book-length works edited by other authors, and wrote at least one section of a work on paintings. His ecclesiastical duties continued throughout his lifetime also. Two years after the death in 1618 of his patron and protector, Cardinal Sandoval y Rojas, he was to become the Chaplain of an even more illustrious figure, don Fernando, the son of Philip III.

It was generally conceded by his contemporaries, as well as scholar-critics today, that Valdivielso was unrivaled as a writer of sacramental plays, and great praise was given to his powers of versification and versatility. Even Calderón, whose *autos* have received much more critical attention than those of Valdivielso, had to alter the focus in his plays to redemption through Dogma, as Valdivielso himself had fairly well exhausted the possibilities of the genre as he had cultivated it, with emphasis on redemption through repentance. This stressing of the infinite possibilities of redemption through repentance gives Valdivielso's *autos* a unique and incomparable character and humane dimension which he exploited to the fullest extent of the genre's potential. Furthermore, it is a concept which fits well with the descriptions of Valdivielso by his contemporaries who saw in him a singularly kind, thoughtful, and modest man of great talent and ability.

El Hospital de los Locos was among the plays included by Valdivielso himself in the volume of 1622. The play itself dates from 1602, however. It was not until 1916, in a collection of *autos sacramentales* complied and edited by Eduardo Gonzales Pedroso in the "Biblioteca de Autores Españoles" series that Valdivielso's works became available for twentieth century readers or performers. Pedroso included fifty-one *autos* in the volume, eighteen of which are anonymous, and others by Gil Vicente, Juan de Pedraza, Juan de Timoneda, Lope de Vega, "Maestro Josef de Valdivielso," Fray Gabriel Téllez (Tirso de Molina), Pedro Calderón de la Barca, Agustín Moreto, and Francisco Bances Candamo. The five works of Valdivielso that are included are *El peregrino (The Pilgrim)*, *El hijo pródigo (The Prodigal Son)*, *La amistad en el peligro (Friendship in Time of Danger)*, *De la Serrana de Plasencia (About the Highland Girl from Plascencia)*, and *El Hospital de los Locos (Madmen's Hospital)*. More recently, in 1975, Professors Ricardo Arias y Arias of Fordham University and Robert V. Piluso of SUNY at New Paltz edited the complete works of Valdivielso in two volumes, and these include the twelve plays of the 1622 edition, plus others that have been identified as belonging to Valdivielso.

The title of the *auto*, *Madmen's Hospital*, or in the IASTA production, *The House of Fools*, could also be translated as Insane Asylum. As the title clearly indicates, this particular work is about madness. The question is, of course, what kind of madness does Valdivielso mean in writing a sacramental drama on this specific subject. The title also includes the word *hospital*, the same as the English word, but certainly with a far different sense and concept from what we mean by the word today. Furthermore, Valdivielso has a specific idea in mind, both for the *locos*, "mad people," and for the hospital itself. They are a part and parcel of the allegory of the work, and fundamental to its meaning.

The theme of madness has had wide treatment in Spanish literature. We have only to mention that most famous madman of all times, Don Quixote, to evoke the theme, but many other characters and works could be cited as well. One of Cervantes' finest and most provocative *novellas* is *El licenciado vidriera* or *Man of Glass* whose protagonist is singularly wise as long as he is judged insane, but loses all insight once he is cured, which is essentially the story of

Don Quixote also. Their insanities are akin to the "divine madness" of saints and visionaries whose "derangement" removes the blindness to fundamental truth created by the material realities of this world, but ecclesiastical authorities - the famed curate of the *Quixote*, for example—as well as the "sane" public who marvelled at and ridiculed them, sought their return to the realities of this world, to "cure" them.

Furthermore, there is that other madness which smacks of devils and aberrations that stem from and lead to evil. It is this madness of unclean spirits and devils to be cast out that the Gospels speak of repeatedly in terms of possession. Christ casts out the evil spirits and heals the souls of troubled men.

It is to this concept that we must relate the "locos" of Valdivielso's play. Their "hospital," as Guilt tells Madness, is a prison, and it is a Hell to which such evil figures as Guilt, Deceit, Lust (or Pleasure), Lucifer, Gluttony, Flesh, and Envy have been irrevocably condemned. Unlike these, however, World is a figure whose salvation is possible. Consequently, the Hospital may be interpreted on two levels, the Cárcel or Jail, and a place where a cure, through the means of the Divine Apothecary and the Church, can take place. The dramatic conflict grows out of the pursuit of Soul by the forces of evil whose agent is Lust. Reason's attempts at saving her are futile, as Lust's seduction has been complete. It is Inspiration (i.e. Divine Inspiration) that comes to liberate Soul, the "image of God," and the bride of Christ's soul, and whose salvation is brought about through Christ and the Church's redemptive powers, and through Soul's penance.

There is a clearly established rhythm between scenes which has been admirably studied by Professor Ricardo Arias, a rhythm well suited to moments of lyrical or conversational levels, while others invite action, dance, and movement.

Sources and Acknowledgments

Spanish literary theoreticians of the Enlightenment, the Age of Reason, saw the *auto sacramental* as a dramatic expression that was not acceptable either esthetically or rationally. They objected to the use of Allegory on the stage, and to various anachronisms that went counter to "reasonable" theatrical expectations. The *auto sacramental* was duly banished from the stage from mid-eighteenth century on by decree of King Carlos III, and that prohibition affected publication of *autos* as well.

Consequently, it was not until the 1916 publication of the "Biblioteca de Autores Españoles" edition, mentioned earlier, that attention was given to the genre. During the Spanish Civil War, however, the *auto* was seen as a vehicle admirably fitting the Franco dictatorship's view of Spain, one corresponding surprisingly to the concept of Ferdinand and Isabella's: all political power in the hands of the Caudillo, the Army, and the Church. Redemption was possible through repentance; political and religious orthodoxy, however, had to be total. The *auto* was a visual spectacle that conveniently coincided with the super-nationalism of the thirties and forties under Franco, resulting in productions such as that given at the Cathedral of Segovia in 1938, or in Madrid somewhat later. More recent secular productions have undoubtedly come about through the newer emphases brought about through the theories surrounding such playwrights as Antonin Artuad.

Two book-length studies of the *auto sacramental* have been published in recent years. One of them is in English, Professor Ricardo Arias's *The Spanish Sacramental Plays*, in the Twayne series published by G.K. Hall and Company of Boston in 1980. The other is in Spanish, Professor Bruce W. Wardropper's *Introduccion al teatro religioso del siglo de oro. Evolucion del Auto Sacramental antes de Calderón*, published by Ediciones Anaya in Salamanca, Spain, in 1967. Both books have extensive bibliographical references for persons wishing to pursue study of the *auto* as genre and as dramatic phenomenon. Also valuable as a source of information concerning staging in particular are sections of Professor N. D. Shergold's *A History of the Spanish Stage From Medieval Times Until the End of the Seventeenth Century*, published at the Clarendon Press in Oxford, England in 1967. Professor Arias has also written a monograph on the *Hospital de los Locos* published by *Insula* in Madrid in 1977. The aforementioned two-volume edition of Valdivielso's *Teatro completo*, by Ricardo Arias and Robert V. Piluso, Ediciones y Distribuciones Isla, Madrid, 1975, has a scholarly introduction and extensive bibliography. Histories of Spanish literature vary considerably in their treatment of the *auto sacramental*, but generally are far less informative or reliable than the works cited above.

INTRODUCTION

by

John D. Mitchell

The decision for the Institute for Advanced Studies in the Theatre Arts (IASTA) to stage for a third time a Spanish Classic was made a long time ago.

I had come to know Miguel Narros, the director for IASTA's production of *THE HOUSE OF FOOLS* [*EL HOSPITAL DE LOS LOCOS*], in June 1964, at the World's Fair in New York, where he was Artistic Director and Company Manager for the Flamenco dance group in the Spanish Pavilion. The highlight of the Pavilion was the Vargas Dance Troupe, which had deservedly won the admiration and enthusiasm of New Yorkers and out-of-town audiences alike. I attended their dance performances numerous times. As I came to know Miguel Narros during our various meetings, he spoke of a form of theatre I was only vaguely aware of - the *auto sacramental*.

"Might that not be a project for IASTA, an *auto* by Valdivielso, for example, *EL HOSPITAL DE LOS LOCOS*?," he asked. "Its roots are in the Middle Ages, but it was a form of Spanish theatre at the time of Lope de Vega and Calderón de la Barca. As a matter of fact, Calderón wrote a number of *autos*."

My next meeting with Miguel Narros was in September of 1966 in Madrid. In the interim, master Spanish stage director Jose Luis Alonso had come to IASTA to direct Calderón's THE PHANTOM LADY [*LA DAMA DUENDE*]. My trip to Madrid had been prompted to visit our first Spanish director, Jose Tamayo, as well as to meet with Jose Luis Alonso. Accompanied by Alonso, I went to the Teatro Nacional Español to see some of the rehearsals of Cervantes' play, *NUMANCIA*, directed by Miguel Narros. Miguel was not doing a traditional production; the style of scenery and costumes was abstract. It was, for me, evocative of the late drawings of Picasso. It was an elaborate production with a large cast. The theme of *NUMANCIA* is of the Roman Conquest of Spain. During a rehearsal break, we talked with Miguel Narros, seeking confirmation of his coming one day to IASTA.

By the 1970's, IASTA had given up doing International Theatre Festivals due to a marked decline in the quality of 42nd Street. We decided to relinquish our Studio Theatre there because more and more people, and potential contributors, were unwilling to brave the neighborhood in order to attend an invited performance of a classic directed by a master director from abroad. (During one benefit performance, audience's coats were stolen, some of them mink. Fortunately, they were later recovered from a trash can).

Sometime after our move, business manager, C. George Willard, came to know Gilberto Zaldivar, head of a Spanish theatre troupe that had settled into the Greenwich Mews Theatre on 13th Street in Greenwich Village. He began exploring with him the possibility of IASTA's collaboration with their resident Spanish-language company. They sought a project of mutual interest.

The Greenwich Mews Theatre had a deep personal history for the Institute, since, in 1966, we had moved IASTA's successful workshop production of Racine's *PHEDRE* there for public performances. Subsequently, the production was performed in London; at Dartington Hall, Devon; and later in Denver and in Aspen, Colorado. There were even more happy associations with the Greenwich Mews Theatre for we had also staged there a Peking Opera in English, *THE BUTTERFLY DREAM.*

Recalling my earlier conversations with Miguel Narros, I wrote a letter inviting him to come and direct the very *auto sacramental* for which he had expressed enthusiasm, *EL HOSPITAL DE LOS LOCOS.* An exchange of letters fixing dates for the production followed.

Another trip to Spain was made to meet with Miguel Narros regarding aspects of the production which he would direct. On September 11, 1971, in Madrid, he agreed to come to the Institute early the following year.

In Madrid, we met with him in a dance studio. He was not busy with his own rehearsals; but he was advising the flamenco dancers for Señorita Vargas, who was rehearsing her dance troupe for an opening in Madrid followed by a tour of South America. It was a curious, noisy place to work out the details of a production in New York! The staccato sounds of the dancing were great, but my conversation with Miguel went on amidst this exciting and distracting rehearsal. At the same time, I also interviewed him and taped his views on styles of theatre, especially Spanish theatre. (The interview was later incorporated into *THEATRE: THE SEARCH FOR STYLE.*)

In early spring of 1972, Miguel Narros arrived in New York. As agreed upon in advance, he brought with him from Madrid a designer, Andrea D'Odorico, an Italian practicing his craft in Spain. Andrea arrived with completed costume designs for the Institute's production of *THE HOUSE OF FOOLS.*

An invitation to audition was sent out to all the actors who had worked in previous IASTA productions, as well as to actors whose resumés were in our files. Actors we knew spread the word that we were casting a Spanish play with a director from Spain. The heads of the Spanish Theatre urged their actors, as well as friends of their actors, to audition. Spanish-speaking actors, from all over Latin America, now residents of New York, came to audition.

After several days had been spent auditioning actors at the Greenwich Mews Theatre, rehearsals commenced. Associate director on the production was Rene Buch; he was the director for the resident Spanish troupe at the Greenwich Mews Theatre.

Since we had not found an English translation of *EL HOSPITAL DE LOS LOCOS,* by Joseph de Valdivielso, over the course of several weeks, Aida Alvarez and I made a translation into English of the play.

For the first time in its history, the Institute's production was to be performed in two languages, English and the original language of the classic, the Spanish of playwright Valdivielso. The IASTA actors were to perform the English translation; the Hispanic actors would perform the original language of Spanish.

As early as 1962, I had become aware of the high quality of speech of all actors performing in theatres of Madrid. The accent on stages there was that of Madrileño, to *cecear,* [1] as it were. However, not all of Spain speaks with the accent of Madrid. Additionally, the accents of Central and South America and Mexico vary, sometimes greatly, although their manner of speaking Spanish is akin, some would say, to that of Southern Spain.

While in Madrid, the plan for a dual language production appealed to Miguel Narros; I was keen for the bilingual theatrical innovation as well. However, neither Miguel nor I had anticipated that there would be this diversity of accents once the production began rehearsals.

For Miguel, some Spanish accents, being harsh and staccato, were as irritating as the sound of a fingernail on a blackboard. His ear had been attuned to the quality of speech of the classical actors of Madrid's stages.

Perhaps Miguel could have been more accepting of his actors who were to perform the play in Spanish; his troupe had performed in South America. However, he was a flexible and friendly man, and the Spanish-speaking actors were very enthusiastic about being directed by a master director from Madrid. Was Miguel's ultimate rejection of his Spanish actors due to the behavior of associate director, Rene Buch? According to C. George Willard, IASTA's business manager, Rene Buch strove to undermine the authority and the directorial style of Miguel Narros. This created a great deal of tension among both the English-language company as well as the Spanish-language company. The outcome was that eventually, deep into rehearsals, Miguel Narros refused to have anything more to do with rehearsing the Spanish-speaking actors. This may very well have been exactly what Rene Buch wanted to achieve.

As in all of IASTA's double casting experiences, the nature of this workshop production was that it was not always possible to have the same company of actors throughout rehearsal and later throughout the performances. There were times when, during the twelve performances given by the IASTA English-speaking actors, a certain role would be covered by another IASTA actor, or by one of the Spanish-speaking actors who could also handle the English and knew the English text.

What prompted Miguel Narros in 1964 to tell me about THE HOUSE OF FOOLS was that he had already directed this play once before. The American actor and star, Mel Ferrer, had been cast in a commercial Hollywood film, EL GRECO. Filming took place throughout Spain. For inclusion in the film, Miguel Narros was asked to stage and direct, in front of the Cathedral of Toledo, on a platform, a production of EL HOSPITAL DE LOS LOCOS.

Miguel Narros received full credit in the film titles for his direction of this stage production within the EL GRECO film; as might be expected, the full play was not incorporated into the body of the American film. Early in the film, however, part of the play is used for local color and serves as background to some verbal exchanges between the Spanish nobles and El Greco, all of whom are attending the performance in front of the cathedral.

The costumes in the film for the characters of Valdivielso's play differ

---

1 *Cecear* is the Spanish verb which designates certain letters are pronounced with a 'th' rather than as an 's' sound.

from the costumes designed for IASTA's New York production; they are period costumes of the time of Valdivielso and El Greco. The film's costume designs are not as abstract and elaborate as those of Andrea D'Odorico. (His drawings of the costumes are included in this book.)

Miguel Narros relates that one day, as he was rehearsing the actors on the platform in front of the Cathedral of Toledo, a group of religious men from the Cathedral were observing and listening to the play. In a very short time, they began to react to the dialogue they were hearing from the actors. One man began to shout and to gesticulate that the play be stopped, that such a scandalous play should not be permitted to play in front of the Cathedral. (These were the repressive days of Franco's total control of all activities throughout Spain.) Narros signaled the actors to continue, then he strode up to the ringleader of the religious set saying loudly and very firmly, "This is a 16th Century play by your fellow Jesuit master, Valdivielso." Without a word, the men turned on their heels and withdrew into the Cathedral. From that moment on, no word of censure or protest about *EL HOSPITAL DE LOS LOCOS* was heard from the religious leaders of Toledo's Cathedral.

The staging of the play for the film had a great deal of vitality; ironically, as edited for incorporation into the film, the play appears to end at a point where the various vices and sins in this morality play triumph in seducing Soul. (In truth, at the end of the play, Soul is **saved**.) The audience within the film, consisting of highly Catholic and upright nobles and aristocrats, as well as townspeople, applaud this false ending of the play. [The scene, performed in Spanish, obviously has cinematic effectiveness, without due thought to the wrongness of ending *THE HOUSE OF FOOLS* thus!] I'm certain this distressed Miguel Narros.

Although the film was not a commercial success in the United States, it is available on videocassette and often turns up on cable television.

As may be seen from the text, *EL HOSPITAL DE LOS LOCOS* ends as a very Christian metaphor in which Soul is rescued by Reason, Inspiration, Christ and St. Peter. The play closes with a celebration of the Mass, as was the custom in the 16th and 17th Centuries when the Jesuit priest, Valdivielso, wrote the play.

It was always a goal of IASTA, in producing a world classic with a master director from abroad, to try to recapture the style appropriate to the play, a style which would have been used at the time of its original production. In 1971, in Madrid, this **had** been discussed at length with Miguel Narros. However, directors have strong wills. By the time Narros reached New York, he and his designer had decided to stage *THE HOUSE OF FOOLS* in an expressionistic style. Perhaps Miguel had wearied of the traditional style he had used for the film, or perhaps he thought the limitations of the Greenwich Mews stage in depth and height prompted a different staging.

Italian contemporary sculpture inspired Andrea D'Odorico for the style of the scenery to be used in the Institute's production at the Greenwich Mews Theatre. Miguel and Andrea purchased sheets of plastic and burned holes in the plastic to use as scenery. The setting was evocative expressionistically of an asylum for the Locos and was, at the same moment, evocative of Hell.

Not being aware of the health risks from burning plastic, their burning it inside the theatre itself precipitated a crisis. The designer and crew had to take the plastic out into the alley, for the fumes are toxic and even deadly. Fortunately, nobody got sick from the fumes.

By studying the footage that is in the film *EL GRECO*, one can see that there is not an exact, but a considerable similarity between the way it was staged in Toledo in front of the Cathedral, and the way it was staged in New York.

Miguel Narros contributed the following program notes for the IASTA production: "Master Joseph de Valdivielso, post-dramatist of *THE HOUSE OF FOOLS*, was born in Toledo about 1560, and died in 1638. He was a priest and chaplain to Cardinal Sandoval y Rojas. Among his friends were Lope de Vega and Cervantes, who were full of praise for his dramatic works. Although a master of the *auto*, Valdivielso is still largely unknown, even in Spain. [2] But his ingenuity and exploiting of form is without equal; each of his plays is characterized by grace, delicacy, and fidelity to the Bible. When his *autos* are contrasted with others, one notes his skill in making the form appealing to large, popular audiences. Valdivielso entered into the great human adventure and the mystery of existence; he got behind the mask of Man and penetrated what we now recognize as the unconscious. Whereas Calderón stressed the theological at the expense of the theatrical, Valdivielso placed Man in timeless space to confront him with all human emotions and drive. Thus, each of his works rises to dramatic heights with the sinner finally coming to God. In his time, performed as they were on platforms before the church, the Ritual of the Mass and the full splendor and panoply of the Catholic Church, provided the ultimate climax following the end of the play.'

"The Mystery and Morality plays of the Middle Ages in Europe flourished and waned, ultimately disappearing except in Spain, where the form continued to develop on into the Golden Age of Spanish drama. The great giants of Spanish dramatic literature, Lope de Vega and Calderón, wrote *autos sacramentales* which treated religious themes and ideas allegorically rather than literally. The *auto* is the only symbolist theatre that has survived from the past. At this moment of theatre history, it seems to have been the harbinger of the theatres of the absurd and cruelty."

After the twelve invited performances had been given by the IASTA actors, the play, performed in Spanish, continued to run for a length of time for public audiences at the Greenwich Mews Theatre.

IASTA's Chairman of the Board, John F. Wharton, invited his friend, drama critic of *The New York Times*, Brooks Atkinson, to a performance of THE HOUSE OF FOOLS. Mr. Atkinson did not write a review of the production, for the *Times* during this period would not publicize a play which did not take ads in *The New York Times*; However, Atkinson told John Wharton that he had found the play, "very fascinating, indeed."

Despite the passage of years, I recently interviewed the actors who had

---

[2] Of late, in the 1980's more and more productions of *THE HOUSE OF FOOLS* are turning up in Spain.

performed in the IASTA production of *THE HOUSE OF FOOLS*. One actress interviewed is bilingual, and had been able to perform both in the English company as well as in the Spanish company in the role of Guilt. Robert Main (or Santos Ramos), stage manager for the production, had retained his stage manager's copy of the script and had it xeroxed for me, making it possible to recapture the *mise-en-scène* for inclusion in this book. A taped interview with Miguel Narros enabled me to provide, beneath the English translation, directorial notes and much of Narros' interpretation of the play.

My hope is that *STAGING A SPANISH CLASSIC: EL HOSPITAL DE LOS LOCOS* will make the remarkable play, *THE HOUSE OF FOOLS*, more accessible to English and Spanish audiences. It is a unique staging of an *auto sacramental* by a Spanish master director, Miguel Narros. Equipped with *mise-en-scènes* and directorial notes on the text, my hope is that the IASTA production will inspire additional productions. Certainly *THE HOUSE OF FOOLS* is a play that merits being heard and seen. Despite their excellence, Valdivielso's works have been neglected in Spain and abroad, although Professor Hugh A. Harter makes known that this particular play of Valdivielso's has been gaining more attention and productions of it are currently being staged in Spain.

The object of a work of art is to arouse emotion and to engender aesthetic perception. As W. Somerset Maugham has written, "The value of emotion lies in its effects. Santa Teresa insisted on this over and over again: the ecstasy of union with the Godhead was precious **only** if it resulted in greater capacity for works. The aesthetic emotion, however delightful and however subtle, has worth only if it leads to action... For the work of art is a diversion, an escape from the bitterness of life and a solace in the world's inevitable cruelty, a rest from its turmoil and a relief from labor. This is much, and if a work of art has only this communication to make it justifies itself. But great works speak with another voice too; they enrich the soul so that it is capable of a nobler and more fruitful activity. Their effects are worthy deeds."

THE HOUSE OF FOOLS
[El Hospital de los Locos]

by

Joseph de Valdivielso

"*Y aquí, ceñida de laurel y oliva, sacras historias Valdivielso escriba.*" [1]
—Lope de Vega (Canto xix, *Jerusalén conquistada*)

---

1 And here, crowned with wreath of laurel and olive, Valdivielso writes his sacred tales.

LEGEND

G = *CULPA / GUILT*

MD = *LOCURA / MADNESS*

D = *ENGAÑO / DECEIT*

LS = *DELEITE / LUST*

LR = *LUZBEL / LUCIFER*

W = *MUNDO / WORLD*

FL = *CARNE / FLESH*

GL = *GULA / GLUTTONY*

MN = *GÉNERO HUMANO / MANKIND*

EN = *INVIDIA / ENVY*

RE = *RAZON / REASON*

S = *ALMA / SOUL*

I = *INSPIRACION / INSPIRATION*

SP = *SAN PEDRO / ST. PETER*

CH = *CRISTO / CHRIST*

A1 = *ACOLYTE*

A2 = *ACOLYTE*

ESCENA PRIMERA

Sale LA CULPA, de hombre, con espada y daga y una escopeta al hombro, y EL DELEITE, de villano, y EL ENGAÑO, de viejo; LA LOCURA, de loco, con un baston y llaves en la mano, como alcaide de locos.

CULPA.
Locura, engañada estás,
Si de la empresa que sigo
En ser sospechosa das.

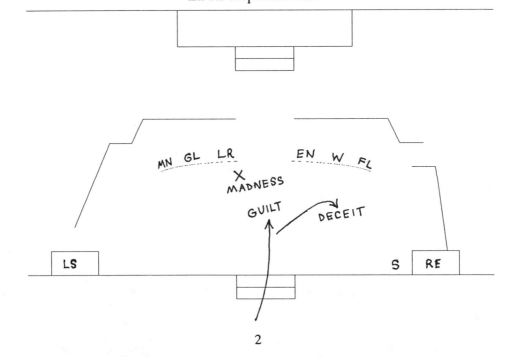

2

HOUSE OF FOOLS

SCENE I

GUILT, DECEIT, LUST and MADNESS

The platform stage represents an asylum; there are doors with grilled openings. Recorded music (composed and conducted by Carmelo Bernaola) starts with the dimming of the house lights and continues until total darkness. Music then fades as stage light then bursts on suddenly.

Carrying a shotgun, GUILT, carried on the shoulders of DECEIT, as an old man, enters at the rear of the auditorium; they rush hurriedly down the center aisle to the stage. LUST, as a youth, follows. He takes up a statuesque pose on the down stage right platform. MADNESS is awaiting them on stage. Jumping down from DECEIT's shoulders, GUILT takes center stage; DECEIT dresses stage down left.

> GUILT.
> *(Music fully out.)*
> Madness, /2 you are mistaken
> In suspecting the intentions
> Of my undertaking.
> *(Taking whip from MADNESS, driving him down stage right.)*

> *So full of artless jealousy is Guilt...*
> Shakespeare: *HAMLET*

It is doubtful that Valdivielso and Shakespeare knew of each other's theatre and writings. As youths, most likely, both had seen Medieval plays performed in towns and villages; hence, their conscious and unconscious tendency to think of attributes as characters.

The director told the actress, playing GUILT, that her character is the best role in the play, wonderful and exciting. The part requires an actress capable of strong bodily movement, a vivid imagination for the powerful images, and most important of all is strong voice. He stressed that actors, English speaking as well as Spanish speaking, work for clear and mellifluous diction, paying heed throughout to consonants and vowels. (From his Spanish cast he sought a quality comparable to that of the actors of the stages of Madrid.)

REASON, down left, is standing. SOUL is in a fetal position on the stage. REASON takes SOUL's hands, and then sits as if to give her counsel.

---

2 / and / / markings indicate the beats of pause, before continuing the verse lines.

LOCURA.

Es muy fuerte tu enemigo,
5   Y muy desarmada vas.

CULPA.

Dime, ¿al Engaño no llevo,
Con que al más santo me atrevo,
Y al mal logrado Deleite,
Cuyo fantástico afeite
10   Es de los necios el cebo?

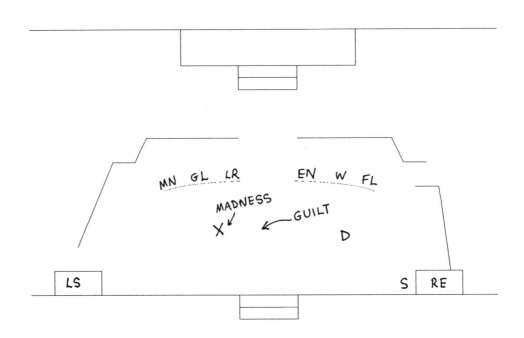

MADNESS.
*(He is servile, as he fingers his keys at his belt
and as he toys with his whip.)*

Your enemy is very strong, /
5   And / you are not well armed.

GUILT.

Tell me, do I not come with Deceit
(A gesture in DECEIT's direction.)
With whom I dare against the most saintly;
And / with ill-gotten Lust
*(Looking over shoulder down right to LUST
who is posed as a wax works.)*
Whose fantastic appearance
10   Is a trap for fools.

Fetter strong Madness in a silken thread.
Shakespeare: *MUCH ADO ABOUT NOTHING*

GUILT maintains and rules this asylum, the House of Fools. Her image is one of control, of manipulating the other characters; she desires power and maintaining it through the other characters; e.g. LUST. As a metaphor, GUILT enjoys vicariously passions and pleasures of the world through the *locos*: FLESH, GLUTTONY, ENVY etc. She abates and keeps active these vices.

The actress found GUILT's costume a challenge. Large boots with platform soles and oversized heels, a high wig bearing a full skull, and a voluminous dress of leather and metal trim, as designated by the designer, made the costume seem to the actress to be both overpowering and cumbersome and heavy. The director said to her, "The costume adds much to the character. It makes the actor playing GUILT feel more powerful, because the actor now is taller, heavier, more magnificent, taking up more room on the stage."

GUILT, go as far as you like in some passages and hold back in others; enjoy the speech in the sense of enjoying the emotional release. The actor needs the words to get release.

MADNESS, be articulate; don't let the feelings get between you and the meaning. Both, play the meaning of the thoughts as strongly as the feelings.

(*CULPA.*)
¿No llevo aquesta escopeta,
En favor de Apetito,
A quien la Razon sujeta,
Con que los rayos imito
15   Que vibra el sexto planeta?
¿No llevo á este sabio, mudo, [3]
Y á este cortesano, rudo,
Entre esta nieve, mi fuego?
¿No llevo á este lince, ciego,
20   Y acqueste armado, desnudo?

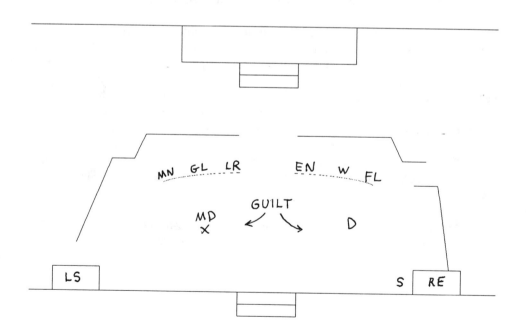

[3] Equivale á: *¿no llevo á los sabios mudos*, etc.

(GUILT.)

Do I not carry this gun
To protect Appetite,
Whom Reason maintains in check?
This gun gives out lightning

> *(For her it is the earth, pointing to ground beneath her feet.)*

15 Which comes from Saturn.
Have I not made the wise man silent
And the courtier crude? /
And do I not carry in this snow my fire? /

> *(Pointing to the ermine.)*

Do I not have with me this sharp-eyed lynx, blind;

> *(Referring to the gun.)*

20 And this armed knight, naked? /

> *(Referring to herself.)*

Since REASON has Appetite captive and under her control; as a character Appetite never appears on stage.

The language has to be made to seem real since it is written in an old Spanish. The biblical allusions have first to be researched and become meaningful to the actor; then his command of the image will make them seem relevant to the audience. When the audience is enjoying the play, the difficulty with images disappears.

The actors' being zestful, using their wits, spending energy and enjoying themselves makes for effective acting. Then, the audience will enjoy the acting too.

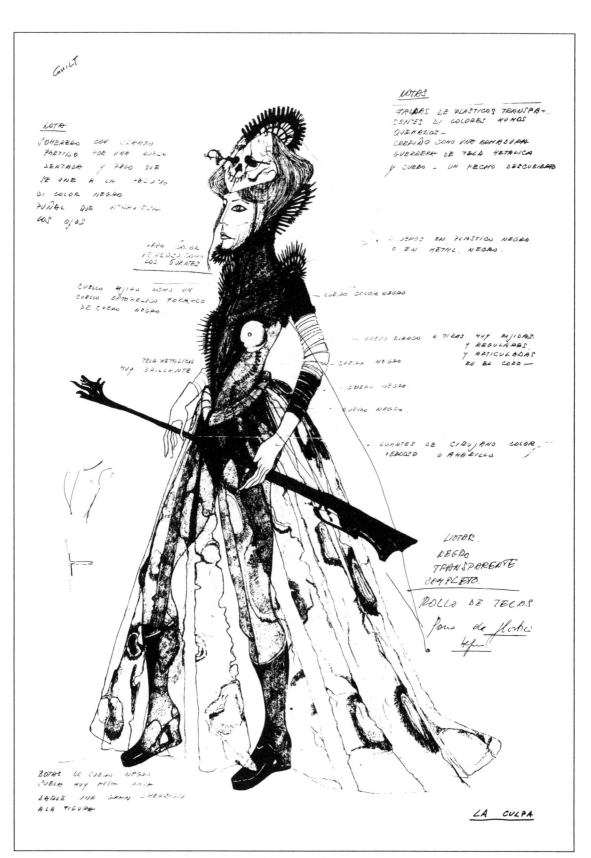

GUILT/CULPA

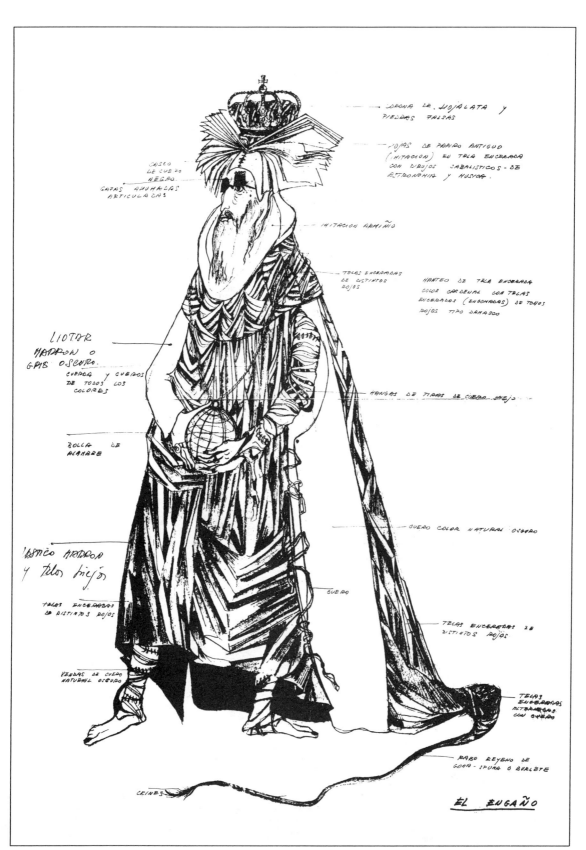

CORONA LE HOJALATA Y
PIEDRAS FALSAS

HOJAS DE PAPIRO ANTIGUO
(IMITACION) EN TELA ENCERADA
CON DIBUJOS SABALISTICOS DE
ASTRONOMIA Y MUSICA.

IMITACION ARMIÑO

COSCO
LE CUERO
NEGRO
GAFAS AHUMADAS
ARTICULADAS

TELAS ENCERADAS
DE DISTINTOS
ROJOS

MANTEO DE TELA ENCERADA
COLOR CARDENAL CON TELAS
ENCERADAS (ENGOMADAS) DE TONOS
ROJOS TIPO DAMASCO

LIOTAR
MADRON O
GRIS OSCURO.
CUERDA Y CUEROS
DE TODOS LOS
COLORES

MANGAS DE TIRAS DE CUERO VIEJO

BOLLA DE
ALAMBRE

CUERO COLOR NATURAL OSCURO

'ASTICO MADRON
Y telas viejas

CUERO

TELAS ENCERADAS
DE DISTINTOS ROJOS

TELAS ENCERADAS DE
DISTINTOS ROJOS

VENDAS DE CUERO
NATURAL OSCURO

TELAS
ENCERADAS
ALTERADAS
CON CUERO

RABO RELLENO DE
GOMA - ESPUMA O BURLETE

CRINES

EL ENGAÑO

DECEIT/ENGAÑO

(CULPA.)
¿No llevo en mi pecho tierno
Todo el poder del infierno,
Con que sabes que he vencido
Cuanto una mujer no ha sido,
25   Y un Niño, que lo es Eterno?
Que uno y otro se libró,
El, por ser Dios encubierto,
Y ella, porque alas tomó,
Con que, volanda al desierto,
30   De mis aguas se escapó.

LOCURA.
No es bien, Culpa, que te enojes
Con quien tu gusto procura.

CULPA.
Ni tú es bien que así te arrojes,
Si no es que, como Locura,
35   Conmigo te desencoges.

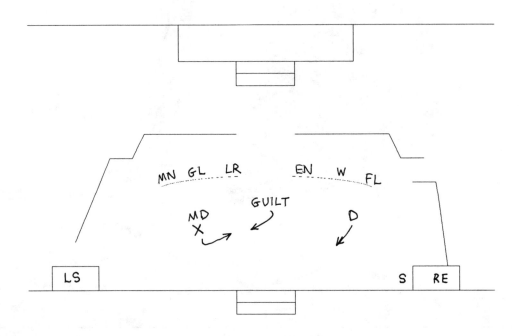

10

(GUILT).

Do I not carry in my tender breast,
All the power of Hell? / /
As you know I have conquered
All but a woman, who is blessed among women
25 And a Child that is eternal.
[That one and the other were saved:
He, by being God in disguise,
And she, taking wing,
Flew away to the deserts
30 *To escape from my waters.]* [4]

MADNESS.

It is not fair, Guilt, that you should be
Annoyed with one who tries to please you.

GUILT.

It is not *fair* to doubt my purpose,
But because you are angry,
35 You grow too bold with me.
(Kicking him fiercely.)

GUILT's motivation is to make sure that MADNESS keeps a strong control in her jail.

The *auto sacramental* THE HOUSE OF FOOLS was one of a series of religious ceremonies over a half century in Toledo, which was the primate church of all Spain. Cardinal Archbishop of Toledo, Bernardo Sandoval y Rojas was a favorite of the King, Phillip the III, and he was as well the Counselor to the King, Lord High Chancellor of Castile and Inquisitor General in the government. From 1604 until his death in December of 1618, the Archbishop was served loyally by the same *cappelán* — the versatile man of letters — Joseph de Valdivielso.

---

4 These lines were not used in the English-language production of the play.

LOCURA.
Pues mi buen ánimo ves,
No hay por qué tan bravo estés.
Cese tu furia y enojo.

CULPA.
Rabia escupo, fuego arrojo
40 De que consejo me dés.
Y pues eres la portera
De los locos que aquí están,
Guarda acquesa cárcel fiera;
Que estas manos te traerán
45 Al Alma por prisionera.

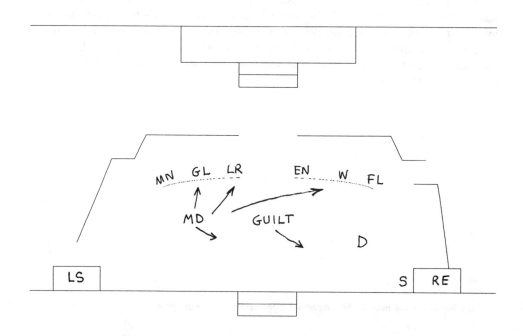

MADNESS.
My intentions are good,
So do not be so angry with me;
Stay your fury and annoyance.

GUILT.
Your giving me advice
40 Makes me spit fire and anger! / /
(Throws down whip.)
And since you are keeper
(MADNESS grabs the whip.)
Of the insane that are here,
You should guard that fierce jail. /
These hands will bring you / /
(Showing hands.)
45 Soul / as a prisoner.

On *'These hands will bring you,'* lights up on the grilles of the asylum cells; on *'Soul as a prisoner,'* loud, harsh laughter from the *locos*. GLUTTONY is crazily demonstrative.

MADNESS flails his whip at the grilles. Laughter subsides.

In this instance, and on subsequent outbursts, the actors must create an illusion of reality, but at the same time achieve balance. Excessive loudness, for its own sake (actor indulgence) can alienate an audience.

With GUILT's speech, the goal of the action is announced. It is of supreme importance that the last line must be projected out to the audience. The line that is not thought is not heard. The *locos* must wait a full beat before reacting to the line as their cue for laughter.

LOCURA.
Parto, Culpa, á obedecerte,
Como á mi rey y señor.

CULPA.
Parte, Locura, y advierte
No echen ménos su rector.

LOCURA.
50   Guardaré tu cárcel fuerte.
(*Vase.*)

ESCENA II

LA CULPA, EL DELEITE, EL ENGAÑO

CULPA
Gusto, Deleite, me das,
Mirando cuán otro estás
Con el disfraz que has tomado.

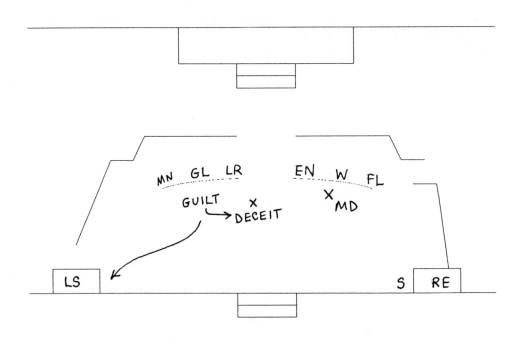

MADNESS.
I go, Guilt, to obey you,
As my king and lord.

GUILT.
Go Madness, / and make sure
To keep a strong control.
>>**(Looking to left and right.)**

MADNESS.
50   I will guard your jail well.
>>**(Crosses up left; sleeps in front of ENVY's and
WORLD's cells.)**
>>**(Music up.)**

SCENE II

GUILT, LUST, DECEIT
[SOUL, REASON, MADNESS]
>>**(Music fades.)**

GUILT.
>>**(Giving gun to DECEIT and crossing right to
LUST.)**
It is a pleasure, Lust, you give to me,
To see how your disguise
Makes you look / like someone else.

Good Lord, what Madness rules in brainsick men.
>>Shakespeare: *I HENRY VI*

Careless Lust stirs up a desperate courage.
>>Shakespeare: *VENUS AND ADONIS*

The *locos* in their cells begin to stir at the awakening of LUST. Fearful
of the whip of MADNESS, their swaying and rocking movements are hushed,
up stage of the grilles of their cells.

GUILT's awakening of LUST is rough and passionate, seeking to arouse
every part of him. Staring into his eyes, and with gestures and glance from the
floor up, she sweeps the length of his body.

On '*To see how your disguise...,*' GUILT steps up stage of him and
whispers in his ear.

15

DELEITE.
¿No voy bien disimulado?

CULPA.

55 Tan bien, que me engañarás.

DELEITE.
De niño me disfracé
Con aqueste sayo tosco.

CULPA.
Extremada traza fué.

DELEITE.
Cual culebra, aquí me enrosco;
60 Más allá me soltaré.
Nadie se teme de un niño,
Y aqueste rústico aliño
A amor y á gusto provoca;
Pondré veneno en mi boca
65 Y zarzas entre el armiño.

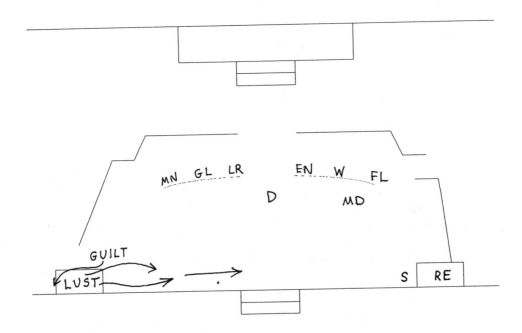

LUST.
Don't you find me well disguised?
> (*DECEIT, nodding approval, crosses up center stage.*)

GUILT.
55   / / So well, that you could ensnare me.
> (*Laughs delightedly.*)

LUST.
I disguised myself as a boy /
> (*Preening.*)

With this rustic smock.

GUILT.
A drastic change it is.

LUST.
Like a snake, I coil in here;
60   Later on I will unwind. /
No one fears a boy,
> (*Crosses left toward SOUL.*)

And this rustic exterior
Provokes love and delight.
I will hide poison in my mouth
65   And brambles in the soft ermine.

Beware of prophets who come to you in sheeps clothing but inwardly are ravenous wolves. —MATTHEW

On *'No one fears a boy,'* at down stage left spotlights reveal SOUL (lying in a fetal position at the feet of REASON, seated on the down left platform). She looks like a painted figure from Botticelli's *La Primavera.*

The sudden appearance of SOUL catches the attention of GUILT, who laughs knowingly. Her glance to the audience connotes: SOUL will be caught.

[Companies of touring actors kept the theatre alive in Spain despite a retrogressive church in respect to the theatre which frequently considered the theatre sinful and licentious. Even Lope de Vega was attacked vehemently in his own time by the clergy who said that he was a sinful friar, a monk possessed of the devil.] —Jose Luis Alonso

17

CULPA.
Y tú, cauteloso Engaño,
Letrado de mi consejo,
¡Cuán bien, entre el pobre paño,
Te finges un grave viejo,
70   Encubridor de mi daño!

ENGAÑO.
Llevo armado un fuerte lazo
Entre este pobre sayal;
De Jael la leche y brazo,

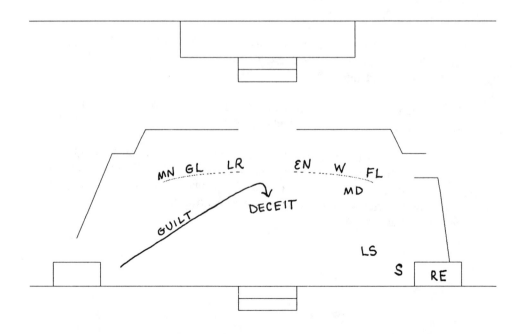

GUILT.
(Crossing up to DECEIT.)
And you, cautious Deceit,
Advisor of my council, /
How well you conceal my evil
In the guise of an old man,
70   In humble clothing.

DECEIT.
Under this coarse sack cloth
I carry a strong noose,
The milk and hand of Jael,

...that Deceit should still such gentle shape.
Shakespeare: *RICHARD III*

Having crossed up to DECEIT, GUILT places her arm comradely on his shoulder, but looks to the audience. She conveys her disgust with DECEIT as she is speaking.

With this speech, DECEIT introduces himself. The actor needs to shape and clarify his thoughts, picking out what is most important and what is less important. The biblical references may be lost upon the audience, but is important for the actor to know who the biblical characters are and what the incident is.

Sisera fled on foot to the tent of Jael, the wife of Heber... Jael came out to meet Sisera, saying... "Have no fear." So he turned aside into the tent, and she covered him with a rug. "Pray, give me a little water to drink," he said, "for I am thirsty." So she opened a skin of milk and gave him a drink. "Stand at the door of the tent," he told her, "and if any man comes and asks you, 'Is anyone here?' say no."... As Sisera was lying fast asleep from weariness, Jael took a tent peg and a hammer in her hand, went softly to him, and drove the peg into his temple, till it went down into the ground. So he died. —JUDGES

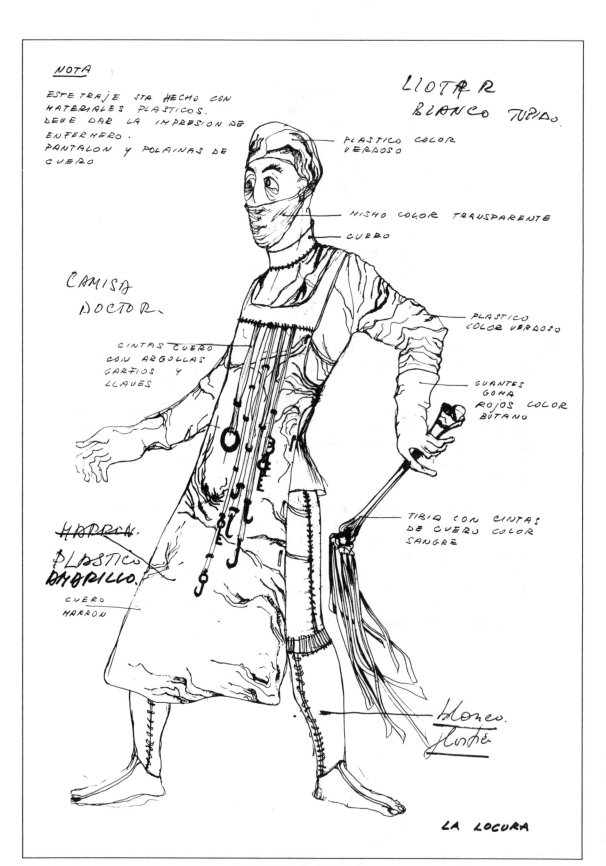

MADNESS/LOCURA

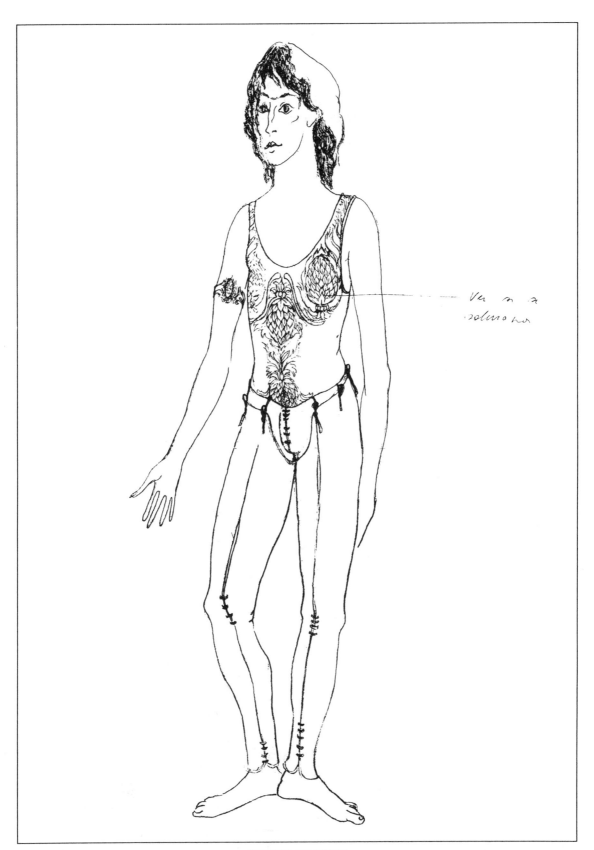

LUST/DELEITE

(ENGANO.)
De Joab llevo el puñal
75   Y de Dalida el regazo.

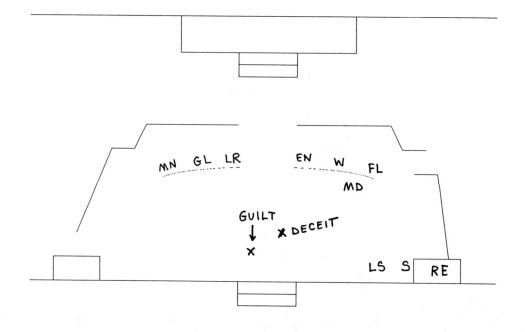

(DECEIT.)

75 The dagger of Joab,
And the lap of Delilah.

When he came out from David's presence, Joab sent messengers after Abner, and they brought him back to Hebron. Joab and Abishai, his brother, took Abner into the inner part of the gate to speak to him privately, and they smote him in the belly and he died. —2 SAMUEL

Absalom was riding upon his mule; Absalom's head caught fast in the branches, and he was left hanging... One of David's servants saw it, and told Joab. Joab... took three darts and went and thrust them into Absalom's heart while he was still alive in the oak. —2 SAMUEL

She made Samson sleep on her knees; and she called a man to shave off... the locks of his hair, and his strength left him. ...the Philistines seized him and gouged out his eyes, and they brought him down to Gaza. There they bound him with bronze fetters, and put him in prison where he ground at the mill. —JUDGES

(*ENGAÑO.*)
Del Alma, que solicito,
La victoria facilito,
Si vence en esta ocasion
El Engaño á la Razon,
80 Y el Deleite al Apetito.

DELEITE.
Pues partamos, porque creo
Que saca al Alma el Deseo,
Como suele, á recrealla.

CULPA.
Vamos; que desta batalla
85 Espero el lauro y trofeo.
*(Vanse todos por el lado torreon. Decubrese
lo interior del hospital.)*

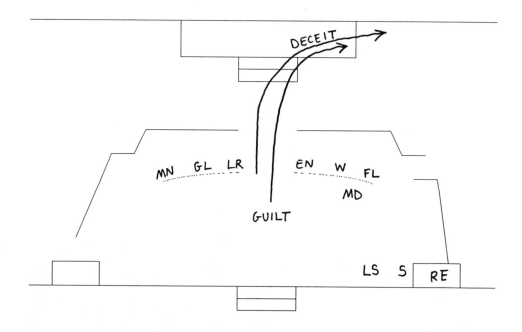

(DECEIT.)
Let Soul be seduced: / /
If, Deceit, defeats Reason,
And Lust defeats Appetite,
Soul's conquest
80   Will be made easier.

LUST.
(Crossing up to GUILT.)
Then let us go, because it seems
That Desire is already enticing Soul
To indulge in pleasures.

GUILT.
Let us go; from this battle
85   I expect laurels and trophies.
> *(Looking to SOUL down stage left.)*
> *(GUILT exits up stage center. The platform represents the tower.)*

Appetite, and an universal wolf...
Shakespeare: *TROILUS AND CRESSIDA*

Each actor in the play must keep in the forefront of his imagination that attributes; e.g. REASON, LUST, Appetite are being referred to as characters. (Appetite, as a character, does not appear in *THE HOUSE OF FOOLS*.) Failure to do so will lead to confusion for the audience.

Religious confraternities at one point took over the Corrales Theatres and gave plays for charity. What they took in at the box office from a public performance went to charity. Thus it may be said that in some respects religious confraternities gave birth to the theatre of Spain. On the other hand, at the time of the Inquisition in Spain, the theatre was much controlled and even bridled by the Inquisition.

ESCENA III

Sale LUZBEL, LA GULA y EL GÉNERO HUMANO, de locos, con acciones de tales y con capirotes de locos. 5

LUZBEL.
Tres partes habia de estrellas
Encima la impírea bola,
Siendo yo de las más bellas;
Mas derribé con la cola

90   La tercera parte dellas.

5 Puede que sea errata. En la escena XV dice: con capirotes de *locos.*

SCENE III
LUCIFER, GLUTTONY, MANKIND, MADNESS.
[SOUL, REASON, ENVY, WORLD, FLESH, LUST]

LUCIFER.
Over the imperial globe,
The stars were divided in three parts;
I was one of the most beautiful stars;
And with my tail
90   I knocked down one third of them.
(Music fades.)

Lucifer shines more brightly than all the other stars. [Quanto splendidor quam cetera sidera fulget Lucifer.]
Ovid: *METAMORPHOSES II*

The interior of the cells becomes brighter. *Locos:* LUCIFER, GLUTTONY, MANKIND break out. First of the three, LUCIFER strides down stage center declaiming.

LUCIFER is proud, boastful; he swings between pride for his actions and bitter remembrance. The challenge to the actor is to make the most of the heightened language, but he must avoid its becoming self-indulgent sound and fury.

[*How art thou fallen, from heaven, oh Lucifer,*
son of the morning!... for thou have said in
thine heart, I will ascend into heaven, I will
exalt my throne above the stars of God... I
will ascend above the heights of the clouds; I
will be like the most high.] —ISAIAH

[*...forever damned with Lucifer...*
Think'est thou that I who saw the face of God,
And tasted the eternal joys of heaven,
Am not tormented with ten thousand hells,
And being deprived of everlasting bliss?]
    Christopher Marlowe (1564-1593): *THE TRAGICAL HISTORY OF DOCTOR FAUSTUS*

[*Him the Almighty Power,*
Hurled headlong flaming from th' ethereal sky
With hideous ruin and combustion down
To bottomless perdition, there to dwell
In adamantine chains and penal fire,
Who durst defy th's omnipotent to arms.]
    John Milton (1608-1674): *PARADISE LOST*

27

GÉNERO HUMANO.
¿Con Dios te pones, ingrato?

LUZBEL.
Pues vos lo quisistes ser
Cuando comistes sin plato.

GÉNERO HUMANO.
Hechizóme una mujer.

LUZBEL.
95   Diós con la mano del gato.

GULA.
Yo me hallé en esa reyerta,
Enmascarada y cubierta.

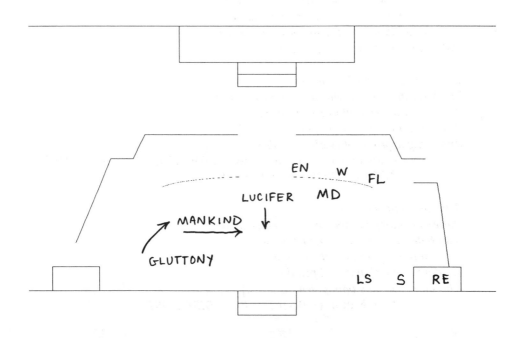

MANKIND.
And you oppose God, ingrate?

LUCIFER.
You also were an ingrate,
When you ate without a plate.

MANKIND.
I was bewitched by a woman.
(Rising.)

LUCIFER.
95   She served you with the hand of a cat.

GLUTTONY.
(Grabbing MANKIND.)
I took part in that encounter,
Well-masked and hidden.

Gluttony and diseases make them. I [Doll Tearsheet] make them not.
Shakespeare: *II HENRY IV*

LUCIFER has explained his role and then goes on to speak of how each loco (vice) comes to be in GUILT's asylum. LUCIFER recalls to MANKIND that he was Adam, saying, *'When you ate without a plate.'* referring to the Garden of Eden. MANKIND's response is a reference to Eve.

GLUTTONY, bedecked with fruit on head and breasts, is thus able to say, *'I took part in that encounter,'* of Adam and Eve.

Each of Valdivielso's characters speaks in metaphors or similes, often biblical images; he provides the actor with heightened language. If the actor has done his homework, has come to understand the biblical references, speaking them with feeling and conviction grounded in knowledge, the Biblical references will not trouble today's audience because of their obscurity for them.

LUZBEL.
Verdad es; bien dices, Gula,
Pues quedó como una mula,
100 Y echáronle de la huerta.

GÉNERO HUMANO.
Habrá en mí arrepentimiento,
Que no le habrá en vos, ni en vos;
Y acabarse ha mi tormento. [6]

LUZBEL.
De querer yo ser par Dios,
105 No lloro, ni me arrepiento.

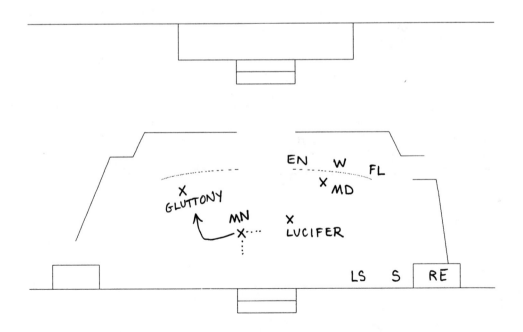

[6] Y acabarse mi tormento.

LUCIFER.

It is true, what you say, Gluttony, /
Because he was like the mule
100   And he was expelled from the Garden.

MANKIND.
(Throws GLUTTONY up center right.)

In me there will be repentance,
But neither in you nor in you will there be repentance;
(Pointing to each in turn.)
And so there will be an end to my torment.

LUCIFER.

Neither do I cry nor repent
105   My wanting to be equal to God.

The actor need not fear expressing emotion. But, it requires his thoughtful analysis as to when it predominates, and when, as Hamlet says to the players, *'In the .. whirlwind of your passion you must acquire and beget a temperance that may give it smoothness.'*

[Moderación en todo, pues hasta en medio del mismo torrente, tempestad y aun podria decir torbellino de tu pasión, debes tener y motrar aquella templanja que hace suave y elegante la expresión.] [7] —*HAMLET, Act III, Sc. 2*

THE HOUSE OF FOOLS is a classic of the Golden Age of Spanish Theatre. Its language requires resonance, or the verse loses all its essence, evaporating if focus and concentration are lacking. Classical plays need a platform or thrust stage, because almost all have elements of the spectacular.

---

7 Shakespeare, W. *HAMLET* [tr. Astrana Marin] Buenos Aires: Espasa-Calpe; Argentina, S.A. 1968

ESCENA IV

Dichos.—*Sale LA INVIDIA de viejo y loco.*

INVIDIA.
¡Qué buena trinca ha salido!

GÉNERO HUMANO.
¿Dónde vas, viejo podrido?

LUZBEL.
¿De qué es, Invidia, el pesar?

INVIDIA.
En los tres no hay qué invidiar.

LUZBEL.
110   ¿De eso la tristeza ha sido?

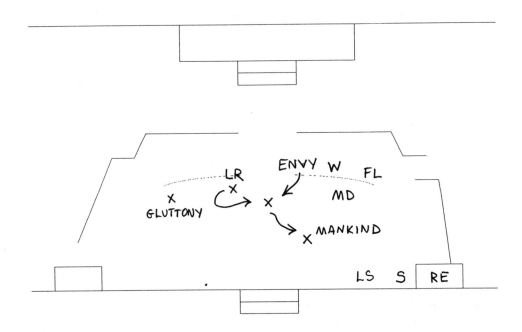

SCENE IV

ENVY, MANKIND, LUCIFER, GLUTTONY
[SOUL, REASON, MADNESS, WORLD, FLESH]

ENVY.
(Enters.)
What a trio we have here!

MANKIND.
Where are you going, rotten old man?

LUCIFER.
(Twisting ENVY's arm behind his back.)
What is your complaint? / Tell me, Envy?

ENVY.
In the three of you there is nothing to envy.

LUCIFER.
(Throwing ENVY across left to MANKIND.)
110   And that is what makes you sad?

As lean-faced Envy in her loathsome cave...
Shakespeare: *II HENRY VI*

ENVY arrives as a very old decayed man, wearing a bejeweled crown with obviously false stones and a ruff of fake ermine.

Valdivielso's characters, as metaphors for human beings, are universal. There is mirrored here the age-old problem of a lack of respect of one human being for another. In *THE HOUSE OF FOOLS* there is something that is contemporary, true for all times: man's struggles, his debates between his instincts and appetites. To give a classical work of today's world, it is necessary that there be a point of contact; the anxieties and the passions of modern man are to be made evident. Hence the simple, abstract style.

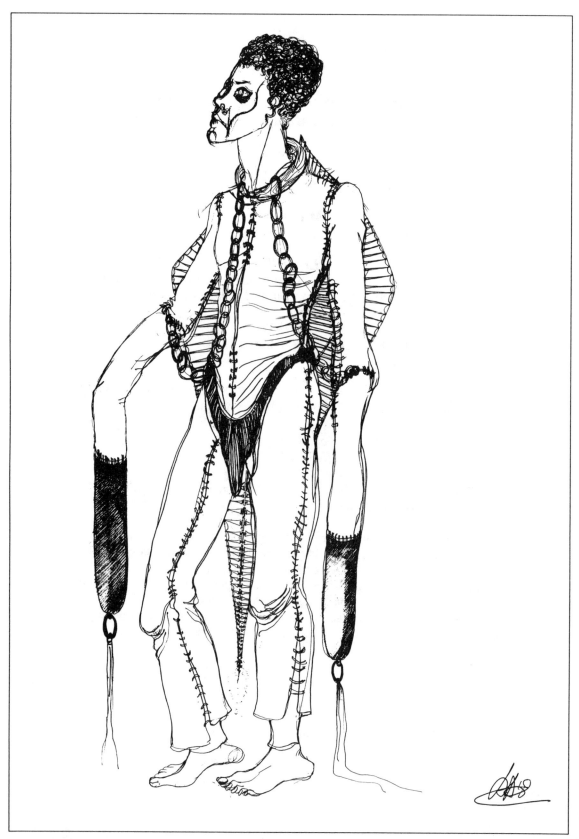

LUCIFER/LUZBEL

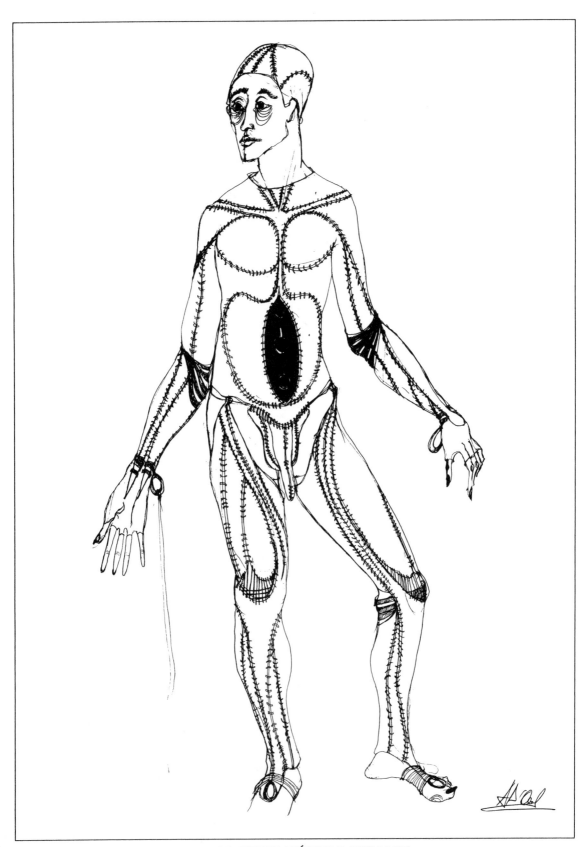

MANKIND/GÉNERO HUMANO

GÉNERO HUMANO.

Véte, Invidia, á los desiertos,
Y haz allá tus desconciertos.
Deja estos tristes cautivos.

GULA.

Viejo, vé á enterrar los vivos
115   Y á desenterrar los muertos.

INVIDIA.

Pues, si una culebra saco,
Yo haré al borracho gloton
Vomite á Céres y á Baco.

GULA.

No me cómo el corazon,
120   Como vos, viejo bellaco.

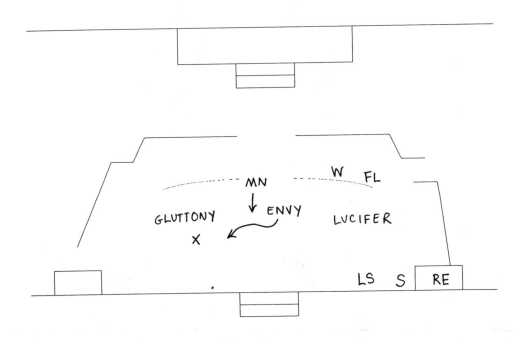

MANKIND.
(Throwing ENVY on top of GLUTTONY's back.)

Go, Envy, / to the desert,
And stir up trouble there. / /
Leave alone these poor captives.

GLUTTONY.

Go, Old Man, bury the living,
115   And unbury the dead.

ENVY.
(Beating GLUTTONY.)

Well, when I take out the snake,
I will make the gluttonous drunkard vomit
Food and wine.

GLUTTONY.

I do not eat my own heart,
120   As you, you sly old man.

Autos sacramentales treat religious themes and ideas allegorically rather than literally. The *auto* is the only symbolist theatre that has survived from the past: it seems to have been the harbinger of the theatres of the absurd and cruelty. In the setting for *THE HOUSE OF FOOLS* it's a completely free style. "I encourage improvisation by you actors; once a theme is created, resolve it. Use nothing more than the physical part of the setting, the levels, the platforms. The atmosphere that envelopes the actor is to be ignored completely, the setting is symbolical."

ESCENA V

Dichos.—*Sale EL MUNDO IMAGINATIVO, con una copa de vino.*

MUNDO.
Bien mi intento trazo y fundo:
Si tantas riquezas tengo
Y es mi poder sin segundo,
A ser emperador vengo.

GÉNERO HUMANO.
125   ¡Qué perdido viene el Mundo!

MUNDO.
¡Hola! ¿no me repondeis?
Es que no me conoceis.
¿Quién ha soltado estos locos?

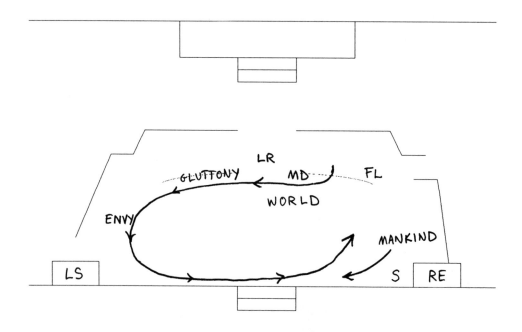

SCENE V

ENVY, MANKIND, LUCIFER, GLUTTONY, WORLD
[SOUL, REASON, MADNESS]

WORLD.
(Enters, circling right to left.)
My intentions are well planned and founded: /
In having the riches I have
And the power without equal.
I have come to be emperor.

MANKIND.
(On his knees crossing right.)
125   How the World has gone astray!

WORLD.
What! Do you not answer me?
Can it be that you do not recognize me?
Who has let these madmen loose?

WORLD crawls around feeling the clothing of the other characters, whatever they're wearing. He feels the fabric and kisses the fabric.

"The *autos sacramentales* were performed at the command of municipalities of the various cities and towns at the festival of Corpus Christi. They were at the height of their success in the age of Lope de Vega... and had become an important part of the religious ceremonies arranged for the solemn sacramental festival to which they were devoted, not only in Madrid, but throughout Spain... *Autos* were acted upon movable cars (*carros*) which passed through the city to the various stations where the representation was to take place... theatres were closed while the *autos* were being presented..." [8]

---

[8] Rennert, H. A. The Spanish Stage During the Time of Lope de Vega. New York: Dover Publications, Inc., 1963.

INVIDIA.
Manda-potros y da-pocos,
130   ¡Qué poco seso teneis!

MUNDO.
¿Qué hace aqui este llora-duelos,
Padre infame de los celos?
¡Vaya fuera, que me enfada!-
Gula, tu cara me agrada;
135   Dame tus brazos.

GULA.
Darélos.

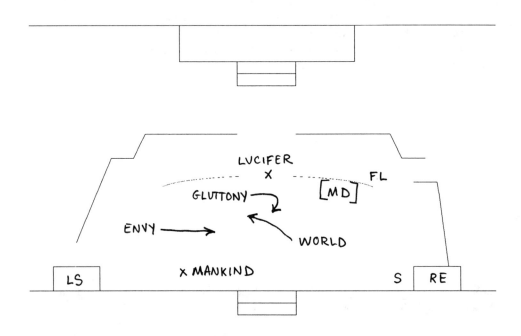

ENVY.
(Crossing to WORLD.)
You talk big and say nothing. /
130   What little brains you have!

WORLD.
(Chasing ENVY back left.)
What is this mourner doing here?
Infamous father of Jealousy!
Get out! You make me angry!- / /
Gluttony, your face pleases me;
135   Embrace me!

GLUTTONY.
(Crossing to WORLD.)
I embrace you!

A Dutch travelers description of a performance of an *auto* in the 17th century included this comment "... Two companies of Players that belonged to Madrid... shut the theatres and for a month represent these Holy Poems [*autos*];... every evening in public on scaffolds erected to that purpose in the streets... in the streets and open air they uses torches to those pieces [*autos*], which in the daily Theatres and within doors they represent without other light than that of the Sun..." [9]

9 Rennert, H. A. The Spanish Stage During the Time of Lope de Vega. New York: Dover Publications, Inc., 1963.

INVIDIA.
Pues, si yo me quito el freno,
Mezclaré al loco poltron
En su gloria mi veneno.

MUNDO.
¡Bríndis!

GULA.
Faró la razon.
(Toma la copa.)

MUNDO.
140   ¡Bueno, á fe de Mundo, bueno!

LUZBEL.
Locos, ¿veis que estoy aquí,
Que casi el mismo Dios fuí?

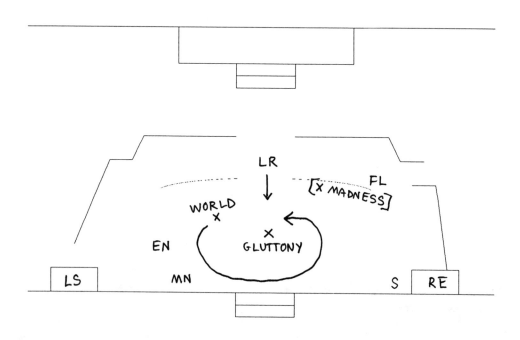

ENVY.
Well, if I take the bit out of my mouth,
I will mix my poison
In the glory of this crazy idler.

WORLD.
*(Crossing past ENVY, picking up GLUTTONY,
he spins around.)*

A toast!

GLUTTONY.
Down with Reason!

WORLD.
(He drinks off the goblet of wine.)

140   Good, / / to the faith of World, good!

LUCIFER.
(Crossing to WORLD and GLUTTONY.)
Fools, don't you see I am here,
Who almost was God?

The *autos sacramentales* are uniquely plays of the Spanish Theatre. Hence the personages of *THE HOUSE OF FOOLS* are at heart Spanish characters, which normally are closed in. True it depends on which play is involved. If it is a work of Garcia Lorca, the conflict is internal. It is a question of a character shutting himself up. Thus the actor must shut himself up in the character's problems, contain them until the character explodes. We have in this *auto* another type; e.g. LUCIFER whose pride causes him to shout out, passion from the inside out. All the fire contained inside explodes, because its force has been constrained inside. [Narros]

Gluttony *La Gula*

GLUTTONY/GULA

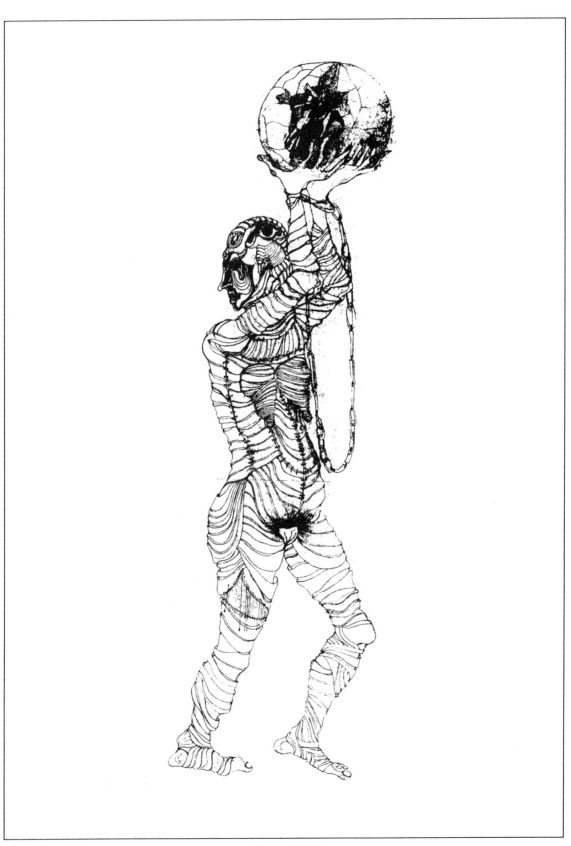

ENVY/INVIDIA

MUNDO.

¿Y tú no ves que aquí estoy,
Y que todo el Mundo soy?

LUZBEL.

145 Pues ¿y qué se me da á mi?
No me debes conocer,
Pues que conmigo te igualas.
¿Sabes lo que quise ser?

MUNDO.

Bien lo muestran esas alas,
150 Sobradas para caer.

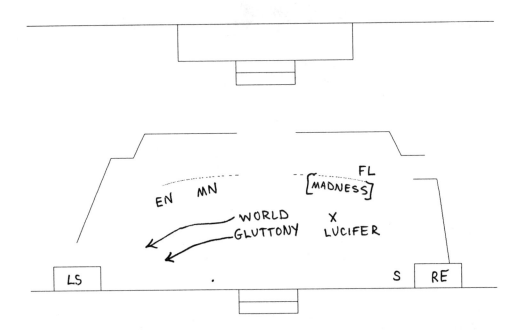

WORLD.
Don't you see that I am here,
And that I am the whole world?

LUCIFER.
(WORLD and GLUTTONY cross right.)

145   Well, what is that to me? /
Should you not know me,
Since you tried to make yourself equal to me,
Don't you know who I tried to be?

WORLD.
Those wings indicate it only too well, since
150   In spite of them you fell.

*Lucifer had banished night and ushered in the shining day, the East wind fell
and moist clouds rose.*
>*[...Nitidum retegente diem noctisque fugante*
>*Tempora Lucifero cadit Eurus, et umida surgunt /Nubila...]*
>Ovid: *METAMORPHOSES VIII*

The language of the original is not naturalistic. The style dictates a very
theatrical form of acting, in key with the costume; e.g. WORLD's costume was
bright yellow, fantastic in design [the actors found the far-out acting style fun!]

>*O Prince, O chief of many throned powers...*
>*...in dreadful deeds*
>*Fearless, endanger'd Heav'ns perpetual King:*
>*And put to proof His High Supremacy...*
>Milton: *PARADISE LOST*

LUZBEL.
¿Querrás decir que caí?

MUNDO.
Pues ¿eso yo no lo vi,
Que te recibí en mis faldas
Cuando, cayendo de espaldas,
155   Veniste á dar sobre mí?

LUZBEL.
Caduco y afeminado,
Azotodo en el diluvio,
Y en Sodoma chamuscado,
Enriza el copete rubio,
160   Que tú morirás quemado.

ESCENA VI

Dichos.—*Sale LA CARNE, con guitarra, loca.*

CARNE.
¡Afuera, afuera! apartad;

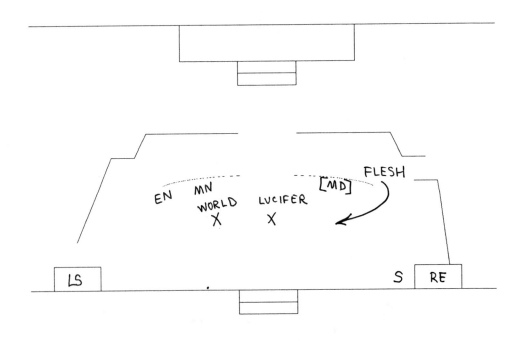

LUCIFER.
Do you dare to say that I fell?

WORLD.
Well, did I not see that?
I caught you in my lap
When you fell on your back
155　Upon me?

LUCIFER.
Decrepit effeminate,
Lashed by the flood,
And scorched in Sodom,
The red summit of Hell will come around you
160　And you will die burning in flames.
(Music up.)

The WORLD tries to make himself the equal to LUCIFER.

SCENE VI

FLESH, WORLD, ENVY, GLUTTONY, LUCIFER, MANKIND
[MADNESS, LUST, SOUL, REASON]

FLESH.
*(Crossing from her cell, crossing down center,
followed by ENVY, WORLD and MANKIND.)*
Get away, get away, go!

Then the Lord rained on Sodom...
brinestone and fire out of heaven. —GENESIS

turning the cities of Sodom and Gomorrah to ashes. —2 PETER

Sodom...undergoing a punishment of eternal fire. —JUDE

...there to dwell (47)
In adamatine chains and penal fire...
Lay vanquished, rowling in the fiery quef...(52)
A dungeon horrible, on all sides round (61)
As great furnace flam'd, yet those flames
No light...
　　　　　　Milton: *PARADISE LOST*

49

(CARNE.)
Pasará mi majestad,
Y adoraréis mi hermosura,
Mi gracia y desenvoltura,
165   Mi donaire y libertad.

MUNDO.
¡Ah Carne! seas bien venida.

INVIDIA.
Despliega, loca, la rueda
Para quitarme la vida;
Que entre perlas, oro y seda,
170   Mi muerte traes escondida.

GLUTTONY

MANKIND   [MADNESS]

WORLD

FLESH   LUCIFER

ENVY

X

LS   S   RE

(FLESH.)
My majesty is going to pass
And you will adore my beauty,
My charm, my ease,
165   My elegance and freedom.
(During the above speech music is down and under by end of speech.)

WORLD.
Ah, Flesh, you are welcome here.

ENVY.
Loose the wheel, Madman,
To take away my life,
Because among the pearls, gold and silk,
170   You carry my death well hidden.

(FLESH, crazed, enters carrying a guitar made from a plastic rib cage. Her costume is rose colored. The colors of the costumes for the individual characters often are symbolic of their different aspects: e.g. hence the pink color predominates for FLESH.)

Flesh stays no farther reason...
Shakespeare: *SONNET IVI*

As a director my goal is to liberate the actor, to create a state of mind, a special explosion of a state of mind. [Narros]

GÉNERO HUMANO.
¡Oh mi mayor enemigo,
De mis pecados castigo,
Pues, que quiera, que no quiera,
Abrazado á esta hechicera,
175   He de llevarla conmigo!

GULA.
Carne, de abrazarte tengo.

CARNE.
Dame, Gula, mil abrazos,
Que contigo mi entretengo,
Y en acquestos bellos lazos
180   A estar en mi esfera vengo.

INVIDIA.
¡Qué trae de galas lá loca,
Con que á los necios provoca!
¡Y entre sus afeites vanos,
Trae más podre y más gusanos
185   Que tiene listas su toca!

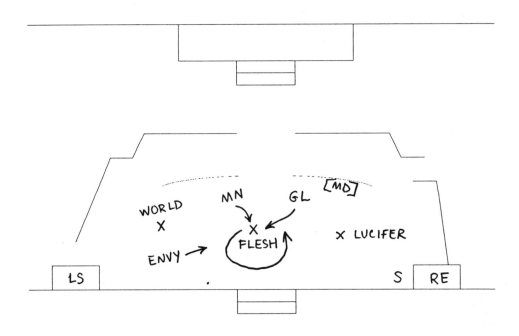

52

MANKIND.
(Holding FLESH from behind.)
Oh, my greatest enemy,
I am punished for my sins
Because, whether she likes it or not,
I must go arm in arm with this witch,
175 And I will have to take her with me!

GLUTTONY.
(Crossing center.)
Flesh, I throw my arms around you.

FLESH.
(Going seductively to GLUTTONY.)
Gluttony, give me a thousand embraces,
I will amuse myself with you,
And in those lovely entwinings,
180 I will come into my own world.

ENVY.
(Crossing to FLESH)
What finery the crazy one wears,
With which to tempt the dunces
And among her vain adornments
She carries more pus and more worms
185 That she has laid up in her headdress.

MANKIND reveals his addiction to FLESH. Likewise, GLUTTONY loves FLESH, who in turn responds to GLUTTONY. The action demonstrates the metaphor.

We're working with a translation of a classic text by a poet whom Lope de Vega not only respected but admired. However, the actor may find in the text, for example, onomatopoeia; verbal effects he can use and exploit to his advantage.

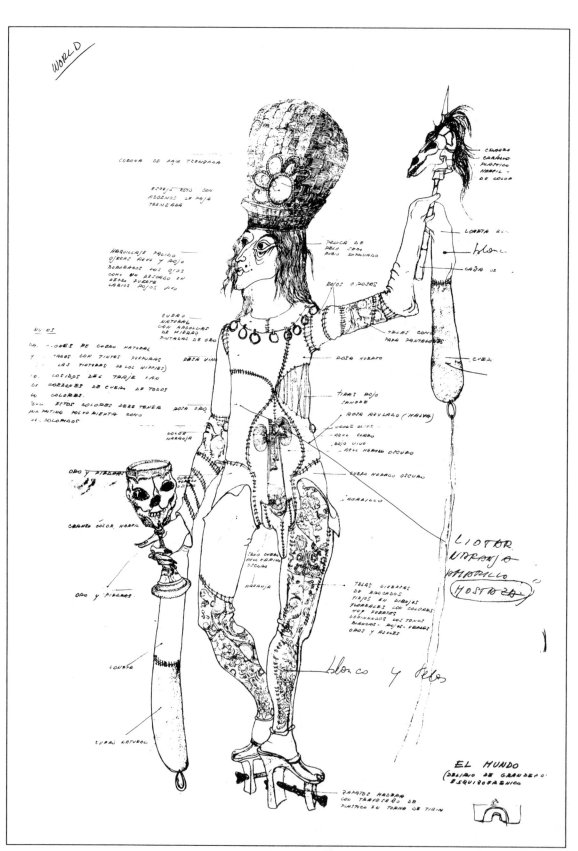

WORLD/MUNDO

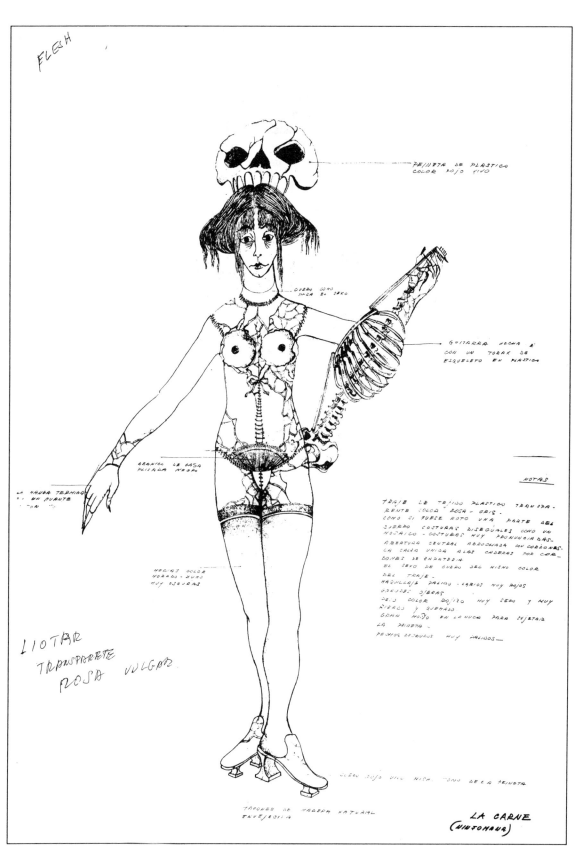

FLESH/CARNE

CARNE.

¿Eché yo á Adan del vergel,
Y dí favor á Caín
Para que matase á Abel?
¿O como vos, viejo ruin,
190   Vendí al hijo de Raquel?

INVIDIA.

No; mas ¿quién quedó burlada,
Cuando, en lascivia abrasada
De acquese Josef hebreo,
Halló, en vez de su deseo,
195   Una capa con nonada? [10]

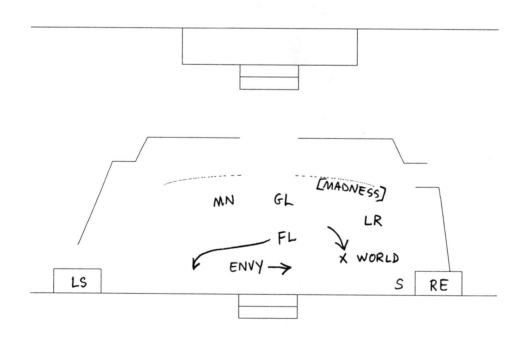

[10] Una copa con nonada.

FLESH.
(Chasing ENVY left.)

Did I not throw Adam
      Out of the Garden of Flowers /
Or give favor to Cain,
In order that he could kill Abel? / /
Or like you, vile Old Man,
190   I sold the son of Rachel?

ENVY.

No. More than that, who was left deceived?
When lewdness, Potiphar's wife burned
For that Hebrew Joseph,
His brothers found, instead of what they expected,
195   An empty cup.

Flesh pridefully, attributes to herself involvement in the eating of the Tree of Knowledge in the Garden of Eden. ... the woman, seeing that the tree was good for food... ate of it's fruit, she gave some to her husband, and he also ate... the Lord God drove man out of the Garden of Eden... —GENESIS

Cain said to Abel, "let us go out to the field," and when they were there, Cain rose up against his his brother and killed him. —GENESIS

Rachel conceived and bore a son, and she called his name Joseph... "let us sell our brother to the Ishmaelites," Judah said,... his brothers heeded him, and when the caravan passed by, they drew Joseph out of the pit, and sold him to the Ishmaelites for shekels of silver. —GENESIS

The images in Spanish in respect to Joseph are troublesome. In their compactness they refer to the efforts of Potiphar's wife who had lewdly attempted to seduce Joseph. Joseph, indeed, had resisted. For rejecting her he was thrown into prison. Later after he'd been restored and raised up by the Pharaoh he had received his brothers during the famine and there is the reference above to the silver cup.

... Joseph commanded the steward of his house, "fill the men's [his brothers] sacks with food, as much as they can carry, and put my cup, the silver cup, in the sack of the youngest." —GENESIS

MUNDO.

De tu discrecion me espanto,
Carne, y del caso que has hecho
De quien está loco tanto.
Entrate en mi blando pecho,
200   Rendido á tu dulce canto.

INVIDIA.

Fanfarron, mucho me enfada
Ver tu atrevimiento loco,
Por tu apariencia dorado.
Hablas mucho y haces poco;
205   Prometes, y no das nada.
¡Habla el vano cascabel,
Muy vestido de oropel,
Con que á los bobos engaña;
Siendo su cetro de caña, [11]
210   Su corona de papel!

MUNDO.

Eres tú mayor tormento,
Y quien colgó del saúco
Al apóstol avariento.

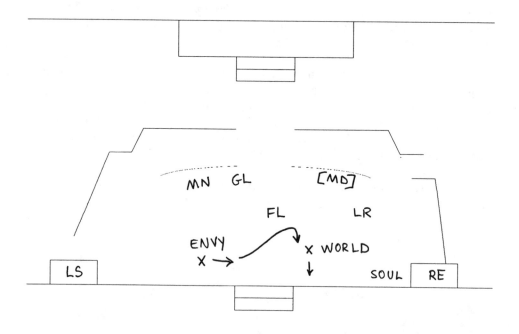

[11] Siendo su centro de caña.

WORLD.

(Crossing down right.)

I am astonished at your wit, Flesh,
And at the point you have made,
Of one who is so mad.
Enter into my tender heart,
200   Spent by your sweet song.

ENVY.

(Crossing to WORLD.)

Braggart, your insane daring
Makes me angry
With your golden appearance.
You talk too much and do too little;
205   You promise much and give little. /
The vain tinkle bell speaks,
Dressed to the hilt in tinsel,
With which to deceive fools,
But your scepter is a reed,

(Knocking off WORLD's crown,)

210   And your crown is only paper!

WORLD.

(Kneeling and getting crown.)

You are your greatest torment,
And the one who hung from the elderberry
The avaricious apostle Judas.

An introspective actor tends to be slow. A serious flaw. Think as you speak, not before! [Narros]

[Judas] *...throwing down the pieces of silver in the temple, he departed; and he went and hanged himself.* —MATTHEW

The costumes worn by the players were of the richest and costliest stuffs. In 1624, when Antonio de Prado presented two of the *autos* at Madrid, it was especially stipulated that he provide the costumes for the said *autos* and that they be of brocade and velvet and damask and satan, trimmed with gold. All to be new. [12]

---

[12] Rennert, H. A. The Spanish Stage During the Time of Lope de Vega. New York: Dover Publications, Inc., 1963.

INVIDIA.
¿Quién sois vos, galan caduco?

MUNDO.
215   Quien soy.

INVIDIA.
Un loco hace ciento.
¿Quiéste conmigo igualar,
Que hasta el cielo me subí,
Y hice á Luzbel levantar?

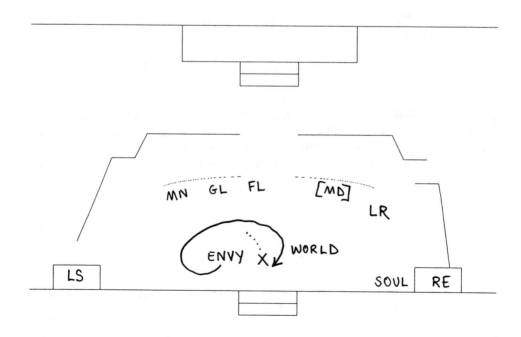

ENVY.
Who do you think you are, decrepit lover?

WORLD.
(Kneeling center.)
215   Decrepit Lover: that's me!

ENVY.
(Circling WORLD.)
One madman makes a hundred. / /
Do you want to make yourself equal
(Crossing center.)
With me, / who rose to the Heavens,
And made Lucifer rise also?

Cervantes gives a description of a traveling company which was presenting an *auto:...* "*The first figure that presented itself to Don Quixote's eyes was that of Death itself with a human face; next to it was an angel with large painted wings, and at one side an emperor, with a crown, to all appearance of gold, on his head... Belonging to this company was a clown and a mummer's dress with a great number of bells and armed with three blown ox-bladders at the end of a stick.*" [13]

For a description of the actors trials and sufferings, an actor speaks from experience: "*A slave in Algiers has a better life than the actor. A slave works all day, but he sleeps at night; he has only one or two masters to please. When he does what he is commanded, he has fulfilled his duty. But actors are up at dawn and write and study from five o'clock till nine, and from nine till twelve they are constantly rehearsing. They dine and then go to the Comedia; leave the theatre at seven, and when they want rest they may be called by the council or the mayors whom they must serve whenever it pleases them.*" [14]

[13] Rennert, H. A. The Spanish Stage During the Time of Lope de Vega. New York: Dover Publications, Inc., 1963.

[14] Ibid.

LUZBEL.

220   Y áun, para abrazarte á tí,
Vino el cielo á reventar. [15]
Tanto mi culpa le carga,
Que no la pudo tener,
Por ser culpa que le amarga.

GULA.

Pesada debió de ser,
225   Pues que se echó con la carga.—

CARNE.

¿Quieres conmigo danzar,
Mundo?

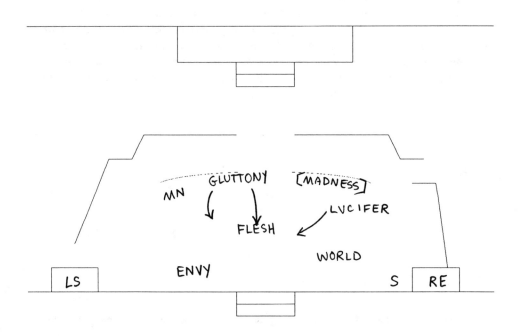

[15] Vino el cielo reventar.

LUCIFER.

I embraced you
220   The Heavens burst open.
So big a crime it was.
My sin weighted down upon God so much
That He could not hold it,

GLUTTONY.
(Music up.)

It must have weighed a lot,
225   For they threw you out with the load.

FLESH.
(Crossing down center.)

Would you like to dance with me,
World?

Music and dancing seem to have been indispensable accompaniments of the *commedia* from the earliest times. They were also a necessary part of all religious festivals and representations, and we'd be sure no *auto* was performed without music and dancing for the delectation of the spectators... As early as the beginning of the Christian era Spanish women were celebrated as dancers... Most of the players in a theatrical company also sang and danced besides acting..., and many of the contracts between manager and player stipulated that the players act, sing, and dance (*Pararepresentar, cantar y bailar*). [16]

---

[16] Rennert, H. A. The Spanish Stage During the Time of Lope de Vega. New York: Dover Publications, Inc., 1963.

MUNDO.
　　Si, mi amada: empieza.—
Gula, ¿quiéresme ayudar?

GULA.
Andaseme la cabeza.

INVIDIA.
230　¡No hicieras tu vientre altar!

CARNE.
Pues da quien dance por tí.

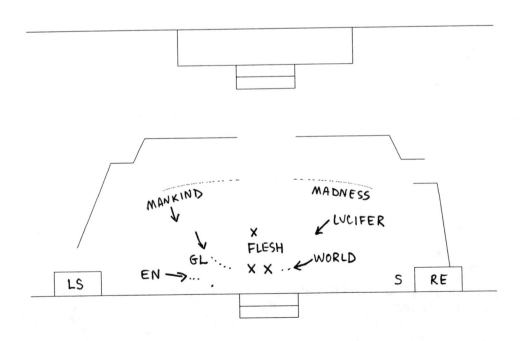

WORLD.
Yes, my love, begin —
Gluttony, would you like to help me?

GLUTTONY.
My head is spinning!

ENVY.
230   Don't make an altar of your belly!

FLESH.
Then choose who will dance for you.

The dances were frequently of such a loose and licentious nature that they caused great scandal and obliged the authorities to intervene and suppress them. Of these *Bayles* the most famous as well as the most voluptuous and indecent, it seems was the *Zarabanda*, first introduced about 1588.

Sarabande, "a stately and courtly dance of Spanish origin, 17th century" [Webster's Dictionary] also familiarly "a noisy and tumultuous dance of Spanish origin." [Larousse]

"It is therefore most strange that, in spite of its notorious immorality, the *Zarabanda* should have been danced at the festival of Corpus Christi in Seville in 1593, when the *autos* were represented by the company of the celebrated Jerónimo Velazquez. Many were the remonstrances against this dance, especially by churches." [17]

17 Rennert, H. A. The Spanish Stage During the Time of Lope de Vega. New York: Dover Publications, Inc., 1963.

GULA.

Sí haré; danzará por mí,
A la abajada de un cerro,
Al rededor de un becerro,
235   Todo un pueblo, á quien rendi.
Y si no, daré una dama,
Que es la hija de Herodías,
Que sabe un baile de fama.

CARNE.

Ésas son hazañas mias:
240   Tales el mundo las llama.—
¿Quiés danzar?
           (A LUZBEL.)

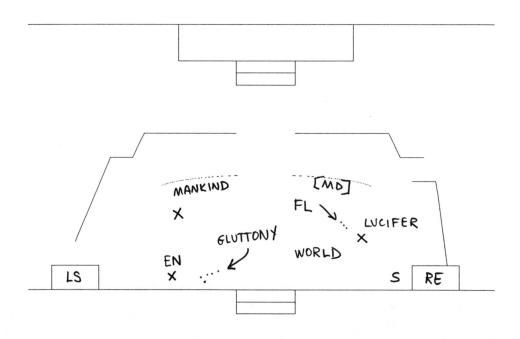

GLUTTONY.
(To ENVY.)

Yes, I choose it,
All the people whom I conquered will dance for me,
On the slopes of a hill,
235   Around a Golden Calf,
And if not, I will bring forth a lady
Who is the daughter of Herodias,
Who knows a famous dance.
(Music up.)

FLESH.

Those are *my* deeds: / /
240   Such as the world calls them —
(To LUCIFER.)
Do you wish to dance?

"*It is not shouting for victory, or the cry of defeat, but the sound of singing I hear*" [said Moses]. *As he came near the camp and saw the calf and the dancing, Moses' anger grew hot... He took the calf they had made, burnt it, ground it to powder, scattered it upon the water, and made the people of Israel drink it.* — GENESIS

The daughter of Herodias danced before the company, and pleased Herod, so that he promised with an oath to give her whatever she might ask. Prompted by her mother, she said, "Give me the head of John the Baptist on a platter." — MATTHEW

LUZBEL.
El *Saltarelo.*

INVIDIA.
¿Ya no saltaste del cielo?

LUZBEL.
¿Quién es el vil que me ultraja?

INVIDIA.
Mejor es danzar la *Baja.*

LUZBEL.
245   Danzaréisla vos, mochuelo.

GÉNERO HUMANO.
Una vez me hiciste el són,
Y, con Eva de la mano,
Danzamos el *estordion.*

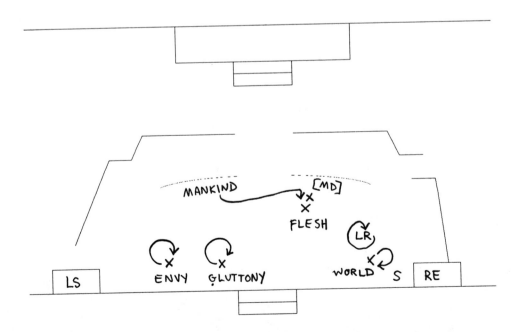

LUCIFER.
The *Saltarelo*. The jumping jig!

ENVY.
Have you not already leaped from Heaven?

LUCIFER.
Who is the villain who insults me?

ENVY.
It is better that you dance the *Baja* a LOW one!

LUCIFER.
245   Dance it yourself, you harpy.
(Music.)

MANKIND.
(Behind FLESH.)
Once you called the tune
And, with Eve's hand in mine
We danced the *Estordion*.

MANKIND with his speech identifies himself with Adam, husband to Eve in the Garden of Eden, and since the dances were sometimes thought of as being too secular and even lewd; there is a metaphor here with the sinning and expulsion from the Garden of Eden.

The *Salterelo* is a skipping and jumping dance, thus the comparison with what happened to LUCIFER in his falling from Heaven. The *Baja*, as indicated, is a low bowing dance. The *Estordion* is a pre-classic Spanish dance. [18]

18 Rennert, H. A. The Spanish Stage During the Time of Lope de Vega, New York: Dover Publications, Inc., 1963.

INVIDIA.
Y os volvieron el *Villano*
250   Con la azada y azadon.

GÉNERO HUMANO.
¡Hola, loco! poco á poco.

INVIDIA.
Yo no sé quién es más loco
Que el que, rompiendo sus fueros,
Sin pensallo se halló en cueros,
255   Y un ángel que le hacia el coco.

CARNE.
¿Qué quiés, Mundo?

MUNDO.
    La Pabana,
Y sé el *Caballero* bien.

INVIDIA.
Pavon de presuncion vana
Y caballero tambien;
260   Pero soislo de agua y lana.

70

ENVY.
And they ended up dancing the rustic dance,
250   Digging and delving.

MANKIND.
Hey, fool! Take it easy.

ENVY.
(To MANKIND)
I don't know who is more insane
Than the one who, throwing away his pride,
And without caring, finds himself stark naked,
255   And with an angel flirting with him.

FLESH.
What do *you* want, World?

WORLD.
The *Pavan*.
And I know a courtly dance well, the *Caballero*.

ENVY.
(Trips WORLD.)
A big peacock of vain presumption;
And a gentleman too!
260   But you've feet of clay.

The Lord God drove man out of the Garden of Eden, to till the ground from which he was taken. —GENESIS

The *Caballero* and the *Pavan* are all dances. The *Pavan* can be a court dance for couples, noble and slow at 2/4 time followed by a *gaillarde*, a lively dance. [Larousse]

The original score was recorded in Spain by musicians of the *Orquesta Nacional de Madrid*. Music had been composed and conducted by Carmelo Bernaola.

71

MUNDO.
¿No harémos que acquéste calle?

CARNE.
¿Quieres conmigo salir,
Y mostrarnos tu buen talle?

INVIDIA.
Por vos se puede decir:
265   *La loca lo tañe y lo saca á la calle.*

CARNE.
La *Zarabanda* inventé
Y la *Chacoha* saqué;
Pero todo me es cansado.

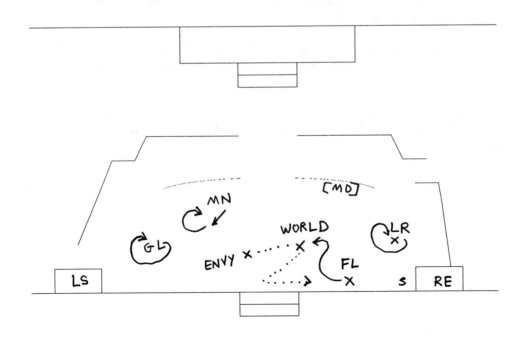

> ### WORLD.
> Can't we make this fellow shut up?
>
> ### FLESH.
> *(Dancing right to left with WORLD, followed by ENVY.)*
> Do you want to start off with me
> And show us your fine figure?
>
> ### ENVY.
> Of you it could be said:
> 265 Flesh plays the Guitar
>   And dances then out into the street.
>
> ### FLESH.
> I invented the *Sarabande*
> And I brought out the *Chaconne*;
> But I'm tired of them all.

The *Zarabanda* [*Sarabande*] was followed by other, and, it is to be feared, not much more decorous dances. Among the most celebrated were the *Chacona* [*Chaconne*]... Cervantes and Lope de Vega were both great admirers of the popular dances, and the former has introduced a *Chacone* in his novel *THE ILLUSTRIOUS KITCHEN MAID*, which is danced by Muleters and Galician Girls, the refrain of which is:

> *The Chacona is a treasure:*
> *Makes of life a real pleasure...*
> *Oft Chacona makes its entry*
> *Through the chinks of convent cell,*
> *And that tranquil virtue flutters*
> *Which in sacred haunts should dwell.* [19]

Urban and rustic dances are contrasted. The directors goal was to have the actors learn the basic different dance forms and then execute them in character. A Madman doesn't have to dance accurate steps, but the dance form within disorder must be apparent. [Narros]

[19] Rennert, H. A. The Spanish Stage During the Time of Lope de Vega. New York: Dover Publications, Inc., 1963.

GULA.
Vaya el *Arre acá, Pienado.*

CARNE.
270   Ése un carretero fué.
           (*Bailan, y dice LUCIFER.*)

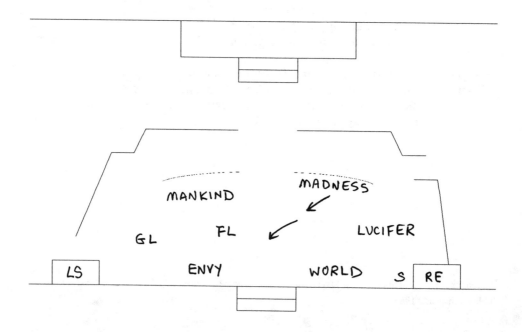

GLUTTONY.
Let's do a livelier jig.

FLESH.
270   That was a dance for mule drivers!
(As they dance, MADNESS awakes and rises, brandishing his whips.)
(Music stops.)

...The *Chacona*... was no less vigorously opposed by the clergy than the *Sarabande* had been. In 1613 we find the Catalan Jesuit... speaking of them in these terms: 'In a certain city in Spain there was current at one time one of those songs which they call the Chacona of such licentiousness that it created the greatest scandal... '

...The lascivious dances... , making their appearance about 1588 became one of the most powerful attractions... urged on by the applause of the dreaded groundlings and of the dissolute 'noble', these dances were carried to a point which sorely tried the conservers of the public morals, which latter were by no means exalted in that not overscrupulous age." [20]

The *Chaconne* is in 3-time; its origins attributed to Mexico, appearing in Spain in the 16th century. [Larousse]

---

[20] Rennert, H. A. The Spanish Stage During the Time of Lope de Vega. New York: Dover Publications, Inc., 1963.

LUZBEL.
¡Hola! la Locura viene
Con el rebenque en la mano,
Y de sacudir nos tiene.

GULA.
¡Podrá esperalla un alano!

CARNE.
275   ¡A huir, que huir nos conviene!

ESCENA VII

Dichos.—*Sale LA LOCURA, con un azote, y dales.*

LOCURA.
¡Oh locos desvanecidos,
Temerarios, atrevidos!

LUZBEL.
¡Mata-perros, no nos des!

LOCURA.
Yo os castigaré despues,
280   En vuestras jaulas metidos.
        (*Vanse todos.* Ciérrase el hospital.)

[MADNESS]

LR
GL   ENVY   WORLD
  MN MADNESS FL
       X

LS   S RE

LUCIFER.
Hey! Madness comes
With whip in hand.
He'll beat us!

GLUTTONY.
We can probably expect a Mastiff next.
(All begin to run.)

FLESH.
275   Let's get out of here; it's best
To get out of here!

SCENE VII

MADNESS, LUCIFER, FLESH, GLUTTONY, MANKIND, WORLD,
ENVY
[LUST, SOUL, REASON]

MADNESS.
(MADNESS flails about.)
(whipping, whipping, whipping)
Oh you vain locos, /
Reckless ones, impudent ones!

LUCIFER.
Rat catcher, stop hitting us!
(MADNESS chases the madmen into their
cells.)

MADNESS.
I'll punish you later
280   As soon as you're locked up in your cells.
(MADNESS hits MANKIND's hand.)
(He sleeps up center.)
(All locos returned to their cells: the asylum is
closed.)

MADNESS has flailed about him, threatening punishment to all; his goal
is to lock them up in their cells. The *locos* scatter, and before his assault they
fly to their cells. They may be seen by the audience behind their grilles at all
times, although locked in their cells.

ESCENA VIII

Sale EL ENGAÑO, por la parte del torreon, y LA CULPA, en traje de mujer, con la escopeta cargada al hombro.

ENGAÑO.

Culpa, sin tí mal me va,
Porque sin tí nada valgo;
Que la Razon voces da.
Y necio y corrido salgo
285   De que rendida no está.

CULPA.

No quise llegarme cerca,
Sino andarme por la cerca,
Para en hallando ocasion,
Poner la cuerda al fogon
290   Y deslumbrar esta terca.
¿Cómo el Deleite lo ha hecho

ENGAÑO.

Al Apetito movió
Con el gusto y el provecho;
Mas la Razon nunca dió
295   A sus hechizos el pecho.

SCENE VIII

GUILT, DECEIT, LUST, SOUL, REASON
[MADNESS, GLUTTONY MANKIND, LUCIFER, ENVY, WORLD, FLESH]

DECEIT.
(To GUILT, who appears on upstage center platform.)
Guilt, without you all goes badly for me, /
Because without you I am good for nothing;
Reason has more power over Soul
And I look like a fool,
280   Ashamed, for not having conquered her.

GUILT.
(Crossing down center.)
I did not wish to come near,
But walked around the wall,
In order to find the chance
To light the fire
(Gestures down left to where REASON sits.)
285   And dazzle this stubborn one.
How did Lust do?

DECEIT.
He moved Appetite
With pleasure and profit;
But Reason never gave
290   Her heart to his charms

DECEIT is ashamed for not having conquered SOUL. GUILT reacts with fury, crossing down stage from the platform and steps. Then GUILT crosses on a diagonal to down left to REASON. GUILT fumes.

CULPA.
De aquesa necia presumo
Que, por bachillera y sábia,
Levanta esas torres de humo,
Pues abrásala la rabia. [21]

295   Con que al infierno perfumo.
Llama, Engaño, á la razon,
Que se asome al torreon,
Y déjame hacer á mí,
Pues armada traigo acquí

300   La escopeta *sugestion*.

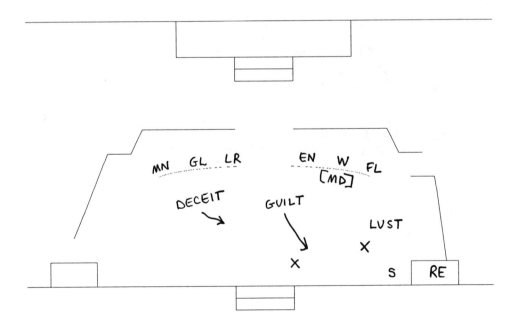

[21] Pues abrasalla la rabia.

GUILT.
(Moving closer to REASON.)
Of that Foolish One, I presume that,
Being a Bachelor of Arts and a sage,
She builds castles in the air,
Then her rage sets her on fire,
295   With which I perfume hell. / /
(GUILT has reached SOUL.)
Call Reason,
To appear at the turret,
And / / leave it to me,
For I am armed here /
300   With the gun, *Suggestion.*

With this scene of overt action, the issue is joined. There is open confrontation between opposing factions: GUILT pits herself against REASON. DECEIT has failed; LUST, alone, has been too weak to capture and subvert SOUL.

As GUILT moves toward REASON, she bristles with rage. With an elongated *'and'* followed by *'leave it to me,'* she is resolved to act. Spurring herself on, she is boastful of her gun and its powers.

The challenge to the actor is to achieve balance. In the whirlwind of the character's passion, rage (to paraphrase Shakespeare) [*turbellino de tu passión*], the text may get strangulated and the intention of the speech lost to the audience. Physical movement helps the actor as GUILT takes center stage, moving down stage, crossing right to take aim at REASON *on the speech.*

(*CULPA.*)

Trae esta fiera escopeta,
Entre lascivas pelotas,
Pólvora infernal secreta,
De las regiones remotas
305 Que mi grandeza sujeta;
Y trae de Dios el olvido,
Y el papel de amor rompido;
Trae el desprecio del cielo,
Que sirve al necio de velo,
310 Que encubre lo que ha perdido.

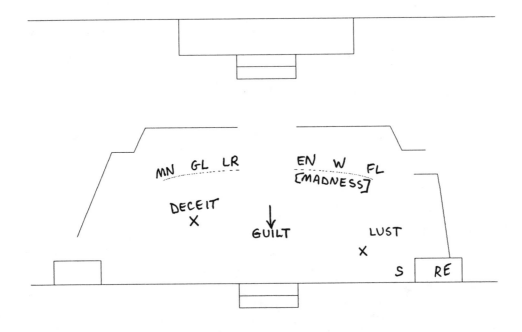

(*GUILT.*)
(Crossing left center, with gun raised.)

This fierce gun carries
In its lascivious pellets
Infernal / secret gun powder
From remote regions,
305   Only my strength keeps it in check.
It brings from God forgetfulness
And the Power of betrayed love. /
It brings scorn from Heaven,
Which is of use to the stupid
310   To hide what has been lost.
(Kneeling on downstage knee.)

The character GUILT as characterized by Valdivielso, is cynical, selfish, and sly. DECEIT is only too clever by half; he feels privileged to be in service to GUILT.

Valdivielso demonstrates artistic foresight in the way in which he anticipates an action, then presents it, and, finally, harkens back to it. At the opening of the play GUILT had set in motion an action; then she left the stage, but her presence is felt throughout the scene of the dancing *locos*. The anticipation of what GUILT will do ends when she returns to the scene of action.

Valdivielso exerts special dramatic expertise in versification... his greatest range is evident in his pieces for the theatre.

83

ENGAÑO.
¡Ah Razon!

RAZON.
(Dentro.)
¿Llamas, Engaño?

ENGAÑO.
Al homenaje te asoma. [22]

RAZON.
(Dentro.)
Querrás hacerme algun daño.

CULPA.
(Al ENGAÑO.)
Caerá la simple paloma,
315   Aunque pese al Desengaño.

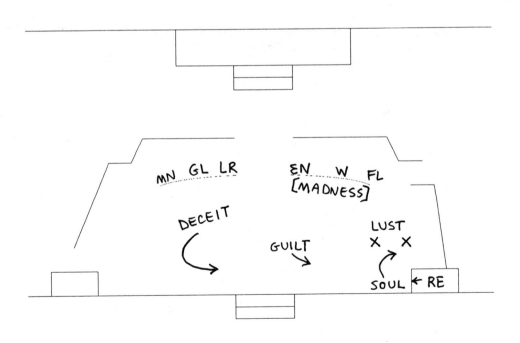

[22] Al homenaje asoma.

DECEIT.
(Crossing down right.)

Ah, Reason.

REASON.
(Stands.)

Do you call, Deceit?

DECEIT.

Appear for homage.

REASON.

You will do me some harm.

GUILT.
(An aside to DECEIT.)

The naïve dove will fall,
315   Although it grieves Disillusion.

DECEIT is hesitant. GUILT reacts to his timidity, gestures to him to get on with it. On GUILT's aside to DECEIT, less intensity, less voice.

REASON down right has been seated, immobile throughout the previous scenes; she stirs as if awakened by DECEIT's call. She is suspicious, fearful for SOUL, and is on guard.

[Disillusion is referred to as a character, but she does not appear.]

[In the film *EL GRECO*, this scene of calling to REASON is where the performance of *THE HOUSE OF FOOLS* begins. Miguel Narros staged Valdivielso's *auto*, for the film, in front of the cathedral of Toledo.]

ESCENA IX

EL ENGAÑO, LA CULPA.— *Asómase LA RAZON á las almenas.*

RAZON.
Entre esa inocente piel
He visto disimulado
Un basilisco cruel,
La muerte en vaso dorado,
320   Y el absintio entre la miel.

ENGAÑO.
A fe, que eres muy discreta.

RAZON.
¿Por soberbia quiés cogerme?

ENGAÑO.
    (Ap. á LA CULPA.)
Requiere aquesa escopeta.—
¿Que hace el Alma?
        (A LA RAZON.)

RAZON.
Holgarse en verme.

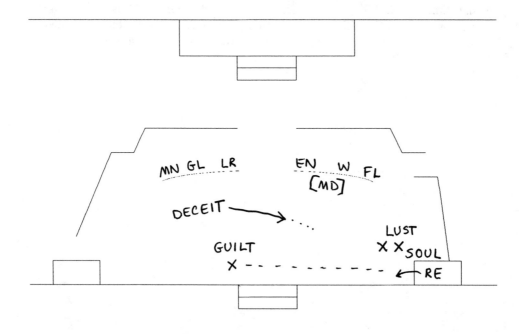

86

SCENE IX

DECEIT, GUILT, REASON, LUST, SOUL
[MADNESS, GLUTTONY, MANKIND, LUCIFER, ENVY, WORLD,
FLESH]

REASON.
Within that innocent fur
I have seen hidden
A cruel basilisk,
Death in a golden glass,
320   An absinthe among the honey.

DECEIT.
(Crossing right.)
By my faith, you are very witty.

REASON.
Do you want to catch me being proud?

DECEIT
(Crossing to make an aside to GUILT.)
Ready that gun —-
(Stopping; then crossing down center to REA-SON.)
What is Soul doing?

REASON.
Rejoicing to see me.

Lines are sometimes divided between two characters, emphasizing a certain snappiness in the dialogue and lightening the weight of the verse at the same time.

ENGAÑO.

325   ¿Y el Deleite?

RAZON.
La inquieta.

ENGAÑO.
¿Está con ella abrazado?

RAZON.
No, ni el cielo lo permita.

ENGAÑO.
¿Un niño te da cuidado?
(Ruido dentro.)

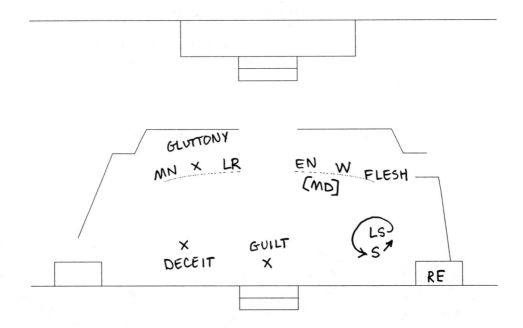

DECEIT.

325   And Lust?

REASON.
He disturbs her.

DECEIT.
Has he his arms around her?

REASON.

No, / / nor would Heaven permit it.

DECEIT.
You are afraid of the Christ child?

LUST and SOUL laugh shrilly, provoking laughter from GLUTTONY and FLESH within their cells. All up stage behind their grilles are observing the action down stage, intensely awaiting the outcome of the contest between GUILT and REASON. Though they are mostly silent out of fear for MADNESS and his whip, (who is fast asleep), they are rooting for LUST to seduce SOUL. Thus there would be a new inmate in the asylum.

RAZON.

330 ¡Ay, que dentro suena grita!
¡Triste! burlada he quedado.
El Deleite la enamora.

ENGAÑO.

Buena ocasion es agora;
¡Dispara, Culpa, dispara!
(Dispara LA CULPA, y se ve al ALMA y al DELEITE atravesar el cercado.)

RAZON.

Alma querida, repara...

CULPA.

335 Y tú presumida, llora.

RAZON.

¡Ah, Deleite, de error lleno!
¿Así, infame, das veneno
A quien tu gusto celebra?

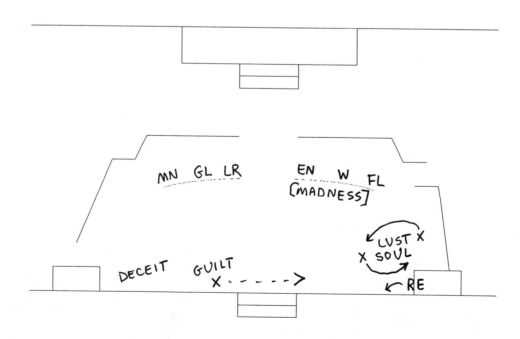

REASON.

330 Ay! I hear cries from within!
How sad! I have been tricked,
Lust is making love to her.

DECEIT.
(Crossing to GUILT.)
Now is a good chance,
Shoot, Guilt, shoot!
(GUILT shoots.)

REASON.
Soul, my dear, stop...
(REASON is shot.)

GUILT.
(Rising.)
335 And you, conceited fool, weep.

REASON.
(Falling to her knees.)
Ah, Lust, full of sin!
Is that the way you give poison
To whomever you please, vile one?

Having shot REASON, wounding her, GUILT rises arrogantly and laughs.

LUST has drawn SOUL to him. She is entranced, he waltzes her around, he embraces her, he kisses her on the neck. He pulls her to the ground as he embraces her.

Avoid taking the words of speech faster than you, the actor, can think. The response of the audience begins to direct you.

(*RAZON.*)

¡Sacude, Alma, la culebra

340   Que se te ha entrado en el seno!

Mira cercadas de espinas

Esas flores engañosas,

A quien ciega te avecinas;

El cuchillo entre las rosas,

345   El fuego entre clavellinas.

Deja aquese amigo aleve,

Muladar lleno de nieve,

Enhechizada manzana,

Muerte dulce, sombra vana,

350   Falsa risa, sueño breve.

¡Que te abrasas! ¡que te quemas,

Y, el pobre barquillo roto,

Por un mar de fuego remas!

Ciego llevas el piloto;

355   ¡Bien es que perderte temas!

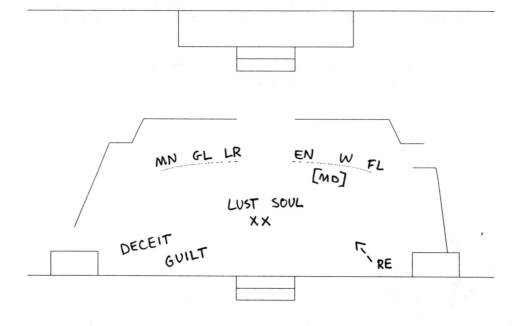

(REASON.)

(Falling to her knees.)

Soul, shake off the snake
340   Which has entered your breast!
See how enclosed by thorns are
Those deceitful flowers,
Which you blindly live by;
A knife among the roses,
345   A fire among Pinks. / /
Leave that treacherous friend,
A dung heap masked with snow,
Bewitched apple, sweet death,
Vain shadow,
350   False laughter, brief dreams.
You will be set afire! You will be burned!
And, the poor little broken boat
You will have to row on a sea of fire! / /
You have a blind pilot with you;
355   Well might you fear you are lost!

The need for variety arises in REASON's long speech, as much a question of balance. REASON is distracted, grieving, but if the character luxuriates in the grief the speech becomes monotonous or worse generalized. The advice is to go as far as may seem in good taste but hold back in other moments.

It's important that however distressed REASON may be, as a character, part of her enjoys the speech in the sense of finding therein emotional release.

Rattling off a long speech, the words remain as something lifeless on a page rather than something the actor, as the character, has found and made his own. Open yourself and try to go over the top.

93

CULPA.
Quítate allá, porfiada.

RAZON.
¡Alma triste y desdichada!...
(Éntrase.)

ENGAÑO.
¿Quién hay, Culpa, que te iguale?

CULPA.
Calla, porque el Alma sale,
360   Con el Deleite abrazada.

ESCENA X

EL ENGAÑO, LA CULPA.— *Sale EL ALMA y DELEITE, de las manos.*

ALMA.
Digo que eres como un oro.

DELEITE.
¿Y un abrazo no me da?

ALMA.
Tu gracia y donaire adoro.

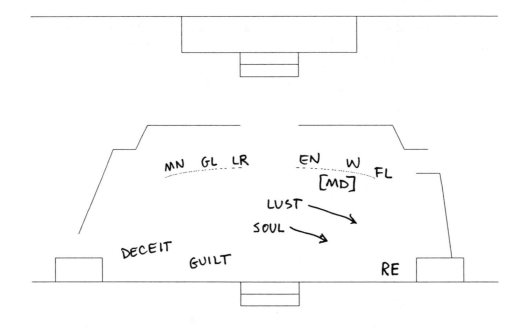

GUILT.
Get out of here, stubborn one!!

REASON.
Poor unfortunate Soul!...

DECEIT.
Who is there, Guilt, who is equal to you?
(LUST crosses down left.)

GUILT.
Be quiet, because Soul enters,
360   With her arms around Lust.

SCENE X

LUST, SOUL., DECEIT, GUILT
[MANKIND, GLUTTONY, LUCIFER, ENVY, WORLD, FLESH, MADNESS]

SOUL.
(Following LUST.)
I say, you are like a piece of gold.

LUST.
And will you not embrace me?

SOUL.
I adore your grace and elegance.

SOUL is a well worked out creation who engages, not withstanding our recognition of all her human weaknesses, our sympathy and understanding.

Valdivielso and Lope de Vega had long been friends. It was, of course, a literary as well as a personal friendship since they were almost equally prolific in least one sense. J. Simon Diaz had written of Valdivielso that in his prodigality Valdivielso was able to compete with Lope de Vega. Lope had temporarily moved to Toledo and his friendship with the Jesuit Valdivielso deepened. On occasion they also were in the company of the painter El Greco.

DELEITE.
Tia, ¿sabe dónde está?

ALMA.
365   ¿Dónde?

DELEITE.
En los cuernos del toro.

ALMA.
Esas manos se me den,
Y aquesos brazos tambien.

DELEITE.
No quiero, que no me quiere.

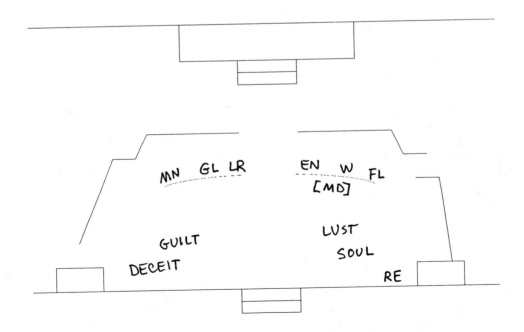

LUST.
Whore, do you know where you are?

SOUL.

365   Where?

LUST.
In great danger on the horns of the bull.
(Crossing down right.)

SOUL.
(Following LUST.)
Give me those hands,
And those arms as well.

LUST.
I don't want to, for you do not love me.

GUILT, of course, is trying to get SOUL into her asylum for *locos*, The House of Fools. SOUL doesn't know that it's an imprisoning asylum; she thinks it's a house where she'll consummate her love affair with whom she thinks is a youth, not realizing it's LUST.

While SOUL and LUST have their amorous scenes together onstage, downstage right GUILT and DECEIT are watching them with keen and meretricious interest.

Valdivielso in 1605 baptized Marcela, the daughter Lope had with Micaela de Lujàn... They met in Madrid, too, for Valdivielso accompanied the archbishop du Phillips court on many occasion. Valdivielso's visits in Madrid were especially frequent after 1609, at a time when Lope and his partisans were the dominant force at court and exerted a strong influence on acceptable tastes in literary output.

ENGAÑO.
Culpa, el corazon la hiere.

DELEITE.
(*Ap. á LA CULPA.*)
370   Hola, madre: ¿hágolo bien? 23

ALMA.
¿No te quiero? ¿ansí te quejas
Cuando el corazon me robas
Y enhechizada me dejas?
Abrázame; ¿que te alejas?

DELEITE.
(*Aparte.*)
375   Así engañan á las bobas.

ALMA.
Por tu dulce amor me muero.

DELEITE.
Aquesa belleza adoro.

ALMA.
¿A dónde voy, hechicero,
Preso entre cadenas de oro?

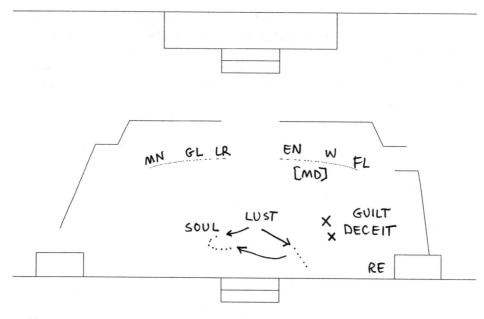

23 Hola, madre, hágolo bien.

DECEIT.
Guilt, how her heart pains her.

LUST.
(Aside to GUILT.)
370   Hey, mother: how am I doing?
(GUILT returns the gesture of approval to LUST.)

SOUL.
I don't love you? You complain thus
When you rob me of my heart
And leave me bewitched? / /
(LUST crosses down left.)
Embrace me; / Why do you move away?

LUST.
(aside to audience.)
375   This is how to deceive fools.

SOUL.
(Crossing center.)
I would die for your sweet love.

LUST.
(Crossing up to SOUL.)
I adore that beauty.

SOUL.
Where am I going, sorcerer,
Imprisoned by golden chains?

There is irony and ambiguity throughout the seduction scene of SOUL by LUST. It has been said as a definition that irony involves saying one thing while meaning something else. Something that is opposite to the surface meaning. It's commonly humerous, but it may at the same time be deadly serious. The speaker enjoys it, sometimes wryly, at his own expense. One of the reasons why irony is difficult is that it's often halfway between thought and feeling.

380   ¿Sabe dónde? al matadero.

ALMA.

¿Qué tienes en esa boca,
Que entre su fuego me abraso,
Si acaso á mis manos toca?
¡Paso, niño, paso, paso...
385   Que harás que me vuelva loca!

DELEITE.

Es, tia, que la retozo.

ALMA.

Digo que tienes donaire,
Y en tus abrazos me gozo. [24]

DELEITE.

Apriete bien, que soy aire.

ALMA.

390   ¿No eres mi gozo?

DELEITE.

En el pozo.

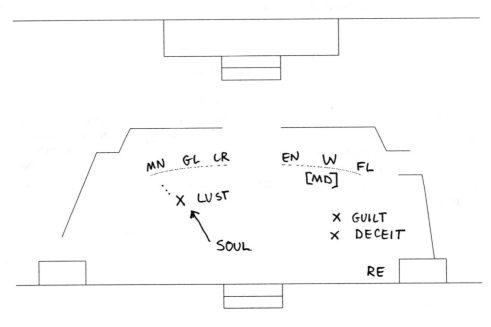

[24] Y en tus brazos me gozo.

LUST.
(Kneeling.)

380 Don't you know where? To the slaughter house.

SOUL.

What do you have in that mouth? /
It envelopes me with your fire
And burns my hands.
Stay, youth, wait. . .

(LUST pulls away, dismissing her with his hand.)

385 For you will drive me crazy.

LUST.

It's because I arouse you, my little whore.

SOUL.

I mean you have wit,
And I delight in your embraces.

LUST.
(Steps back.)

Hold me tight, / for I am air. / /

SOUL.

390 Will you not be my love?

LUST.

I'll leave you at the church.

On LUST's *'hold me tight'* SOUL grabs for him. He drops to the floor. No youth, at all in fact, he is an old hand at seduction. SOUL is naïveté and guileless innocence. At this moment she is totally unaware of the danger she is in. GUILT, with her gun, had immobilized REASON.

Irony involves the character in being at once inside and outside the situation in which the actor finds himself. He must begin by finding the right intention. A certain special tone is involved with irony.

LUST plays two or three contradictory attitudes at once.

SOUL is to go for the spirit as well as the details.

ALMA.
¡Ay mi regalo y mi bien!
Esas dulces manos ten;
Que entre tus gustos me muero.

DELEITE.
Mire, tia, acqueso quiero.—
395 Hola, madre: ¿hágolo bien?
(A LA CULPA..)

CULPA.
Y estás bien entretenido.

ALMA.
¿Es tu madre?

DELEITE.
Y mi ventura.

ALMA.
Dichosa madre habeis sido.
Quien parió tanta hermosura
400 Será madre de Cupido.

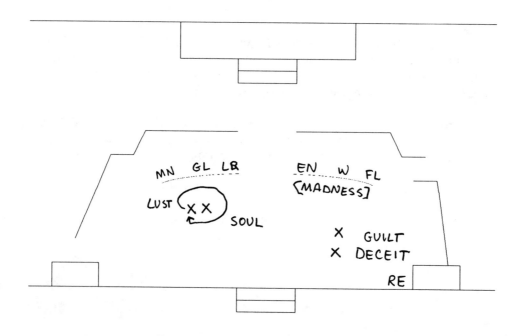

SOUL.
Oh, my joy and pleasure!
Take those sweet hands away,
For in your delights I will die.

LUST.
Look, whore, that is what I want.- - -
(Aside to GUILT, crossing up stage of SOUL.)
395   Hey, mother; how am I doing?

GUILT.
(A mock reverential bow.)
Good! And how you're enjoying it too!
(Bowing, joined by DECEIT in a mocking bow.)

SOUL.
Is that your mother?

LUST.
(A wink to audience, as he bows: down left in direction of GUILT.)
And my good luck.

SOUL.
(Slightly puzzled.)
What a lucky mother to have
Given birth to so much beauty! /
400   She must be the mother to cupid.

During this seduction scene much of it is played on the stage floor in which LUST paws and grapples with SOUL. She is conflicted and is ambivalent about what is taking place for her. From time to time she may look for guidance to REASON, but REASON has been temporarily defeated and without power by the earlier wounding shot delivered by GUILT. Both GUILT and DECEIT are observing this seduction scene on the stage floor, relishing in their feeling of achievement and success. The circling movements of the actors playing GUILT and DECEIT are left largely to the actors discretion.

103

(ALMA.)
Pues ¿y qué haceis por aquí?

CULPA. [25]
Como por vos me perdí,
Vine en vos misma á buscarme.

ALMA.
Por vuestra podeis mandarme;
405   Serviros podeis de mí.

CULPA.
Porque cansada vendréis,
Aquí en una casa mia
Os ruego que descanseis.

DELEITE.
No le diga de no, tia.

ALMA.
410   No haré, si vos lo quereis.

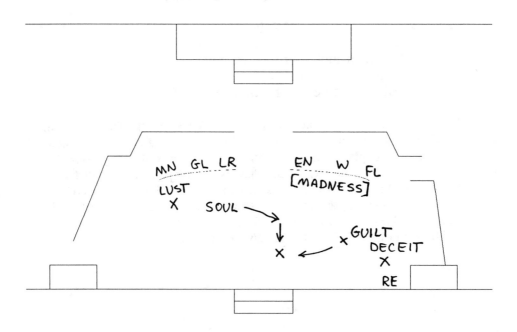

[25] De. (*Deleite*) Pero el alma he dirigido su pregunta á la Culpa.

104

SOUL.
(To GUILT, crossing to her.)
Then what are you doing here?

GUILT.
Due to you / I lost myself / /
I come right back to you / to find myself.

SOUL.
You may ask anything of me;
(Kneeling center stage.)
405   I am at your service.

GUILT.
(Helping her up.)
Because you come tired,
(LUST and GUILT exchange meaningful glances.)
I beg of you rest,
(Raising SOUL.)
Here, in one of my houses.

LUST.
Do not say no to her, whore.
(Directed pointedly to SOUL.)

SOUL.
410   I will do it, if that is what you wish.

Throughout the seduction scene it is not clear to naive SOUL what is happening to her and what is GUILT doing and saying. The rough words he uses are totally lost upon her. There is irony because it isn't clear to SOUL what LUST is actually doing. It is apparent to the audience of course that he is mocking her, that he is pretending to be on SOUL's side but actually he is her *dearest* enemy. There is ambiguity as well because there are words that mean two things.

CULPA.

Es, Alma, un rico hospital,
Del cual ninguno se escapa
Que vió del aire el cristal
Desde el sacristan al Papa,
415   Y desde el Rey al zagal.
Dirás, en viéndote en él,
Que es la torre de Babel;
Y es un hospital de locos,
Donde sanan los más pocos
420   De los que vienen á él.
Soy rector deste hospital. [26]

ALMA.

¿Hay allá enfermos de amor?

CULPA.

Haylos de cualquiera mal.

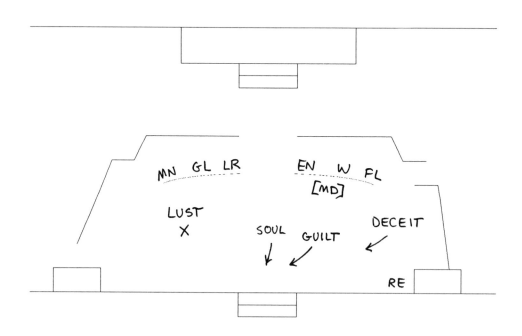

[26] Soy *rector*, dice la Culpa en la misma escena en que se ha presentado como *madre* del Deleite. Este descuido se repite en la escena XV, en que el Alma, dirigiéndose á la Culpa, la llama *señor*.

GUILT.
(Crossing with SOUL down center.)
It is a luxurious house, Soul!
No one / / escapes!
Who has looked upon its crystalline appearance: / /
Neither Sacristan, nor Pope,
415   Neither king nor shepherd boy. / /
You will probably say,
                  In seeing it,
   That it is the Tower of Babel;
             (A spiral gesture.)
Or **The House of Fools**,
Where the least of those are cured
420   Who enter in, /
I am the keeper of this house.

SOUL.
Are there any there, / sick for love?

GUILT.
(Laughing—DECEIT snickers behind his hand.)
There are those of every sickness.

...a tower [of Babel] *with its top in the heavens.* —GENESIS

GUILT, as she walks with SOUL, weaves an hypnotic spell. Her delivery is rythmical and intimate. Her laughter, for SOUL's benefit, is intimate as if sharing a secret. A covert glance to the audience reveals the double meaning, the ambiguity and irony, of her mirth.

GUILT should make the text vigorous and tough, rather than smooth and bland.

ALMA.

Hirióme este encantador
425   Con sus labios de coral.

DELEITE.

Venga, no le dé disgusto.

ALMA.

Ir con los dos me da gusto,
Porque, mirando á los dos,
Me acuerdo poco de Dios,
430   Y mucho de los dos gusto.

CULPA.

Hijo, quiero te ven.

DELEITE.

Más quiero aquesa señora,
Que me ha parecido bien.

ALMA.

Tu belleza me enamora.

DELEITE.
(A LA CULPA..)
435   Hola, madre; ¿hágolo bien?

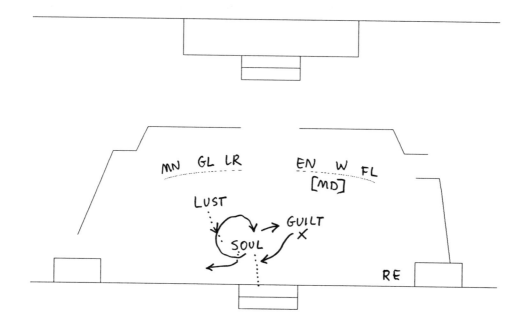

108

SOUL.
(Crossing to LUST.)
425 This Enchanter has wounded me
With his coral lips.

LUST.
Come, don't upset her.

SOUL.
To go with you would please me
Because looking at the two of you
I think little of God
430 And I think much of you two.

GUILT.
(Crossing down center, taking hands of LUST.)
Son, come with me.

LUST.
I would rather go with that lady
Who has pleased me very much.

SOUL.
I am enamoured of your beauty.

LUST.
(To GUILT.)
435 Hey, mother: How am I doing? //

With '*Come*,' LUST whirls SOUL, and then crosses up to GUILT. SOUL follows and falls into their joined arms. SOUL tries to kiss LUST, but GUILT whirls her off. GUILT tries to lead LUST down center steps and into the aisle. LUST breaks away, crossing up left to SOUL.

(*DELEITE.*)
En llegando á la posada
    (Al ALMA..)
Abrirémos la empanada,
Aunque os ha de dar pesar.

ALMA.
¿Por qué?

DELEITE.
    Porque habeis de hallar,
440   Entre dos platos, nonada.

CULPA.
    (Al ENGAÑO.)
Vos á la Razon guardad.

DELEITE.
Puto viejo, allá os quedad;
Que yo no gusto de viejos.

ENGAÑO.
Pues ¿son malos mis consejos?

DELEITE.
445   Mejor es esta beldad.

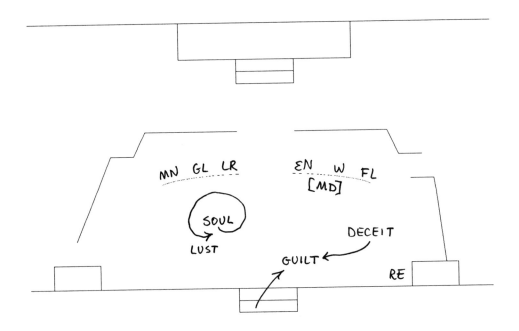

(LUST.)
(To SOUL.)
When we arrive at the inn
(Making a circle with SOUL.)
We'll open the meat pies
Although you may regret it.

SOUL.
Why?

LUST.
Because you're likely to find,
440   Between the two crusts, a trifle!

GUILT.
(Crossing back to the stage from the audience,
as DECEIT crosses down right.)
(To DECEIT.)
Watch out for Reason!

LUST.
Stay there, you old pimp;
I don't like old people.

DECEIT
(Crossing to center stage.)
Well, is my advice bad?

LUST.
445   This beautiful woman is better.

The scene is in general accord with usage of the early 17th century. The verse here has skill, grace, and mastery of speech rhythms. The verses confer to the flow of dialogue a certain elasticity and variation which is pleasant , and a wide range of expression for the actors for changes in tone and mood. A suspension of the highest tone is achieved as SOUL is caught up in ectasy and her thoughts turn away from God earthward.

CULPA.
(Al ENGAÑO.)
Cuenta con la razon ten.

ENGAÑO.
Tus obras fama te den.

DELEITE.
Alma, vos sois alma mia.

ALMA.
Y vos la de mi alegría.

DELEITE.
(A LA CULPA.)
450   Hola, madre: ¿hágolo bien?
(Vanse camino del hospital.)

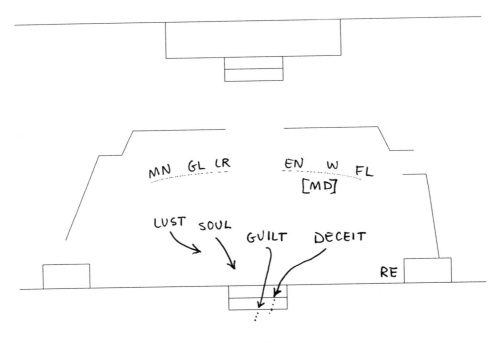

GUILT.
(To DECEIT.)
Keep in mind, Reason.

DECEIT
(Turning back to GUILT at center stage.)
Your works will bring you fame.

LUST.
(Taking SOUL down toward center stage.)
Soul, you are my soul.

SOUL.
And you are my happiness.

LUST.
(To GUILT.)
450   Hey, mother: How am I doing?
(Exeunt.)

LUST and SOUL, embracing as lovers, exit up the aisle, followed by GUILT and DECEIT. GUILT beams with the smiles of a conqueror.

Despite what has been said, above, the actor, acting in Spanish or in English, mustn't just play the poetry and hope for the best.

Marry the onomatopoeia with clear intention and clear characterization.

ESCENA XI

Sale LA RAZON, de viejo, por lo alto del torreon.

RAZON.

Alma, ¿sabes cómo estás
Condenada á eterno fuego,
Si no te vuelves atrás?
Ciega vas tras otro ciego,
455   Y donde él cayó, caerás.
Como simple corderillo,
Das la garganta al cuchillo,
Y en un laberinto estás.
De donde nunca saldrás,
460   Si no te ases de mi ovillo.
Alma, enternézcate el llanto
De aquestos ojos, que dejas
Ciegos por amarte tanto,
Y no cierres las orejas,
465   Como el áspid, al encanto.
(De rodillas.)
¡Soberana Inspiracion,
Que en esa alegre region
Vas coronada de estrellas,
Inclina tus luces bellas
470   A ver tanta perdicion!
Lo que la importa la inspira,
Alumbrando aquestos ojos
A quien cegó la mentira;
¡Mire yo tus rayos rojos,
475   En quien el cielo se mira!

MN GL LR   EN W FL
[MADNESS]

REASON

LS

SCENE XI

[MANKIND, GLUTTONY, LUCIFER, ENVY, WORLD, FLESH, MADNESS (Sleeping.)]

REASON.
(Stirring.)

Soul, you know that you will be
Condemned to eternal fires
If you do not turn back?
Blind, you are led by the sightless Lust.
455   Where he falls / you will fall.
Like an innocent lamb
You give your throat to the knife,
And you remain in a labyrinth,
From which you will never escape
460   If my tangled words do not goad you.
Soul, prolong the weeping from those eyes
Which you have let
Be blinded from loving too much,
And do not close your ears,
465   Like the snake before the charmer. / /
               (INSPIRATION enters up center stage on level.)
Sovereign Inspiration,
               (Turning to INSPIRATION having entered.)
Who in that happy region
Is crowned with stars,
Incline your lovely eyes
470   And look upon so much ruination!
What is important to her,
               Will inspire her,
Enlighten her eyes,
Which lies have blinded;
Turn your enlightenment on me
475   That I may see heaven!

REASON rises and drops her upstage hand from shielding her eyes. She turns downstage looking after the departing SOUL, captured by DECEIT and GUILT. Upon the entrance of INSPIRATION she turns upstage to some degree. She is recovering from the wound from GUILT's gun. 'REASON is not a refined lady; she has the harshness coupled with the simplicity of a peasant woman, her movements are limited because she is wrapped in a costume which suggests swadling clothes.' [Narros]

In the long speech, excite the audience about what is going to happen; grab audience attention by extra stress at the very beginning.

ESCENA XII

LA RAZON.—*Sale LA INSPIRACION, de ángel.*

INSPIRACION.
¿Qué es lo que quieres, Razon?

RAZON.
¡Oh soberana vision!
Dame á besar esos piés;
Y es justo que me los dés,
480   Pues que mi remedio son.
Ya sabes que el alma mia
Tras el deleite se fué,
Viendo lo que á Dios debia;
Ciega y triste me quedé
485   A la sombra escura y fria.
Enmascarado su mal,
La llevan al hospital,
Donde, para rematalla,
Le da contina batalla
490   Un ejército infernal.
Entra allá, que si allá vas,
Y tus consejos la das,
Saldrá á buscar la Razon;
Llevarla he á pedir perdon,
495   Y en mí un esclavo tendrás.

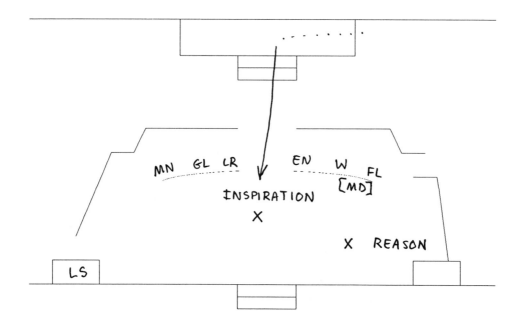

116

SCENE XII

REASON, INSPIRATION
[MANKIND, GLUTTONY, LUCIFER, ENVY, WORLD, FLESH, MADNESS (Sleeping.)]

INSPIRATION.
What is it you want, Reason?

REASON.
Oh sovereign vision!
Give me your feet to kiss;
And just it is that you give them to me,
480   For they are my salvation.
You already know that my Soul
Has gone after Lust.
Knowing what she owes to God
Has left me blind and sad
485   In dark cold shadows.
Masking her sickness,
They take her to the asylum
Were, in order to ruin her
They assault her unceasingly
490   With infernal forces.
Go in there, for if you enter there,
And give her your advice
Perhaps she will leave to look for Reason;
I must take her to beg for pardon;
495   So you will have me for a slave.

INSPIRATION appears as an angel. He crosses down left toward REASON. REASON, as he moves toward her, gradually lifts her head, and pleads with INSPIRATION. INSPIRATION has come to help REASON save SOUL.

On long speeches the silent actor does not move at the same time as the speaking actor; therefore no actor —generally— moves as another speaks. All gestures and movements are weighted and significant in a classical Spanish play; therefore, there is an economy of both.

What the actor must do to make the audience listen to a long descriptive speech, covering pages, is to **make** them attend. For a long speech both actor and audience have to work harder. The audience can be made to think the long story is worth listening to, to feel the story as it moves forward, as long as the actor is deeply inside the situation. He must 'coin' the language symbolically, as it were, as if the lines were coming out for the first time.

INSPIRACION.
Razon, por hacerte gusto,
Y porque mi oficio es,
De hacer lo que pides gusto.

RAZON.
Dame, Inspiracion, los piés.

INSPIRACION.
500   Darte un abrazo es más justo.
De mi aficion está cierta,
Que haré, porque se convierta,
Todo cuanto fuere en mí.

RAZON.
¿Piénsasla hablar luégo?

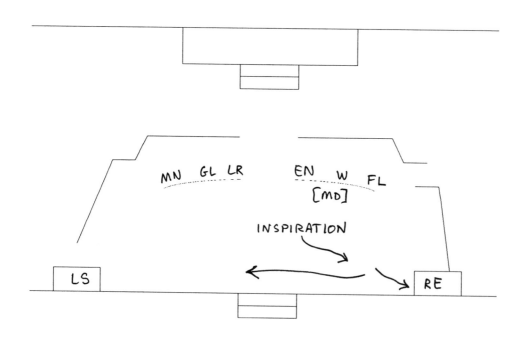

INSPIRATION.
Reason, to please you,
And because it is my duty,
I will do what you ask gladly.

REASON.
Inspiration, let me kiss your feet.

INSPIRATION.
500   It is more fair to give you my arms
You can be sure of my affection. /
(Lifting REASON to her feet; he starts to exit.)
With all the power I have
                    I will do it,
In order to convert her.

REASON.
Will you talk to her?

Valdivielso, a Jesuit, and Lope had long been friends. It was, of course, a literary as well as a personal friendship since they were almost equally prolific in at least one sense, each having written many plays as well as *autos*. Lope had temporairly moved to Toledo and his friendship with Valdivielso deepened. There they met with other Toledo based men of note, and on occasion El Greco.

Despite Valdivielso's friendship with Lope and despite his being chaplin to the Cardinal-Archbishop Sandoval y Rojas the Archbishop was no partisan of Lope de Vega. [Lope de Vega at that time was characterized due to his high productivity as The Phoenix.] There seemed to always be tension between Lope and the Archbishop, not lessened at all by the fact that in 1614 the Archbishop, under pressure from Lope's influential protector, the Duke of Sessa, administered Lope's final vows. [Lope, late in life, had become a religious.]

In 1660 the Archbishop was planning the festivities for the new chapel of the Virgin of Sagario and he chose to exclude Lope, taking advantage of growing tensions between him and the Cordoban Góngora to further that goal. Tensions between Góngora and Lope as poet rivals had been intensified in 1613.

INSPIRACION.

Sí,

505   En el umbral de la puerta.
Véte con Dios.

RAZON.

Él te guie,
Y al Alma, en esta locura, [27]
Su auxilio eficaz la envie,
Pues la sanará esta cura,
510   Aunque la Culpa porfie.

> *(Vase LA INSPIRACION por los aires, y LA RAZON se retira. Tórnase á ver lo interior del hospital.)*

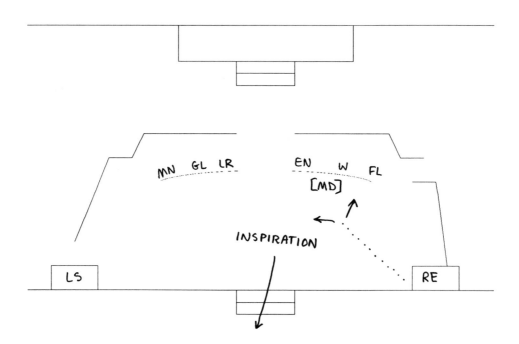

[27] A alma en esta locura.

INSPIRATION.

505 Yes, at the exact crossroads.
Go with God.

(Starting to turn upstage for an exit.)

REASON.

(Speaking to him as he moves.)

May He guide you,
And send His true help to Soul in her madness,
For this cure will restore her health,
510 Even if Guilt may persist.

*(INSPIRATION exits by the aisle, and REA-
SON crosses up stage, pauses to look into the
interior of the asylum. Shudders, and then she
crosses down stage left and resumes her place
on the down stage platform.)*

Lope de Vega served as Captain of a group of Literati hostile to the new
wave of poetry of which Góngora was the chief exponent. Lope's star was on
the wane, and the bitterness of the invective exchange between the two groups
of the strongly partisan poets increased in shrillness. At the time of a literary
competition of a poetical nature held in Toledo in 1616, the Archbishop made
his chaplain Valdivielso acutely uncomfortable by making him serve as secretary
of the literary competition, an assignment which Valdivielso was in no position
to refuse. The Cardinal had been successful in excluding Lope. This put a
decided strain on the friendship of long-standing between Lope de Vega and
Valdivielso. Lope struck back with a vitriotic parody which included a work by
Joseph de Valdivielso.

ESCENA XIII

Sale Los Locos: LUZBEL con unos palos de tambor, LA GULA comiendo, LA INVIDIA mordiéndose las manos, y EL MUNDO con un caballo de caña, y EL GEÑERO HUMANO muy penstivo, LA CARNE con una guitarra.

LUZBEL.
¡Tápala, patan, tan, tan!
¡Guerra, guerra, guerra,
Al cielo y á la tierra!

GEÑERO HUMANO.
Ella la rota me dió,
¿Y tengo la culpa yo?

GULA.
Rector vil, ¿quieres matarme?
515 *¿Que estoy rabiando de hambre!*

CARNE.
Todo el mundo tras mí llevo:—
¿Qué más quiero? ¿qué más quiero?

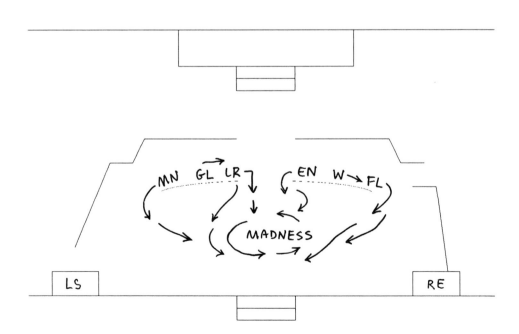

122

SCENE XIII

LUCIFER, GLUTTONY, ENVY, WORLD, MANKIND, FLESH [REASON, MADNESS (Sleeping.)]

LUCIFER.
Tapala patan tan tan!
War, War, War,
In Heaven and on Earth

MANKIND.
Eve gave me the apple
And am I to blame?

GLUTTONY.
Vile keeper, do you want to kill me?
515   *I'm dying of hunger.*

FLESH.
I have all the world with me - -
What more do I want? What more do I want?

> *(LUCIFER, wielding drumsticks on a drum, enters, accompanied by GLUTTONY, eating; ENVY is biting his nails as he enters; WORLD riding a toy horse; MANKIND enters looking pensive; FLESH enters with a guitar.)*

"You will not die," the serpent said, "God knows that when you eat of it your eyes will be opened, and you will be like God knowing good and evil". So the woman [Eve] seeing the tree was good for food and was to be desired to make one wise, ate of its fruit, and she also gave some to her husband, and he also ate some.
—GENESIS

In this scene the vices have broken loose; they indulge in dancing and raging, for they are driven by their wants. As the scene develops they express weariness with their attributes; e.g. GLUTTONY, ENVY, FLESH, etc.

LUCIFER on '*war, war, war,*' looked downstage left in the direction of REASON on her platform. He kneels and blows on a conch type horn to get her attention as he mocks her. [This moment was very vivid in the scene as directed by Narros for the film *EL GRECO*.]

MUNDO.

Que por vos, la mi señora,
                La cara de plata,
Correré yo mi caballo,
520   *A la trápala, trápala, trápala.*

INVIDIA.

¡De mañana están borrachos
Los bellacos, los bellacos!

LUZBEL.

Yo, el mejor de los querubes,
Que nací como el aurora,
525   Que oro esparce y perlas llora,
Con que enriquece las nubes,

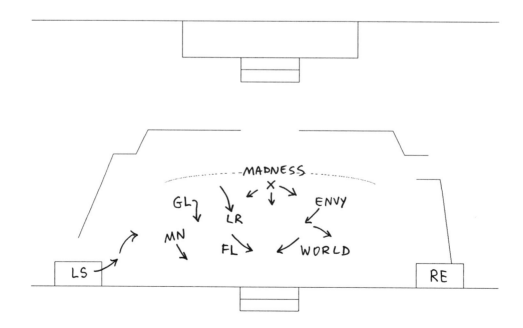

WORLD.

For you My lady
              Of the silver face,
I will ride my horse.
520   *A la trapala, trapala, trapala.*

ENVY.

In the morning, they will be drunk,
The scoundrels, the scoundrels!

LUCIFER.
          (Drum stops.)
I, the best of the cherubs,
Who was born like the dawn,
525   Scattering gold, and weeping pearls,
With which I enrich the clouds,
                    (The inmates circle MADNESS, then stop
                    when the drum stops; they start when the drum
                    starts.)

"*For thou* [Lucifer] *has said in thine heart, I will ascend to heaven, I will exhault my throne above the stars of God: I will sit upon the mount of the congregation, in the sides of the North: I will ascend above the heights of the clouds; I will be like the most high. Yet shall be brought down to hell, to the sides of the pit.*" —*ISAIAH*

Dante's Lucifer is pictured three faced: his red visage betokens love of evil, or hate; the black face is the emblem of ignorance, the opposite of wisdom and the source of pride; the pale yellow one signifies impotance, the opposite of power and the begetter of envy... His Lucifer has six wings; a pair of them sprouts beneath each face, and the three winds produced by their flapping frees Cocytus. Immovable and helpless in the ice of his own making, he holds sway over his *Doloroso Regno* by these winds alone.

Lo'mperador del doloroso regno
Da mezzo'l petto uscia fuor de la ghiaccia:
E più con un gigante io mi convegno,
Che I giganti non fan con le sue braccia:
Vedi oramai quant'esser de quel tutto
Ch'a così fatta parte si confaccia...
Non avean penne, ma di vipistrello
Era lor modo; e quelle svolazzava,
Cì che tre venti si movean da ello.
Quindi Cocito tutto s'aggelava.
Con sei occhi piangeva, e per tre menti
Gocciavail pianto e sanguinosa bava.
                    [Canto XXXIV: *Inferno* (*La Divina Commedia*) —Dante]

(*LUZBEL.*)

¿A un Hombre habia de adorar
Hecho de ceniza y lodo?
¡Pese á mí y al mundo todo,
530   Y á quien más puede pesar!
¿Por un hombre me destierra?
¡Buenas sus justicias van!
Afuera, tapalapatan,
Guerra al cielo y á la tierra!
             (*Repiten.*)

GÉNERO HUMANO.

535   ¡Entre tanto desconsuelo,
Bien es que el llanto no cese, [28]
Como que en cueros me viese
Todo el cielo, todo el cielo!
La mujer me enhechizó
540   Con una manzana bella
Y aunque me hizo morder della, [29]
¡Yo tengo la culpa, yo!
             (*Repiten.*)

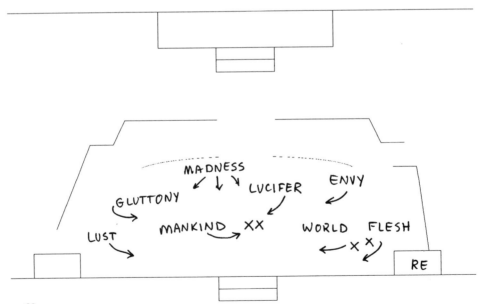

[28] Bien es llanto ne cese.

[29] Acaso:

        Y aunque me hizo morder ella.

LUCIFER.

Should I adore a Man,
Made of ashes and mud?
A burden to me and the whole world.
530   And on whomever else it may weigh!
For one man am I to be exiled?
How blind their justice is!
Away, tapalatan,
War in Heaven and Earth!
                    (Drum.)

                (All repeat the last two lines.)

MANKIND.
                (Drum stops.)
535   Mid such distress,
It is a good thing the weeping does not cease, / /
How naked was I seen,
By all the Heavens, by all the Heavens! /
The woman bewitched me
540   With a beautiful apple.
And although she made me eat of it,
I am to blame, I!
                    (Drum.)

                (All repeat the last two lines.)

Valdivielso would seem to have had a strong identification with the rebel Angel — as did Dante, and a little later in far off England the poet Milton.

Valdevielso has put real passion into LUCIFER's speeches; the actor needs to enter that passion.

LUCIFER's reference is to Jesus, whom he mocks. MANKIND speaks of Eve and of his awareness of nakedness in the Garden of Eden after having eaten of the fruit of the tree of knowledge.

Then the eyes of both were opened, [Adam and Eve] *and they knew that they were naked, and they sewed fig leaves together and made aprons for themselves. —* GENESIS

All is not lost; the' unconquerable Will,
And study of revenge, immortal hate,
And courage never to submit or yield:
                    [Milton]

127

GULA.

Rector vil, de hambre me muero;

Al punto me manda dar

545 Las mesas de Baltasar

Y las comidas de Asuero.

Dame, si tienes, fiambre

Del pueblo ingrato que domas,

El estiércol de palomas,

550 *¡Que estoy rabiando de hambre!*

(*Repiten.*)

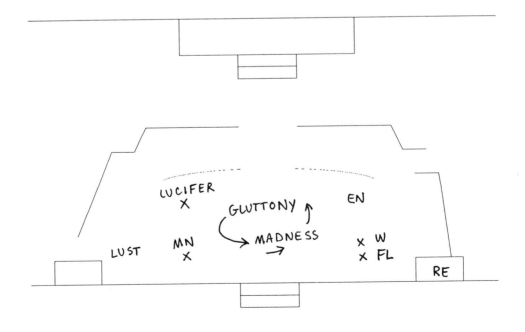

GLUTTONY.

(Kneeling at MADNESS's feet.)

The Vile Guardian, I am dying of hunger.
Instantly set for me
545 The tables for Belshazzar's feast
And the banquets for Ahasuerus
Or, give me, instead the blood
Of the ingrate people you dominate,
Or, the droppings of doves.
550 For I am ravished by hunger.

(MADNESS hurls her back.)
(Drum.)

(All repeat the last line.)

People in a highly psychotic state are very physical, grotesque in their movements; they express themselves in a very physical way. [Narros]

In such a speech of heightened language: metaphor and simile, the actor must freshly mint the words the most. This is very important. This is how the play -a morality- works dramatically.

King Belshazzar of Babylon made a great feast for a thousand of his lords, and he commanded that the vessels of gold and silver which had been taken out of the temple in Jeruselem be brought. Then the king and his lords, his wives, and his concubines drank from them, while they praised their Gods of gold and silver, bronze, iron, wood, and stone. ...That very night Belshazzer was slain, and Darius the Mede received the kingdom. —DANIEL

The king [Alhasuer] and Haman feasted with Esther, and as they were drinking wine, the king said, "What is your petition Queen Esther? It shall be fulfilled." Esther answered, "Oh king, let my life be given me at my petition, and my people at my request. For we are sold, to be slain and to be anhiliated." —ESTHER

"Who is he, and where is he that would presume to do this?" asked the king. "A foe and enemy!" Esther said. "This wicked Haman!" ...The king said, "Hang him on that." So they hanged Haman on the gallows he had prepared for Mordecai, and King Ahasuerus gave Esther the house of Haman. —ESTHER

129

CARNE.
Si entre mi frígido afeite,
Entre mi hechizo y mi encanto,
En el anzuelo del llanto
Pongo el cebo del deleite;
555 Si en él pican los Alcídes,
Los indomables Sansones,

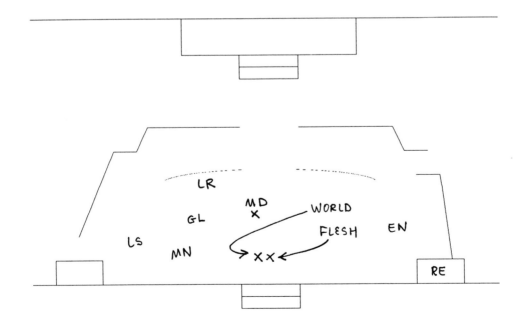

FLESH.
(Drum stops.)
If behind my cold mask,
Amidst enchantment and spells;
And with the lure of weeping,
I place the bait of lust;
555   And, if thus, swallow the bait those Hercules, [30]
Those indomitable Samson's.

[In the English translation, it was decided to keep the Hercules, Samson, Solomon singular.]

The *locos* characters of GUILT's asylum are in *their world*, and they are being exploited by GUILT, controlled, even beaten by MADNESS. WORLD like the other *locos* is oblivious of the machinations of the plot, set in motion by GUILT, for the seduction of SOUL.

[30] Hercules, a celebrated hero, who, after death, was ranked among the gods. Most often, he was considered by the ancients as the son of Jupiter and Alcmena, a mortal. Before he had completed his eighth month as a babe, the jealous Juno, intent upon his distruction sent two large snakes to devour him. The child, not terrified at the sight of the serpents, boldly seized them, one in each hand, and squeezed them to death. This established early his remarkable strength. By decree Hercules was obliged to perform twelve labors. When he indignantly refused, Juno punished him for his disobedience by rendering him so delirious that he killed his own children. When he recovered his senses he consulted the oracle of Apollo and was informed that he must be subservient and perform the labors.

(*CARNE.*)
Los discretos Salomones,
Y los invictos Davidos;
Y si todo el mundo entero,
560 Enlazado en estos ojos, [31]
Es de mis triunfos despojos...
¿Qué más quiero? ¿qué más quiero?
(*Repiten.*)

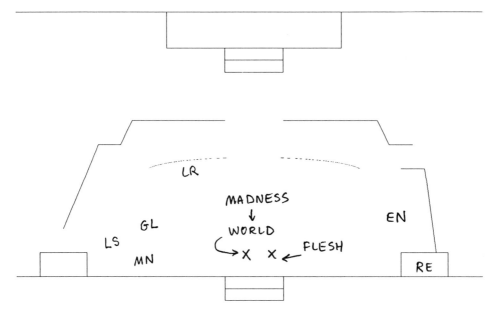

[31] Acaso:

Y si todo este mundo entero.

Enlazados en estos ojos.

(FLESH.)
The ingenious Solomons,
Those invincible Davids / /
Even all the entire world
560   Be bound to these eyes
They be the leftovers of my triumphs...!
What more do I want, what more do I want?
(Drum.)

(All repeat the last line.)

Two women in dispute over to which woman the child belonged came before Solomon the king. The king said, "Bring me a sword." A sword was brought and the king said, "Divide the living child in two and give half to one woman and half to the other." —I KINGS

Then the heart of the first woman yearned for her son, "Oh, my lord," she said, "give her the child, by no means slay it." —I KINGS

"It shall be neither mine nor yours," said the other, "divided." —I KINGS

Then the king answered and said, "Give the living child to the first woman, and by no means slay it: she is its mother". All Israel heard of the judgment the king had rendered, and they stood in awe of him, because they perceived that the wisdom of God was in him. —I KINGS

... David took his staff and his sling and he chose five smooth stones from the brook. Putting them in his shepherd's bag, he drew near to the Philistine. When Goliath saw David, he disdained him. ...He said, ..."You come to me with sticks?" — I SAMUEL

"I come to you in the name of the Lord of hosts,"... said David, "...whom you have defied." Then he put a hand in his bag and took out a stone, and slung it, and struck the Philistine on his forehead. The stone sank in and Goliath fell to the ground. David ran and stood over him and took Goliath's sword out of its sheath and killed him, and cut off his head. —I SAMUEL

MUNDO.

                A aquesas luces, que adoro,
                Consagro aquestos plumajes,
565   Gallas, invenciones, trajes,
                Perlas, piedras, plata y oro;
                Los peces que la mar cría,
                Los animales del suelo,
                Las bellas aves del cielo,
570   Y el cielo del alma mia;
                Los ámbares, los olores,
                Los juegos, cazas y pescas
                Las yerbas y flores frescas,
                Y el fruto de aquestas flores
575   Y, al fin, cuanto el cielo tapa
                Os daré para gozallo,
                Y correré mi caballo
                A la trápala, trápala, trápala.
                        (Repiten.)

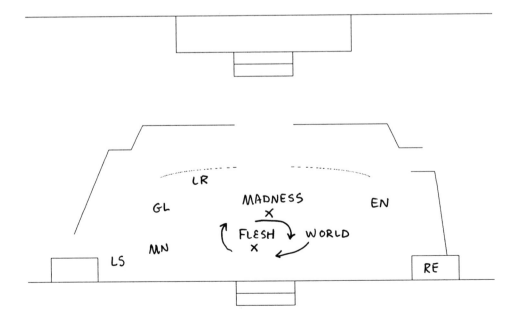

134

WORLD.
(Crossing to FLESH.)
To those lights that I adore,
I consecrate these plums,
565   Finery, inventions, clothing,
Pearls, precious stones, silver and gold;
(Circling FLESH.)
The fish which the seas breed,
The animals of the earth,
The beautiful birds of the sky,
570   And the Heaven of my soul.
The amber, the scents,
Game, hunting and fishing,
Grass, and fresh flowers,
And fruit of these flowers.
575   And finally everything the Heavens cover,
I will give to you to enjoy,
And I will ride my horse,
A la trapala, trapala, trapala.
(Drum.)

(All repeat the last line.)

WORLD rides a toy broomstick horse around the stage.

Images are poetic, sensual. Words work on words qualifying and changing the direction of the thought. The action of the speech is a form of seducing FLESH, enticing her with these images. The speech is to be acted; it's not a recitation. The actual sounds of the words must work on one another.

Valdivielso shows a constant fidelity to bibilical tradition, which is present in all of his theatrical pieces. [Italian Theatrical Encyclopedia]

135

INVIDIA.

　　Mirad al necio Luzbel

580　Dando voces, como loco;

　　Y esotro, necio no poco,

　　Padre del que mató á Abel;

　　Y allá el borracho gloton,

　　Que siempre de hambre se muere;

585　Y la bellaca, que áun quiere [32]

　　Herir á este corazon;

　　Y el Mundo, con sus penachos

　　Haciendo muy del galan;

　　¡Y están todos, como están,

590　*Muy de mañana borrachos!*

　　　　(*Repiten.*)

ESCENA XIV

Dichos.—*Sale LA LOCURA, con el azote.*

LOCURA.

¡Alto, fuera de la sala!

LUZBEL.

¡Arre allá, bestia mayor!

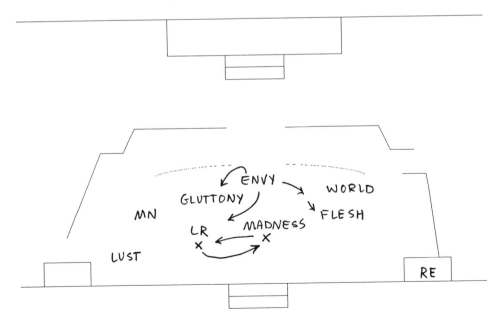

32　Y la bellaca, que aunque quiere.

ENVY.
(Crossing to each madman who cringes.)

Look at the foolish Lucifer
580   Shouting like a madman;
And that other one, no less stupid,
Father of him who slew Abel;
And over there the gluttonous drunkard,
That is always dying of hunger;
585   And the wench, ever wanting
To wound this heart;
And World like a dandy
With his plumes.
And they are all, the way they are,
590   **All, early in the morning, drunk!**
(Drum stops.)

(All repeat the last line.)

SCENE XIV

MANKIND, GLUTTONY, LUCIFER, ENVY, WORLD, FLESH, MAD-NESS
[LUST, REASON, INSPIRATION]

MADNESS.
(Cracking whip at FLESH.)
Stop! Leave the room!

LUCIFER.
(Throwing MADNESS to the floor.)
Gidap — Get along, great beast!

Adam knew Eve his wife, and she conceived and bore Cain. ...again she bore his brother Abel ...the lord had regard for Abel and his offering, but not for Cain ...so Cain was very angry ...Cain rose up against his brother and killed him. —
GENESIS

The riotus behavior of the *locos* rises to a noisy climax which is then abruptly brought to a halt by the awakening of MADNESS who moves among them wielding his whip.

137

LOCURA.

Salid, que viene el Rector.

LUZBEL.

595

¡Venga muy en hora mala
Paya vos y para él,
Y para quien bien le quiere,
Y para quien no dijere:
<<Para vos y para él!>>

LOCURA.

Calla, que trae una loca,

600

Que fué de Dios bella estampa.

LUZBEL.

¿El Alma cayó en la trampa?
Carne, tu instrumento toca.

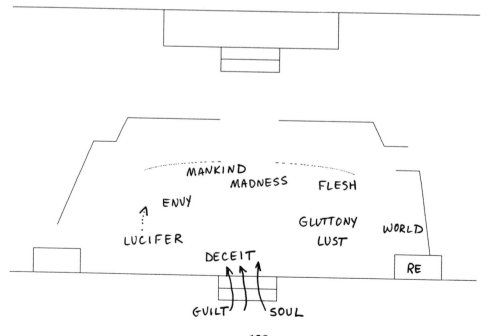

MADNESS.
(GUILT, DECEIT, and SOUL enter down aisle toward the stage.)
Get out, here comes the keeper!

LUCIFER.
Guilt comes at a bad time
595   For you and for her,
And for those who like her well,
And to those to whom I may not have said:
Bad for you and bad for her.
(He angers GUILT, who pushes SOUL toward the stage.)

MADNESS.
Shut up: for she brings a mad woman,
600   Who is God's beautiful image.

LUCIFER.
(Backing upstage 5 steps.)
Has Soul fallen into the trap?
Flesh, play your instrument.
(GUILT takes SOUL onto stage.)

MADNESS acknowledges the sovereignty of GUILT as keeper of the asylum for the *locos*. Both SOUL and GUILT are now wearing the hoods of *locos*. ENVY follows GUILT and SOUL up right center.

GUILT is exulting over her seeming conquest. SOUL is oblivious of what has happened to her. The actors should make the most of an entrance down the center aisle to the stage — as in the film *EL GRECO*.

ESCENA XV

Dichos.—*Sale LA CULPA y EL ALMA. con capirote de loco.* [33]

MUNDO.
Bien os está el capirote.

GULA.
¡Hola! tus brazos me da.

INVIDIA.
605 Alma, huélgome que ya
Os dieron en el cocote.

LUZBEL.
Vuesta venida celebro,
Aunque no me conoceis.

INVIDIA.
Esta noche llevaréis,
610 Alma, un famoso culebro.

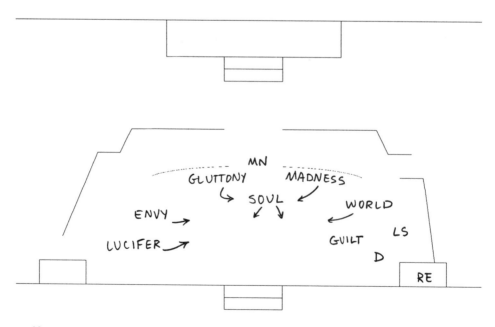

[33] Con capirotes de locos.

SCENE XV

GLUTTONY, ENVY, MANKIND, GUILT, SOUL, LUST, LUCIFER, WORLD, FLESH

[REASON]

WORLD.
The hood fits you well.

GLUTTONY.
Hello! Give me your arms.

ENVY.
605   Soul, I am happy to see
They gave you a blow on the head.

LUCIFER.
(GUILT lets go of SOUL.)
I celebrate your arrival, / /
Although you don't know me.

ENVY.
This night, Soul,
610   You'll wear a famous snake.

GUILT has arrived up stage. SOUL is upstage center, bewildered, soon to be stunned and ashamed. Each *loco* in turn on a speech makes sardonic mock bows; each takes a slight step in the direction of SOUL.

Irony involves saying one thing while meaning something else. Something that is opposite to the surface meaning. It's commonly humorous, but it may at the same time be deadly serious. The speaker enjoys it, sometimes wryly at his own expense. One of the reasons why irony is difficult is that it's often half-way between thought and feeling.

ALMA.
(A LA CULPA.)
No conozco aquesta gente;
Señor, decidme quién son

GULA.
Quien gasta la colacion.
Pagad luégo la patente.

CULPA.
615   Locos, apartáos allá.

LUZBEL.
Apartaránse.

CULPA.
¡Ea, pues!

LOCURA.
(A Luzbel.)
¿Respondes?

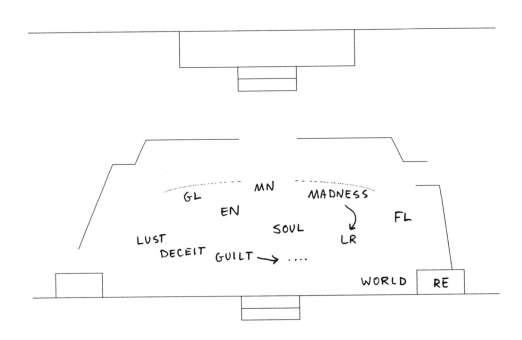

SOUL.
(To GUILT.)
I do not know these people;
Tell me who they are.

GLUTTONY.
Whowever uses up the food,
Will pay the bill.
(All locos laugh.)

GUILT.
(Stopping the laughter.)
615 Fools, move away there.

LUCIFER.
(Crossing center.)
They will move away.

GUILT.
(Crossing to LUCIFER.)
Well! / Do you dare?

MADNESS.
(Crossing closer to LUCIFER.)
(To LUCIFER.)
What do you say to that?

SOUL has become one of them, but she doesn't know who these madmen are. With an imperious gesture GUILT re-establishes control, stopping the madmens laughter.

LUCIFER and GUILT confront each other. *'Do you dare?'* is the subtext of the *'Well!'*. MADNESS and LUCIFER fight fiercely.

Bring it alive at the moment you speak it. Have a relish for the text, the interplay. Play dangerously, walking a tight-rope.

143

LUZBEL.

　　Pues ¿no lo ves?
Y bien respondido está.
¡Pues vuélveme á replicar,
620　　O incítame á que me enoje,
Y, vivo yo, que te arroje
Al abismo del penar!
¿Pretendeis, gente crüe,
Tras mi pena y desconsuelo,
625　　Que arroje aquel monte al cielo,
Y que á Dios le dé con él?

GÉNERO HUMANO.
¡Oh, cómo el traidor blasfema!

LUZBEL.
Decid, ¿no sabeis los dos,
Infames, que soy par Dios?

INVIDIA.
630　　Cada loco con su tema.

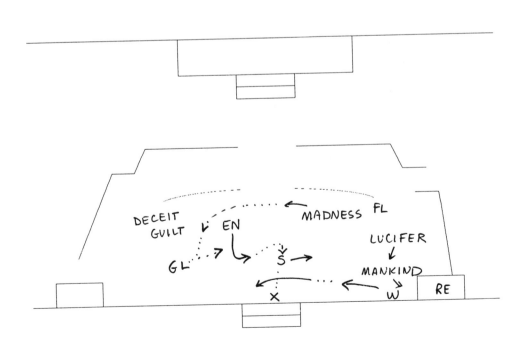

LUCIFER.
(Knocking down MANKIND, who crosses right.)
Well, don't you see?
I answered that!
Well, ask me again to reply.

620 Or incite me until I am annoyed,
On my life I'll hurl you
Into the abyss of Grief.
Cruel people, you solicit
My Grief and distress,

625 So that I may hurl that mountain to the sky
And hit God with it?

MANKIND.
(Crossing behind SOUL who crosses LUST, behind MADNESS.)
Oh! How the traitor blasphemies!
(SOUL is chased back left by MADNESS.)

LUCIFER.
Tell me, don't you two know,
Scoundrels, that I am like God?

ENVY.
(Crossing to SOUL.)
630 Every madman has his mania.

...Him the almighty power
Hurled headlong flaming from th' Ethereal Sky
Milton: *PARADISE LOST*

We may with more successful help resolve
To wage by force or guile eternal war
Irreconcileable, to our grand foe,
Who now triumphs, and th' excess of joy
Soul reigning holds the Tyranny of heav'n
Milton: *PARADISE LOST*

CULPA.
¿Cómo tu lengua se atreve
Delante de mi presencia?...

LUZBEL.
¿Eres tú más que la Escencia
Que adoran los coros nueve?
635   Pues, con temerarios modos,
Cuando mi hermosura vi,
Al mismo Dios me atreví.

INVIDIA.
Ansí me lo paguen todos.

ALMA.
Aquéste loco es de atar.

LUZBEL.
640   Atadme vos, cariharte.

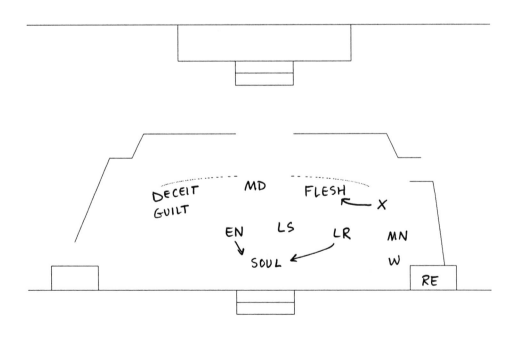

GUILT.
How does your tongue dare
In my presence...?

LUCIFER.
Are you more than the Essence
That the nine muses adore?
635   Well, with reckless ways,
When I saw my beauty,
I dared even God.

ENVY.
(Crossing to SOUL.)
Thus everyone repays me.

SOUL.
(FLESH crosses up.)
This fool is all tied up.

LUCIFER.
(Crossing to SOUL.)
640   Tie me up, yourself Decayed one.

...peace is dispaired,
For who can think submission! War then, war
Open or understood must be resolv'd.
He spake: And to confirm his words, out flew
Millions of flaming swords...
...highly they rage'd
Against the highest, and fierce with grasped arm's
Clash'd on their sounding shields the din of war,
Hurling defiance toward the vault of Heav'n.
          Milton: *PARADISE LOST*

Goddesses who presided over poetry, music, dancing, and all the liberal
arts; they were nine in number.

...O how fall'n! How chang'd
From him, who in the happy Realms of Light
Cloth'd with transcendent brightness dids't thou't shine
Myriads...
          Milton: *PARADISE LOST*

ALMA.

¿Quién eres?

LUZBEL.

¡Cócale, Marta!

INVIDIA.

Monos es que sabe trepar.

CULPA.

Echalde nuevas prisiones.

LUZBEL.

Cuando de diamante fueran,

645   Mis fuerzas las deshicieran,

Y á tí, si á echarlas te pones.

CULPA.

Bellaco, viejo Mal-hagas,

Respetad á esta señora.

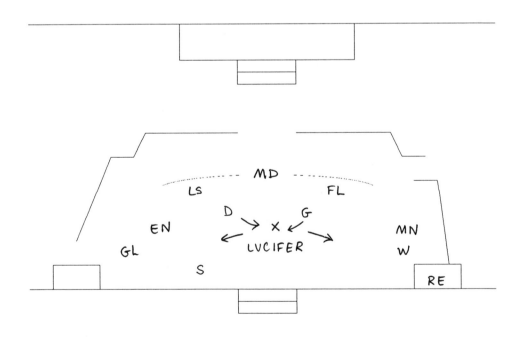

SOUL.
Who are you?

LUCIFER.
Cocale, Marta!

ENVY.
Only a monkey knows how to climb trees.

GUILT.
(With DECEIT, grabbing LUCIFER.)
Put on new shackles.
(To MADNESS.)

LUCIFER.
(Throwing both off, left and right, respectively.)
Then if they were made of diamonds,
(MADNESS crosses around him, up left center.)
645   My forces would destroy them,
And you, if you try to put them on.

GUILT.
(Crossing to LUCIFER in a fury.)
You schemer / old evil doer,
Respect this lady.

GUILT goes to MADNESS to put shackles on LUCIFER. Shackling LUCIFER would have been beneath GUILT. During this scene GUILT maintains a false face to SOUL who still thinks of GUILT as mother to the Youth, LUST. However, GUILT's plans, as we have learned, is for SOUL to be destroyed and eventually for her to be shackled as well. GUILT's binding of LUCIFER is to support her image as protective of SOUL.

149

INVIDIA.
Pues, ¿quién es?

LUZBEL.
    La perra mora,
650   Que viene por vuestras bragas.

ALMA.
Furor tiene.

CULPA.
    Es un furioso,
Que, aunque siempre está enjaulado
Y en llamas encadenado,
No tiene hora de reposo.

ALMA.
655   ¿De qué tan furioso está?

CULPA.
De una soberbia caida.

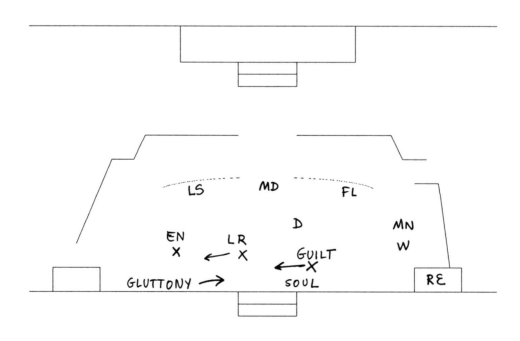

ENVY.
Why, who is she?

LUCIFER
(Crossing to ENVY.)
The Moorish bitch,
650 Who is hanging onto your breeches.

SOUL.
He is in a fury.
(Murmurings and yelping of locos stop.)

GUILT.
(She stamps her foot at GLUTTONY.)
He is a furious man,
Who, was always caged
And chained down in flames,
And has had no time to rest.

SOUL.
655 What has made him so furious?

GUILT.
By an arrogant fall.
(She looks ominously at SOUL.)

GUILT, there is need for balance: if the actor goes too far emotionally, the actor needs to go somewhat in the opposite direction.

...Him the Almighty Power
Hurled headlong flaming...
To bottomless perdition, there to dwell in adamantine
Chains and penal fire...
Milton: *PARADISE LOST*

The Roman poet Ovid was the most widely read Latin poet of the middle ages. We may assume that Ovid's *METAMORPHOSES* was well known to Valdivielso as it had been known and widely read by the Italian poet Dante.

ALMA.
¿Tiene peligro su vida?

CULPA.
Antes nunca morirá.

ALMA.
¿Que siempre vive muriendo?

CULPA.
660   Es su tormento sin fin.

LUZBEL.
Soy un negro serafin,
Que vuestras tachas entiendo.

ALMA.
Lástima me da el mirallo.

LUZBEL.
Yo no la tengo de vos.

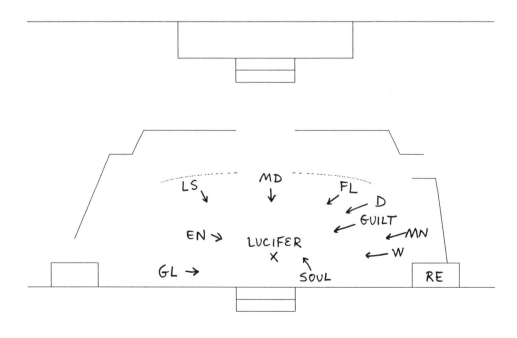

SOUL.
Is his life in danger?

GUILT.
(Looking to LUCIFER.)
Once he would never die.

SOUL.
He always lives, dying?

GUILT.
660   It is his unending torment.

LUCIFER.
I am a black seraph
Who understands your weaknesses.

SOUL.
It pities me to see you.

LUCIFER.
I have no pity for you.

GUILT in some respects is in competition with LUCIFER; both struggle to capture SOUL, to control her for each's own end. Moreover LUCIFER wants to be free of his chains. To that end he tries to get anyone on his side. GUILT had put LUCIFER in chains; he struggles, fights to be outside of her control.

GUILT stamps at GLUTTONY whom she wants to have away from her. Other of the *locos* are testing GUILT, closing in on her. This challange to GUILT's authority makes her furious.

The actor is to make friends with the text, becoming not bound by it, but more free.

Clues and hidden stage directions exist in the text.

(*LUZBEL.*)
665   ¿Sabeis quién soy?

              ALMA.
              ¿Quién?

              LUZBEL.
              Par Dios.
              ¡Par Dios, á pié y á caballo!
              Angel diz que quiso hacerme
              El que á los demas crió,
              Y tan hermoso me vió,
670   Que tuvo envidia de verme.
              Volvióme un fiero avestruz,
              Mi mismo yerro comiendo; 34
              Caí do vivo muriendo,
              Hecho un lucero sin luz.

              GÉNERO HUMANO.
675   Así cae elque se atreve.

Valdivielso, as may be noted, uses in the Spanish text the word
avestruces [ostriches] which colloquially may mean ignoramous. I assume he is
also echoing the line... *become cruel, like the ostriches in the wilderness (...Se han
hecho crueles como las avestruces del desierto.)* —*LAMINTATIONS (4:3).*

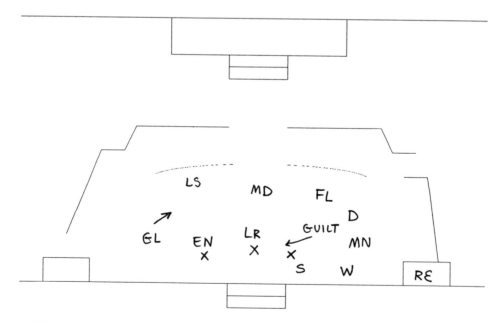

<hr />

34 Recuérdese la creencia vulgar de que los añectreces digiren el hierro.

LUCIFER.

665   Do you know who I am?

SOUL.
Who?

LUCIFER.
Equal to God.
Equal to God on foot and on horseback!
They say that He who created all the others
Wanted to make me an angel
And so beautiful He saw me,
670   That He had envy of me.
He turned me back into a wild ignoramous
Letting me get on with my erring
Alive, my fall was mortal,
Made into a star without light.

MANKIND.

675   Thus falls he who dares.

MANKIND's pithy comment is both poignant and dramatic. It is a one line of dialogue that deserves all that the actor can give it; however, sentensious or solemn delivery is to be expressly avoided. These single lines that are compact are a textual challenge.

I behold Satan as lightening fall from heaven. —LUKE
Yo veía a Satauås coyendo de cialo, como un rayo. —LUKE

...his Pride
Had cast him out from heaven... aspiring
To set himself in Glory above his Peers,
He trusted to have equal'd the most High...
...Him the Almighty Power
Hurld headlong flaming from th' Ethereal Skie
With hideous ruine and combustion down
To bottomless perdition,...
            Milton: *PARADISE LOST*

LUZBEL.
¿Y vos, viejo, no caistes?

ALMA.
En efeto, ¿un ángel fuistes?

LUZBEL.
Y soy el diablo que os lleve.
Soy quien sé beberme un rio
680 Y tragarme entero un monte;
Espantar ese horizonte,
Cuando al cielo desafio.
Soy quien vomita centellas
Del infierno de mi daño,
685 Y soy un dragon, que empaño
Con mi aliento las estrellas.

ALMA.
Locura, á este loco ten.

LOCURA.
No hayais miedo.

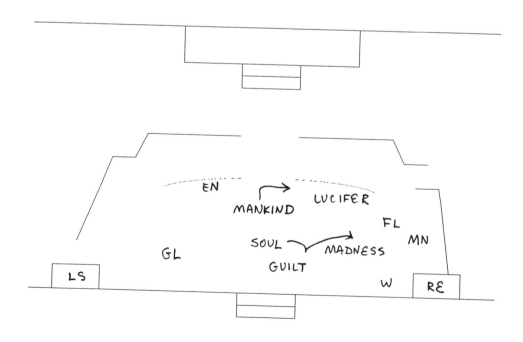

156

LUCIFER.
And you old man, you did not fall?

SOUL.
So indeed you were an angel?

LUCIFER.
And I am the devil who is with you.
I am one who knows how to drink a river
680   And swallow an entire mountain;
To frighten the horizon,
When it defies Heaven.
I am one who vomits lightening
From the Hell of my sorrow.
685   I am a dragon, who tarnishes
The stars with my breath.

SOUL.
(Behind MADNESS.)
Madness, take this fool.

MADNESS.
(Fearfully.)
Don't be afraid.

GUILT watches SOUL's questioning of LUCIFER. GUILT is a very powerful image on stage. Due to her built up boots, she is the tallest, also, the darkest, most elaborately costumed of the characters.

This is a moving and dramatic scene; SOUL, for the moment, is *straight man* to LUCIFER, setting up LUCIFER's responses. The actor playing LUCIFER must avoid working the text too hard. If the actor gets himself too emotionally envolved in a speech of heightened language, he may flatten out his voice, cut off communication. When there is an excess of pain and feeling, the text may get strangulated and cut off.

157

ALMA.
Airado está.

LUZBEL.
Quién os trujo por acá?

ALMA.
690 El Deleite.

LUZBEL.
Hizo él muy bien.

CULPA.
Alma, deja ese insolente,
Y mira al Género Humano.

ALMA.
¿Cuál es?

CULPA.
Mira aquel anciano.

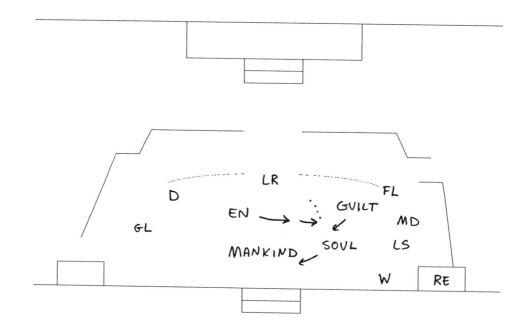

                    SOUL.
                    He is furious.

                    LUCIFER.
          Who has brought you here?

                    SOUL.
690   Lust.

                    LUCIFER.
                    He did well.

                    GUILT.
                    (Crossing to SOUL.)
          Leave the insolent one, Soul, /
          And look at Mankind.
                              *(ENVY intrudes and GUILT pushes him up
                              center.)*

                    SOUL.
                    *(Crossing with GUILT to MANKIND down
                    left.)*
          Which is he?

                    GUILT.
                    (Moving toward MANKIND.)
                    Look at that Ancient One.

     LUCIFER is treating SOUL badly. GUILT stops laughing and she goes
to protect SOUL. She doesn't like LUCIFER treating SOUL in that manner.

     The text should do a great deal of the work.

     If the emotions don't get on top, the text itself will resonate more.

ALMA.

Pues es algo mi pariente.

695   Decid, ¿de qué enloqueció?

CULPA.

De ser muy enamorado;
Dióle su dama un bocado,
Con que el seso le quitó.
Hizo en su estado mudanza.

ALMA.

700   Ya su desgracia imagino.—
¿Quién sois vos?
                (Al GÉNERO HUMANO.)

GÉNERO HUMANO.

        Soy un pollino...
Tras ser de Dios semejanza.
Virey fuí de todo el suelo,
Y allá, por cierta desgracia,

705   Privóme el Rey de su gracia,

SOUL.

695   He seems to be familiar. /
Tell me, of what did he go mad?

GUILT.

Of being too much in love;
His lady gave him a bite
With which he lost his senses.
It changed his whole being.

SOUL.

700   I can well imagine his misfortune —
(Kneeling to MANKIND.)
And who are you?

MANKIND.

I am a young ass...
(All laugh.)
After being in God's image.
I was viceroy of the whole Earth
(Laughing.)
And there, because of a certain misfortune,
705   The King deprived me of his grace.

SOUL is to look at MANKIND, that Ancient One, as a relative. As SOUL says *'Tell me, of what did he go mad?'* and then SOUL learns that it was of love. SOUL is moved and goes closer to MANKIND, slowly and senuously, touching his head. She can understand his misfortune now that she is going through what he went through. She is now infatuated with LUST. In a state of ectasy from being in love SOUL touches all the *locos.*

Then God said, "Let us make man in our image, after our likeness; and let them have dominion over all the earth."... —GENESIS

"Because you... have eaten of the tree of which I commanded you not to eat, cursed is the ground because of you."... So the Lord God drove man out of the Garden of Eden... —GENESIS

(*GÉNERO HUMANO.*)
Y, par diez, dejóme en pelo.
Enojóse la Razon,
Tiró el Apetito coces,
Dieron los dos muchas voces,
710 Y hubo mucho mojicon.
Perdí el ser noble é hidalgo
Por seguir mi antojo ciego;
Vi un cuchillazo de fuego,
Y dí á correr como un galgo.
715 La tierra produjo abrojos,
Frio el aire, el sol calor,
Estas entrañas dolor,
Y lágrimas estos ojos.
Una mujer me brindó
720 (Que esto nunca olvidaré),
Y, aunque ella la causa fué...
¡Yo tuve la culpa, yo!

INVIDIA.
¡Concertadme esas razones!

GÉNERO HUMANO.
Aquesto pasa sin duda.

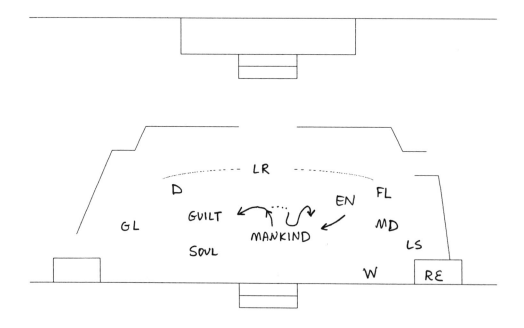

                    (MANKIND.)
          [And, with ten Hail Mary's, left me stripped.
          Reason became irritable,
          And kicked Appetite,
          They both shouted,
710   *And many times they punched each other in the*
          *face.]*35
          I lost the right to be noble and proud
          By following blindly whims
                         (Taking stage: Crossing up right and down
                         right.)
          Then saw I a torrent of fire,
          And I ran like a hound.
715   Rocks sprang from the earth,
          The air became cold; the sun scorching;
          I learned of pain in my entrails,
          Tears in these eyes.
          A woman gave me an apple
720   (This I will never forget),
          And although she was the cause...
          I was to blame, I!

                    ENVY.
                 (Crossing to Man.)
          How can you prove all that!

                    MANKIND.
          That's how it happened without a doubt.

So the woman, seeing that the tree was good for food and was desired to make one wise, ate of its fruit. she gave some to her husband, and he also ate... East of Eden He [the Lord God] placed cherubim and a flaming sword which turned every way, to guard the way to the tree of life. —GENESIS

---

35 These lines were not used in the English-language production of the play.

INVIDIA.

725   Pues la pena será cuerpo suda
El señor Quiebra-terrones.

ALMA.

Pésame de su desgracia,
Por el bien que en ella pierdo.

INVIDIA.

Por la pena será cuerdo.

GÉNERO HUMANO.

730   Mejor diréis por la Gracia.

INVIDIA.

¿Quién soy no me preguntais?

ALMA.

No importa no conoceros.

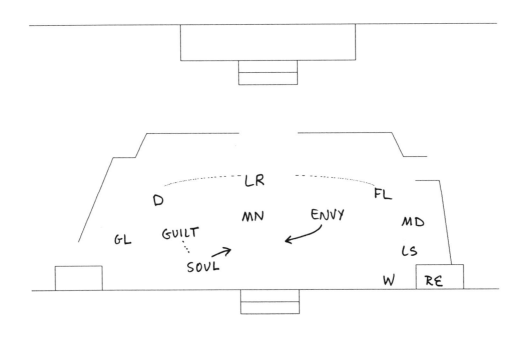

ENVY.
(Crossing center.)
725 So now Man, who plows the earth,
Does so with the sweat of his brow.

SOUL.
My condolences for his midfortune,
For the happiness which he lost.

ENVY.
(To SOUL.)
Through pity he will become sane.

MANKIND.
730 Better you say: through Grace.

ENVY.
(To SOUL.)
Don't you ask me who I am?

SOUL.
It's not important that I know you.

Characters are always inter-reacting physically with each other, thereby seeing that the nearest character gets out of his space. Each is in his own world. At moments they are hitting each other; at other times embracing each other. At all times in these scenes much is going on.

GUILT is insincere. She doesn't let SOUL know that she's a captive in her asylum. Thus, SOUL doesn't realize she's locked in now. She thinks she's meeting these interesting people. GUILT pushes WORLD toward SOUL. GUILT introduces her to all the wonderful pleasures of the WORLD, for SOUL is innocent.

"...In toil you shall eat of it [the tree] *all your life, and it shall bring forth thorns and thisles to you. In the sweat of your face you shall eat bread till you return to the ground..." —GENESIS*

INVIDIA.

Soy quien le pesa de veros
Tan galana como estáis.

ALMA.

735   ¿Cómo me quereis tan bien?

INVIDIA.

Como es en mí natural
Darme gusto vuestro mal,
Y tormento vuestro bien.

MUNDO.

No quieras que te requiebre
740   Quien no deja hueso sano.

INVIDIA.

Haceldo vos, casquivano,
Que vendeis gato por liebre.

MUNDO.

Deja esa melancolía,
Y pues eres bella y moza,
745   Mi riqueza y gustos goza,
Y los de esta hermana mia.
        (Señalando á LA CARNE.)

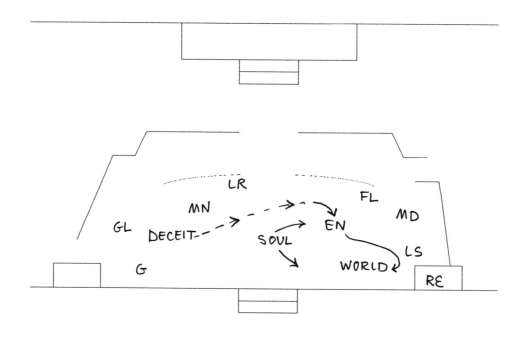

166

ENVY.
I'm the one who regrets to see you
(Gesturing sweepingly to SOUL's costume.)
As elegant as you are.

SOUL.
(To FLESH and then to WORLD.)
735   What would make you like me more?

ENVY.
It is my nature to
Get pleasure from your misfortune,
(Pushing WORLD toward SOUL.)
And torment from your happiness.

WORLD.
You don't want to be wooed by Envy.
740   He'll crush your bones.

ENVY.
(Held in a grip by DECEIT.)
Do it yourself, hare-brain:
You'd sell a sow's ear for a purse.

WORLD.
Leave this melencholy,
And, since you're young and beautiful,
745   Enjoy the riches and pleasures,
Of my sister and me.
(Pointing to FLESH.)

WORLD crosses between SOUL and ENVY. LUST pushes ENVY toward DECEIT; WORLD and SOUL cross down right, followed by LUST.

The actors should stress key words, lift them out. It is important to avoid an overlay of emotion expressed, rather than a realization of the text.

(*MUNDO.*)

Esparciré á esas estrellas,
De rosas y de jazmines
Alhombras de mis jardines,
750   Que pisen tus plantas bellas.
Darete arroyos de plata,
Piedras, diamantes, rubíes,
Los corales carmesíes
Y las telas de escarlata;
755   Las lanas, sedas, brocados,
Plantas, animales, aves,
Dulces músicas süaves
Y extraordinarios guisados.
Del mar te daré el tesoro,
760   De aquellos ojos las perlas
Quc si ésos llegan á verlas,
Las verás cubiertas de oro
Daréte lo que me pidas,
Daréte lo que imagines.

GULA.

765   Y yo haré los matachines
Con las orejas de Mídas.

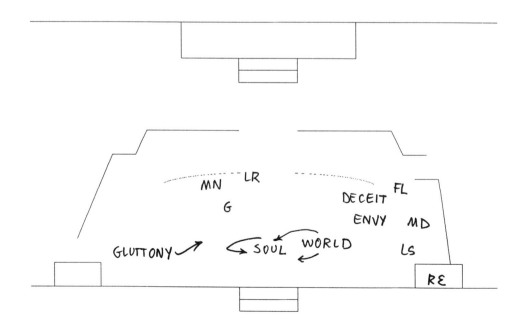

168

(WORLD.)

I will scatter to those stars,
All the petals of rose and jasmine,
Carpets of my gardens,
750   On which your beautiful feet may tread.
I will give you streams of silver,
Precious stones, diamonds, rubies,
Crimson corals;
Cloth of scarlet,
755   Wool, silk, brocades;
Plants, animals, birds;
Sweets, soft music
And wonderous foods.
I will give you the treasures of the sea,
760   Pearls, eyes of the ocean;
Which, if ever seen,
Will be seen covered in gold.
I will give you whatever you ask of me,
I will give you anything that you may imagine.

GLUTTONY.

765   And I will play the clown
With King Midas' donkey ears.

King Midas had the imprudence to assert that Pan was superior to Apollo in singing and in playing on the flute, for which rash opinion the offended God changed his ears into those of an ass, to show his ignorance and stupidity.
Ovid: *METAMORPHOSES*

The Spanish is verse and the English is free verse. Phrase it to have a slight break at the ends of the lines; phrase it with rather than against the verse lines. The actor is to breathe at the end of the verse lines: however, following the verse slavishly is something not to be recommended; likewise, to ignore it totally is most unfortunate.

This is WORLD's seduction with language. It's a poetically tense speech of lush imagery: '... wools, silks, brocades, plants, animals, birds, sweets, soft music and wonderous foods.' The actor should largely experience these images tactilely and thereby communicate to the audience a sensuous experience, for WORLD is offering to SOUL whatever she may ask of him.

Each image should be expressed very sharply as different. Convey the color, the sensation through vocal resources.

169

ALMA.

Mundo, tus brazos me da.
(*Abrázanse.*)

CARNE.

De gusto y contento salto.

LUZBEL.

Deja el cielo.

ALMA.

Está muy alto;
770 Estése el cielo ahora allá.—
¡Ah, Gula! ¿no nos hablamos?

GULA.

De vuestro cuello me cuelgo.
¿Holgaisos?

ALMA.

Mucho me huelgo.

GULA.

Pues comamos y bebamos.

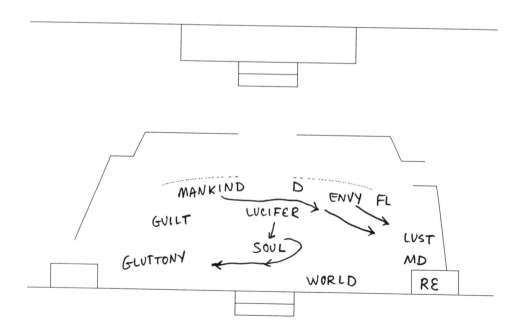

170

SOUL.
World, give me your arm.

(They embrace and MANKIND dances with ENVY up right to LUST.)

FLESH.
I jump with glee and joy.

LUCIFER.
Abandon Heaven.

(LUCIFER whirls SOUL; then he spins her down right to GLUTTONY.)

SOUL.
Heaven is very high

770 May it now remain there. //
Oh, Gluttony are we not speaking?

GLUTTONY.
I hang from your neck.
Does that please you?

SOUL.
It pleases me very much.

GLUTTONY.
Then we will eat and drink.

WORLD is trying to lure SOUL, by feeling her white, filmy dress. All the *locos* are around her, trying to lure her into imprisonment.

The scene is tremendously physical. There is to be no moment of the *locos* just standing around; all are to be very, very, active at all times on stage.

A challenge to the actors in the scene is how to marry the emotional and intellectual demands of the text.

CULPA.

(Ap. á la Carne.)

775   Buenos mis intentos van.
        Carne, al Alma me provoca.

GULA.

¡Ya está loca, ya está loca!

LUZBEL.

¡Loca está! ¡Tapalatan!

CARNE.

        De rosas nos coronemos;
780   Vino oloroso bebamos;
        No haya flor que no cojamos,
        Ni prado que no pisemos.
        Entreguémonos al gusto,
        Al ocio, al ocio, al placer,
785   Al deleite, á la mujer.

ALMA.

Mucho de tus cosas gusto.

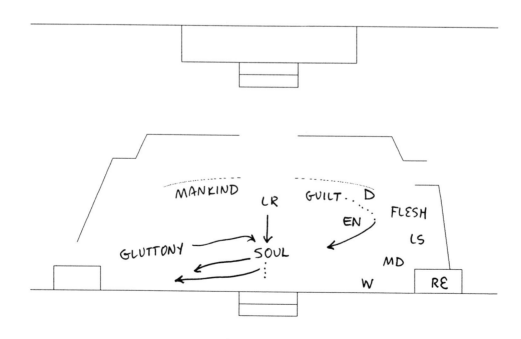

172

GUILT.
(Aside to FLESH.)

775   My plot goes well.
Flesh, flirt with Soul.

GLUTTONY.
(She whirls SOUL up center to FLESH.)

Now she's mad, now she's mad.

LUCIFER.
(Crossing down center.)

She's mad, tapala ta!
(Music.)

FLESH.
(Crossing with SOUL down left.)

We will crown ourselves with roses;
780   We will drink fragrant wine;
There will be no flower we will not pick,
Nor meadow we will not trod.
We will give ourselves to pleasure,
Idleness, vices, delights,
785   To lust, to women.

SOUL.
I like very much what you offer.

As was cited above as a direction to relish WORLD, FLESH is to relish the images of her long speech; she likewise, tactilely, the images that are in the speech. This is to communicate to the audience a sensuous experience.

I was in the third circle of the rain
That falls eternal, heavy, cold, and damned...
Cerberus, strange and ferocious beast...
He tore the spirits, skinned, and quartered them...
For the pernicious vice of gluttony.
    [Dante: HELL]

Io sono al terzo cerchio della piova
Eterna, mala detta, fredda e greve...
Gerbero, fiera crudele e diversa...
Graffia gli spiriti, iscuoia, e disquatra...
Per la damnosa colpa della gola.
    [Dante: INFERNO]

MUNDO.
Vive alegre, Alma divina;
Vive alegre en verte aquí.

GULA.
¡Ésta es vida, pesiamí!
790 No el ayuno y disciplina.

MUNDO.
Ande la fiesta y banquete,
El sarao y la cancion,
El juego y murmuracion,
El baile, el mote, el billete.
795 Ande la gala, el donaire,
La risa y desenvoltura.

ALMA.
¡Ven, ventura, ven y dura!...

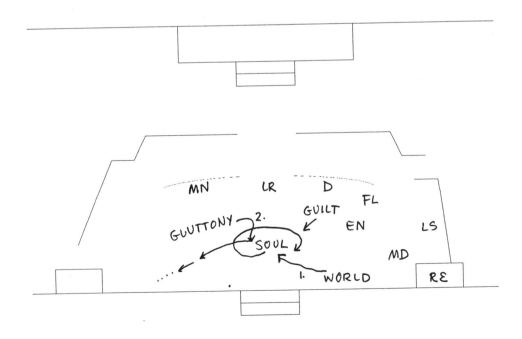

> ### WORLD.
> *(Taking SOUL up stage center with a swirl.)*
> *(Music up.)*
> Live happily, Divine Soul;
> Live happily, in being here.
> > *(GUILT sends GLUTTONY up center stage.)*

> ### GLUTTONY.
> *(Dancing with SOUL.)*
> This is life, dammit!
790   No fasting or dicipline.
> > *(Crossing down right.)*

> ### WORLD.
> *(WORLD and SOUL dance.)*
> May the feast and gaiety go on,
> Wine and song
> Games and gossip,
> Dancing, taunting, billets d' amour.
795   On with splendor, elegance,
> Laughter and abandonment.

> ### SOUL.
> Come, good fortune, come and endure!...

Direction to WORLD: learn to play an action; if you get lost asking yourself what am I doing here, what am I after?, return to the intention of the scene, for WORLD is likely to feel lost at moments.

As with the other *locos*, WORLD is to do certain definite things. But, WORLD, as is true for each *loco*, is to invent *business* not part of the basic plot. For example, WORLD may invent what is going on for him, improvise, but he is to do so as the character, as must each *loco*, in his or her own fantasy.

If the actor plays the action fully, the emotion will come. Always.

MANKIND dances with FLESH. A carousel effect with all actors begins here, gaining in momentum: circling first is MANKIND, then FLESH, LUCIFER, MADNESS, DECEIT, LUST; GLUTTONY with ENVY creates a counter weaving. The carousel stops with SOUL's line.

INVIDIA.
Abre la boca, y paparás aire.

CULPA.
¡Oh, qué bien los dos hacieis!

MUNDO.
800   Toma mi cetro y corona.

ALMA.
¡Ésta sí qué es vida bona!

INVIDIA.
Al freir me lo diréis.

GULA.
¡Hola, venga la comida!

ALMA.
Venga, que comer deseo.

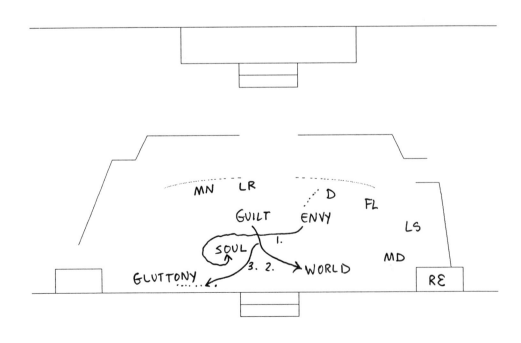

ENVY.
(Singing and dancing with SOUL.)
Open your mouth, and you will gulp air.

GUILT.
(Taking SOUL back to WORLD.)
Oh, how well you both do!

WORLD.
800   Take my scepter and crown.

SOUL.
This is surely the good life.

ENVY.
(Crossing to grilles of the cells for a shawl.)
You will tell me when you are bored to death with it.

GLUTTONY.
(Kneeling.)
Hello, here comes the food!

SOUL.
(Crowning GLUTTONY.)
Let it come, for I wish to eat.

Play two or three contradictory attitudes at once. Go for the spirit as well as the details in the dialogue.

Mariana of Austria (his Queen) upon the death of Philip IV totally prohibited performances of theatre in Spain. She stated that not until the Prince (her son?) would decide, would there be once again performances. Religious committees went to ask the Queen, Mariana, for permission to allow them to have theatres, because theatre was a way of raising money to carry out works of charity. Thanks to the religious, after seven years, there was once again theatre in Spain.

GÉNERO HUMANO.

805   Bebió el agua del Leteo.
Rematada está y perdida.

CULPA.

Repica aquesa guitarra,
    (A LA CARNE.)
Y tú el panderete toca,
    (A LUZBEL.)
Que hoy triunfo del Alma loca.

INVIDIA.

810   Bebió el zumo de tu parra.

ALMA.

Llégate á mí, amada Carne;
Tú, Gula, á mí te avecina.
    (Pónese EL ALMA entre LA GULA y LA
    CARNE.)

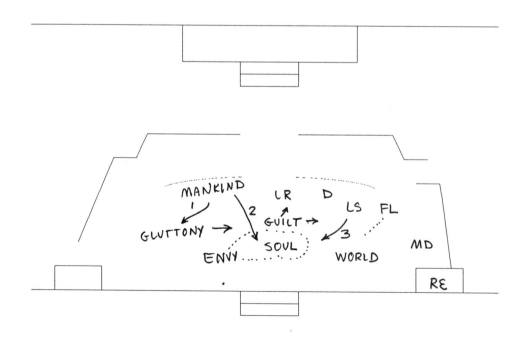

MANKIND.
(Crossing to GLUTTONY.)

805   She drank the water of Lethe
She is ruined and lost.

GUILT.
(To FLESH.)
Play that guitar again,
(To LUCIFER.)
And you, play the tambourine
For today I triumph over crazy Soul.
(Staying behind with DECEIT and LUST.)

ENVY.

810   She drank the wine from your vine.

SOUL.
(LUST and MANKIND swing her.)
(Fade music.)
Come here to me, beloved Flesh;
(She steps between GLUTTONY and FLESH.)
You, Gluttony, come nearer to me.

Lethe: One of the rivers of hell, the waters of which the souls of the dead drank after they had been confined for a certain space of time... it had the power of making them forget whatever they had done, seen, or heard before. [36]

On MANKIND's *'she is ruined and lost;'* SOUL breaks away from his embrace. WORLD claims his crown. ENVY parades about WORLD with his robe.

WORLD carries a bottle of wine. Dancing with WORLD, SOUL is drunk and drunk with pleasure. GUILT notes that she drank wine from WORLD's vine. Inebriated, SOUL calls to FLESH and GLUTTONY. SOUL is beginning to be taken over by both vices.

[36] Lemprierè, J., LEMPRIERE'S CLASSICAL DICTIONARY. London: Bracken Books, 1984

INVIDIA.
Alma, pareceis espina,
Metida entre cuero y carne.

MUNDO.
815   Hoy tu vitoria publico.
GULA.
Andiamo á mangiar, madonna.

ALMA.
¿Dónde vamos?

GULA.
A Chacona.

ALMA.
Pues vámonos por Tambico.

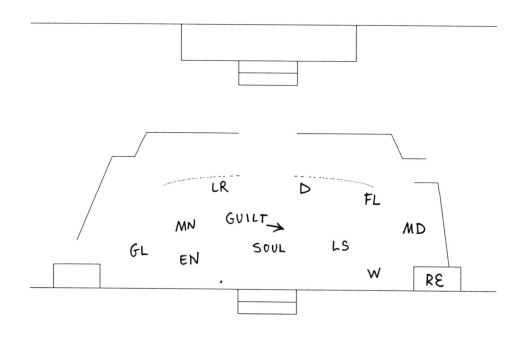

ENVY.
(Throwing shawl over SOUL.)
Soul, you look like a thorn,
Placed between leather and Flesh.

WORLD.
815   I announce your victory today.

GLUTTONY.
[In Italian.]
"Andiamo a magiar madonna."
[Let's go eat, madonna.]

SOUL.
Where are we going?

GLUTTONY.
(As she dances.)
To the *Chaconne.*

SOUL.
Then let us go to dance the *Tambico.*

The climax of the scene is dancing and more dancing. Dance as pleasure represents sexuality symbolically .

At the performances of *autos,* there was much noise and disorder among the motley crowds that thronged the streets and the public squares to see them. Nor was this disorder confined to the mob. Under the date of June 16, 1615, there was a statement emmanating from the council of Madrid declaring that attention is bein g drawn to the disorder which is wont to be created on the stage... On June 10, 1765, a royal decree was issued stating that the theatre's were not proper places and the commedians were unfit and unworthy persons to represent the sacred mystries of which the *autos sacramentales* speak, and that the King had therefore determined to prohibit absolutely all representations of *autos sacramentales...* Thus there passed from the popular stage a kind of religious drama that was peculiar to Spain.

181

RAZON.
(MUSICA.)

<blockquote>

¡Vita, vita, la vita bona!

820   *¡Alma, vámonos á Chacona!*

Al hospital de la Culpa

Vino enferma esta señora,

A quien el sol del Deleite

Dió una terrible modorra.

825   *A la cama de Cupido,*

Que es de espinas entre rosas,

Llevan á la pobre dama,

Que entre sus males se goza.

Es la Gula la enfermera,

830   *Y la Carne la doctora,*

Que, cual médico ignorante, [37]

La manda que beba y coma.

</blockquote>

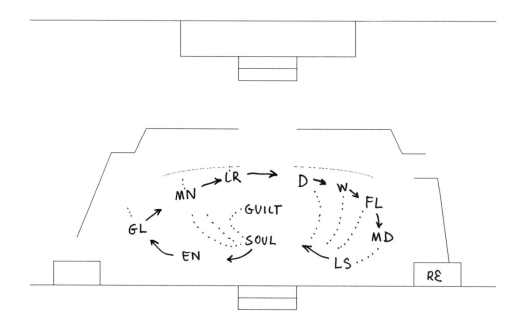

[37] Que cualquier médico ignorante.

REASON.

(Singing.)

Vita, vita, la vita bona
820   *Let us go dance the Chaconne!*
This sick lady came,
To the house of Guilt,
And the heat of Lust
Infected her with a terrible itch.
825   *They brought the poor lady,*
Who rejoices in evil things,
To Cupid's bed
Made with thorns among the roses.
Gluttony is the nurse
830   *And Flesh is the doctor,*
Who, as any ignorant physician does,
Tells her to drink and eat.

REASON sings the song. REASON is to sing the song as a peasant, not as a refined lady. The voice is to be sort of harsh, peasant-like, and simple. REASON is to be a peasant all the way through.

The refrain, *'Vita, vita,'* etc., is repeated, first by SOUL, second by all, third by all *locos* without SOUL.

(*RAZON.*)
Es el Mundo boticario,
Que las píldoras le dora,
835 *Dándole a agua del olvido*
De sus fingidas redomas.
Ella, cual simple cordera,
Lleva arrastrando la soga,
Y, con ir al matadero,
840 *Repite en voces sonoras:*
¡Vida, vida, vida bona!
¡Vida, vámonos á Chacona!
(*Vanse.*)

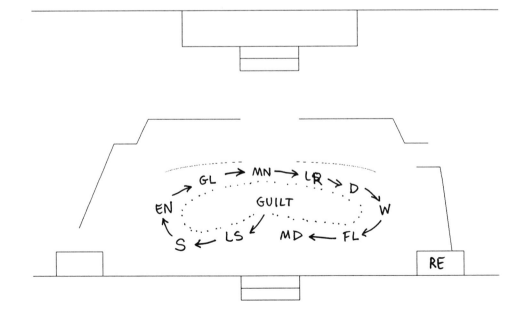

REASON.

World is the apothecary,
Who gives the pills,
835   *Giving her water of forgetfulness*
From his false flasks.
She, like a meek lamb,
Drags at the halter,
And, while off to the slaughter house,
840   *Repeats in a resounding cry:*
Life, life, the good life!
Life, let us go to the Chaconne!
(SOUL screams. All fall asleep.)

All the *locos* circle the stage twice ending on the floor left and they fall asleep.

ESCENA XVI

Quedan LA CULPA, y LA LOCURA.

CULPA.

Locura, cuidado ten,
Y entre aquella gloria falsa
845   Ponle la engañosa salsa
Que hace mal y sabe bien.
En medio de la comida,
Cuando con más gusto coma,
De los cabellos la toma,
850   Pues no habrá quien te lo impida,
Y llevarásla arrastrando
A la más triste prision
Que inventó mi confusion,
Adonde viva penando.
855   Enjaulada en una reja,
Pondrás entre sus prisiones
Tristes desesperaciones
Del bien eterno que deja.
Quítale la luz del cielo;
860   Represéntala su mal.—
Parte, ministro infernal,
Y haz lo que te mando.

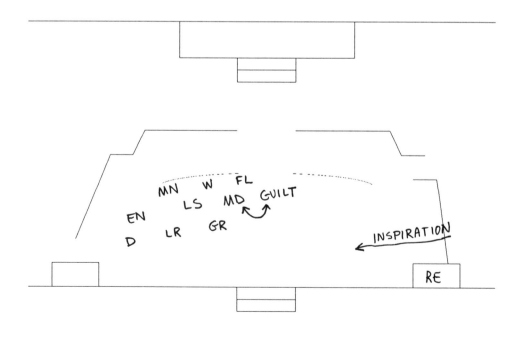

186

SCENE XVI

GUILT.
(Waking MADNESS.)

Madness, be careful,
And within that false song of praise to God
845   Put the deceitful melody
That does evil while it sounds good.
In the midst of the meal,
While she eats with most enjoyment,
Take her unaware,
(Gesturing toward the sleeping SOUL.)
850   For there will be no one to prevent it,
And you will carry her, resisting,
To the saddest prison
That my deliberate confusion created,
Where she may live, punished.
855   Caged behind bars,
You will place among her shackles
Sorrowful reminders
For the eternal good that she leaves behind
Take away from her the light of Heaven;
860   Show her misfortune. / /
Go, infernal minister,
And do what I tell you.

All are asleep except GUILT and MADNESS.

Heaven banished them before they marred it,
And even deepest Hell will not accept them...
An old man white with venerable hair,
Who started shoutng: "Woe to you, base spirits!
Abandon hope of ever seeing Heaven!
I come to take you to the other side,
Into eternal darkness..."
      Dante: *HELL*

Cacciarli i Ciel per non esser men belli:
Nèlo profondo inferno gli riceve...
Un vecchio bianco per antico pelo,
Gridanda: "Guai a voi anime prave:
Non isperate mai veder lo cielo!
I'vegno per menarvi all'altra riva,
Nelle tenebre eterne..."
      Dante: *INFERNO*

LOCURA.

Harélo.

Será su tema crüel,

Tal, que la gloria le quite,

865 Y yo haré que la visite

La Carne, Mundo y Luzbel.

(Vanse, y se cierra el carro del hospital.)

ESCENA XVII

Sale LA INSPIRACION.

INSPIRACION.

Buscando vengo ocasion

De poder al Alma hablar,

Que nunca ha dado lugar

870 A ninguna inspiracion.

Tiénela á su infame mesa

El mundo falso engañada,

La vil Carne enhechizada,

Y el torpe Deleite presa.

875 Mas ¿Qué es lo que adentro suena?

¿Posible es que vengo á vello?

¡Como! ¿que te han puesta al cuello

Una pesada cadena?

La Carne el rostro la arana,

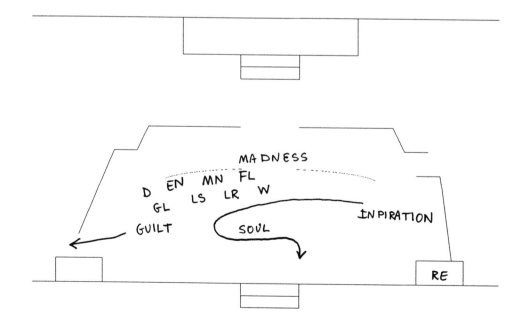

MADNESS.
　　I shall do it.
　　(He rises.)
　　It will give her such a cruel exercise
　　That the Glory of God may be withdrawn,
865　And I will have Flesh, World
　　And Lucifer visit her.
　　　　(GUILT crosses up to platform and exits
　　　　right.)

SCENE XVII
　　(INSPIRATION enters left, crossing to center;
　　then he circles SOUL ending down left.)

INSPIRATION.
　　I am looking for the opportunity
　　To be able to speak to Soul,
　　For none has provided her
870　With Divine influence
　　At his infamous table;
　　False World has deceived her
　　Vile Flesh has bewitched her;
　　Lewd Lust has her captive.
　　　　(SOUL awakens.)
875　But, what is that sound?
　　Is it possible what I see around her neck?
　　What! Have they placed
　　A heavy chain.
　　Flesh scratched her face,

INSPIRATION comes looking for SOUL. His goal is to save her. The actor playing INSPIRATION shoul seek out hidden ingredients of humor and wit, irony perhaps.

At the close of his speech, MADNESS moves up stage returning with a chain which he places around SOUL's neck. He leads her in a somnambulistic state up stage placing her behind one of the grilles.

REASON/RAZON

INSPIRATION/INSPIRACION

(*INSPIRACION.*)

880 El mundo vil la atormenta,
La Culpa penas inventa,
El infierno la acompaña...
No es ésta mala ocasion.
Pues que sola veo que queda
885 Enjaulada, donde pueda
Escuchar mi inspiracion.
Hácia la reja me voy;
Que ella hácia la reja llega.

ESCENA XVIII

LA INSPIRACION, en el escenario.—*Asómase EL ALMA arriba, en una reja, con una cadena, con acciones de loca.*

ALMA.

¿Qué es esto? ¿cómo estoy ciega?
890 ¿Cómo atada y ciega estoy?
¿Qué tristes fieras prisiones
En esta jaula me enlazan?
¿Cómo airadas me amenazan
Negras y horribles visiones?
895 Infierno, la boca cierra;
¿Por qué me quieres tragar?
¡Sorberme quiere la mar!
¡A hogarme quiere la tierra!—

(INSPIRATION.)

880 Vile World torments her,
Guilt invents punishments,
Hell accompanies her...
This is my chance,
For I see that she has been left
885 Caged and alone, where she may
Listen to my inspiration.
Caged as she has been
I will go to her.

SCENE XVIII

SOUL, INSPIRATION
[DECEIT, ENVY MANKIND, FLESH, LUCIFER, MADNESS, GLUTTONY, WORLD, LUST, REASON]

SOUL.

(Gesticulating wildly.)
What is this? Why am I blind?
890 How is it I am tied down and blind?
What sad fierce shackles
Have chained me down in this cave?
How is it angry, black and horrible
Visions threaten me?
895 Hell closes its mouth;
Why do you want to swallow me?
The sea wants to swallow me up!
The earth wants to smother me! //

SOUL is seeking for salvation in vain.

The problem for the actress is how to do justice to the sound and fury of the language and to keep it humanly sympathetic for the sake of the audience. The emotion expressed must not be so great as to obscure the words, leaving them to take care of themselves. To make the spectators both listen to the speech and to empathize feelingly with it the actress must use the words, finding the images and to make them express the emotions.

(ALMA.)

¡Triste! ¿qué es lo que he perdido?
900 ¡Triste! ¿qué es lo que he ganado?
La puerta el cielo ha cerrado,
Y de luto se ha cerrado,
¿Quién se ha muerto? ¿quién se ha muerto
Angeles, ¿de qué llorais?
905 ¿Para qué voces me dais?...
Que es dar voces en desierto.
Buscais mi remedio en vano,
Pues Dios, con ira no poca,
Trae un cuchillo en la boca,
910 Y una navaja en la mano.
Envainad aquesa espada...
¡Angeles, ponéos en medio!
¡No hay remedio! ¡no hay remedio!

INSPIRACION.

¡Alma triste y desdichada!

ALMA.

915 ¿Quién hablaba aparte allá? [38]

INSPIRACION.

Alma amada, ten sosiego.

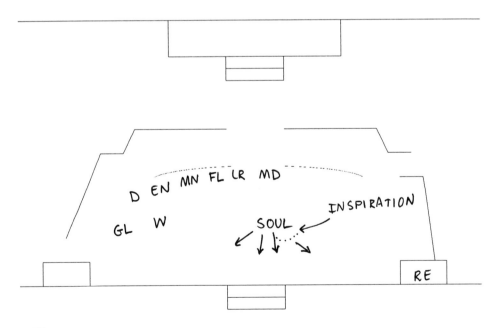

<hr>

38 ¿Quién habla aparte allá?

194

SOUL.
(SOUL moves out from behind the grille on to the stage.)

Woe is me! What have I lost?
900   Woe is me! What have I gained?
The door of Heaven has shut,
And is draped in mourning.
Who has died? Who has died?
Angels, why are you crying?
905   Why do you shout at me? / /
It is like shouting in a desert.
(INSPIRATION kneels beside SOUL.)
You look for my salvation in vain,
For God, with no little anger,
Carries a knife in His mouth,
910   And a dagger in His hand. / /
Sheath that sword...
Angels, place yourselves in the way!
There is no help! There is no help!

INSPIRATION.
Poor unfortunate Soul!

SOUL.
(Rising.)
915   Who is speaking over there?

INSPIRATION.
Beloved Soul, calm yourself.

SOUL's speech is long. In contrast to that of INSPIRATION, there is the need to express grief, anger, remorse. The danger is that the emotion of the character SOUL may get on top of what is being said. Meaningless mellifluous sound never moves an audience. If the actress lets her emotions carry her away, the audience may not listen. The emotions are to be there, yes, but they are to be channeled toward the goal of the speech. What is it SOUL wants?

INSPIRATION is deeply moved by the plight of SOUL. He is calmly and firmly striving now to win her to salvation.

Inspiration: A divine influence or action on a person believed to qualify him to receive and communicate sacred revelation. [WEBSTER'S DICTIONARY]

ALMA.

Temo una espada de fuego,
Que amenazándome está.
Detenla, mancebo rubio;
920   Tenla, del puño la tome...
¡Mira el fuego de Sodoma!
¡Mira el agua del diluvio!
¿Vienes preso, ó estás loco?
Huye, que te prederán
925   Y en cadenas te pondrán.
¡Huye, huye!

INSPIRACION.

Escucha un poco.

ALMA.

¡Que me quemo! ¡Que me abraso!
¡Que me abraso! ¡Que me quemo!
Un monte de alquitran temo,
930   Y una mar de azufre paso.

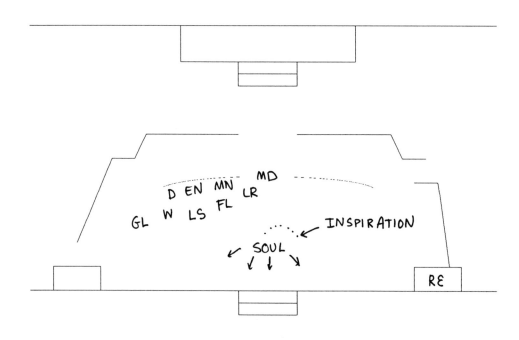

SOUL.

I fear a sword of fire,
That is threatening me.
Hold it back, Golden Youth,
920   Take it, by the hilt //
See the fire of Sodom!
See the waters of the flood!
Do you come as a captive, or are you mad?
Flee, for they will catch you
(INSPIRATION rises.)
925   And place you in chains.
Flee, flee!

INSPIRATION.
(Holding SOUL.)
Listen a moment.

SOUL.

I am burning! I am set on fire!
(Writhing in pain.)
I am on fire! I am burning!
I fear a mountain of tar, and
930   I cross an ocean of brimstone.

This is heightened language: Metaphor and simile must be freshly found. This may be the very most important thing for the actor.

... Then the Lord rained on Sodom and Gomorrah brinstone and fire out of heaven; and he overthrew the valley and all the inhabitants of the cities. But Lot's wife, behind him, looked back, and she became a pillar of salt. —GENESIS

The flood continued. Rain fell upon the earth for forty days and forty nights. The waters increased and... prevailed so mightily that all the high mountains were covered more than twenty feet deep. —GENESIS

INSPIRACION.
Alma, dame atento oido;
Oye sólo una razon.

ALMA.
¿Quién eres?

INSPIRACION.
    La Inspiracion.

ALMA.
Sabe que tarde has venido.

INSPIRACION.
No pierdas la confianza,
Pues, miéntras dura la vida,
Serás de Dios espera:

935

ALMA.
Con alguna espada y lanza.
    (Quédase EL AlMA arrimada á la reja y
    vuelve en si.)

INSPIRACION.
Alma enferma, en Dios espera:
Llama á tu Dios.

940

ALMA.
¡Ay Dios mio!
(Llora.)

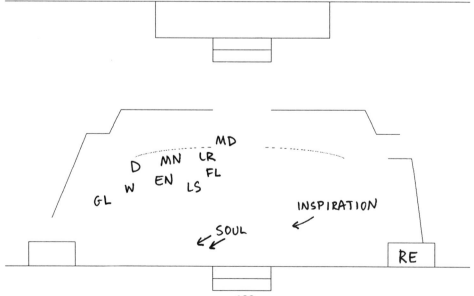

INSPIRATION.
Soul, listen closely.
Listen to one reason alone.

SOUL.
Who are you?

INSPIRATION.
Inspiration.

SOUL.
(Pulling away.)
You know you have come too late.

INSPIRATION.
935   Do not lose hope,
For while there is life
You will be received by God...

SOUL.
With a certain sword and lance.

INSPIRATION.
Ailing Soul, hope in God:
940   Call on your God.

SOUL.
Ah, my God!

Then the Lord God... placed... a flaming sword which turned every way, to guard the way to the tree of life. —GENESIS

It is ever risky for the actor to think of too many things at once — especially in long speeches. However, the lines of the long speech are important, often many meanings at points may be embedded in the lines. The author asks the actor to get all the diverse meanings out of the lines.

INSPIRACION.

De tu remedio confio,
Si lloras desa manera.

ALMA.

¡Ay miserable de mí,
Que ha sido mi culpa mucha!

INSPIRACION.

945 Alma, tu remedio escucha.

ALMA.

Atenta te escucho, di.

INSPIRACION.

Alma, retrato de Dios,
Bello espejo en quien se mira
Para su cielo criada,
950 Para su esposa escogida;
De la casa de tu padre,
Noble en casta, en bienes rica,
Pidiéndole tu porcion,
Saliste á buscar la vida.
955 Del alacran del Deleite,
Que con el extremo pica,
Siendo peste su dulzura,
De peste quedaste herida.

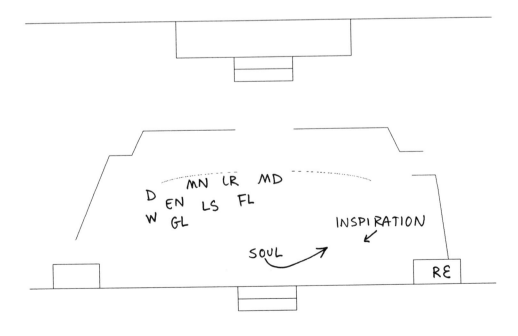

INSPIRATION.
I trust in your salvation
If you weep in that way.

SOUL.
Oh, miserable me,
I have been so much to blame!

INSPIRATION.
945   Soul, listen to your salvation.

SOUL.
I will listen attentively, tell me.

INSPIRATION.
Soul, the image of God,
A beautiful mirror in which one can see
A being created for God's Heaven,
950   Chosen for His bride.
You, noble in breeding, rich in possessions,
Having left your father's house,
Now you ask for your portion,
You look for life.
955   Your gentleness being a plague to
That scorpion Lust,
At the final moment of life, he stings,
And, wounded, you sicken.

God created man in his own image, in the image of God he created him; male and female he created them. And God blessed them... —GENESIS

There was a man who had two sons... The younger son gathered all he had and took his journey into a far country, and there he squandered his property in loose living... When he came to himself he said, ...I perish here with hunger! I will arise and go to my father, and I will say to him, "father, I have sinned against heaven and before you"... He arose and came to his father but while he was yet at a distance, his father saw him and had compassion for him and ran and embraced him and kissed him... The father said... "This my son was dead and is alive again; he was lost and he is found." —LUKE

(*INSPIRACION.*)
Dióte un letargo crüel,
960 Una modorra continua,
Cuyo frenesí furioso
Te tiene loca y cautiva.
Desta fiera enfermedad
Está á peligro tu vida:
965 Si quieres ponerte en cura,
Darte he médico divino
La misma Sabiduría,
Que dió vida, cuerpo y sangre,
Para hacer las medicinas.

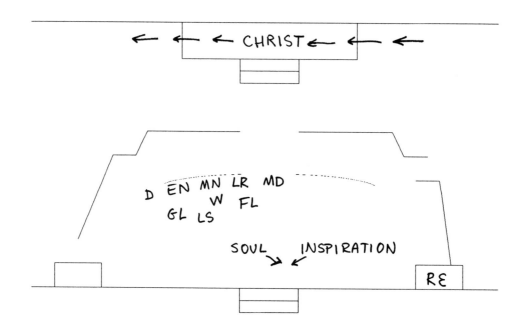

(INSPIRATION.)

960

Lust gave you a cruel lethargy,
A continual drowsiness,
His furious frenzy,
Has you captive and mad. /
By this wild sickness
Your life is endangered:

(CHRIST enters up left.)

965

If you wish to cure yourself,
I can give you physician and apothecary.
It will be the Divine Physician
The same Providence that gave life, body and blood,
To make the medications.

CHRIST, carrying a cross, slowly moves over the up stage platform, head facing down stage. He dows not react to SOUL or to INSPIRATION, dispite the look of suffering and pity on his face. He slowly exits right.

Several characters already have been faced with the challenge of the long speech. REASON, INSPIRATION, and CHRIST must come to terms with very long speeches. These have long been conventions of the comedies and the dramas of the Spanish Golden Age of Theatre. They were not exceptional to the *autos* and for the audience of the times they would have been expected and looked forward to as an opportunity for the actor to thrill them with his voice and command of language.

INSPIRATION is to approach his long speech with the motivation - as if - telling a story. He opens himself to us, works out with the audience what he has to say to SOUL, making it deeply felt. Always in control of his feelings, INSPIRATION is to make the audience think with him.

Jesus took bread, and blessed, and broke it, and gave it to the diciples and said, "Take, eat; this is my body." And he took a cup, and when he had given thanks he gave it to them, saying, "Drink of it, all of you; for this is my blood of the covenant, which is poured out for many for the forgiveness of sins. —MATTHEW

(INSPIRACION.)

970   Es la botica la Iglesia,
            Llena de drogas divinas,
            De aromas, simples, compuestos,
            De yerbas, flores y epítimas,
            De esmeraldas, de rubíes,
975   De topacios, margaritas,
            De jacintos, de bezares,
            De perlas y piedras finas,
            Diacoral que al triste alegra,
            Diamargariton que anima,

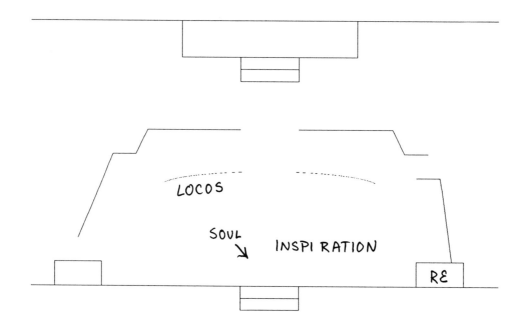

(INSPIRATION.)

970 The Church is the apothecary, /
Having Divine drugs,
[Aromas, simple, compounded
Herbs, flowers and
Emeralds, of rubies
Topazes, of daisies,
Hyacinths, of bezoars [39]
Pearls and fine stones,
Translucent coral [40] *that gladens the sorrow,*
That pelucid pearl [41], *margarite, that gives life,*
The hands of Christ.] [42]

What must an actor do if he is to help and hold an audience? Audiences don't listen to a complex and long speech unless the actor makes them do so. This occurs when the actor is generalizing, emoting a general mood or feeling that the speech suggests to him. An actor must come to gripswith the speech through arduous study, perhaps making a summary of the speech. The actor must discover the speech line by line as it is spoken.

39 Bezoars stones were thought to be antidote to venom and poisons.

40 Translucent coral is introduced here because coral was thought to denote illness or good health when worn.

41 Pelucid pearl magarite is often referred to by early writers as translucent, white and clean.

42 These lines were not used in the English-language production of the play.

(INSPIRACION.)

980	Manos *Christi* siempre abiertas,
	Que amor y perdon destilan,
	Lágrimas que manchas sacan,
	Y sangre que culpas quita.
	Tiene un palo, que, por santo,
985	Es el árbol de la vida;
	Tiene tres clavos de amor,
	Azotes, lanza y espinas,
	Y de su divino rostro
	Bofetadas y salivas.
990	Tiene en un vaso guardado
	Vino mezclado con mirra,
	Una esponja con vinagre,
	Y con hiel una bebida.
	Tiene, en siete cajas de oro,
995	Los tesoros de sus indias,
	Donde en siete Sacramentos
	Su vida y su muerte cifra.
	Es Pedro el dispensador
	Desta celestial botica;
1000	De gracia da sus tesoros... [43]

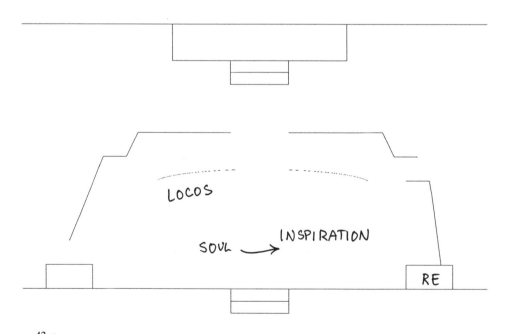

[43] Da gracia de sus tesoros.

980-   *Manos Christi,* always open,
           That dispense love and pardon.
           Tears that draw out stains,
           And blood that takes away sins.
           He has a staff, which, being blessed,
985   Is the tree of life;
           He has three nails of love;
           Whips, lances, thorns,
           And the Divine face,
           Spat upon, slapped.
990   He has kept a chalice:
           Wine mixed with myrrh,
           A sponge with vinegar,
           And a drink with gall.
           He has, in seven golden boxes,
995   The treasures of the Indies,
           Wherein are the seven sacraments,
           Which enumerate his life and his death.
           Peter is the giver,
           The celestial apothecary
1000   He gives the Grace of his treasures...

Actors, and audiences, have to work harder with these very long speeches. Following dialogue is like watching a tennis match; dialogue provides spontaneous activity for audience and actors, alike. Hence, dialogue is relatively easy to follow. The actor must be on the alert that with a very long set speech the play may begin to lose momentum and the action to run aground.

The soldiers took Jesus... They stripped him and put on him a scarlet robe and a crown of thorns, and a reed in his right hand. ... They spat upon him, and took the reed and struck him on the head... and led him away to crucify him... at Golgotha, they offered Jesus wine to drink mingled with gall. ...And one of them at once.. took a sponge, and filled it with vinegar, put it on a reed, and gave it to him to drink. —MATTHEW

... A soldier pierced his [Jesus] side with a spear, and at once there came out blood and water. —JOHN

The foundations of the wall were adorned with every jewel: jasper, sapphire, agate, emerald, onyx, carnelian, chrysolite, beryl, topaz, chrysoprase, jacinth, amethyst. —REVELATIONS

(*INSPIRACION.*)

Alma, llega arrepentida;
Mira que del cielo vengo
A revolver la picina,
Para que, echándote al agua,
1005 Pises con salud su orilla.
Contra el espíritu inmundo,
Que, como á Saúl, te incita
Oye la arpa de mi lengua,
Y huirá á las aguas estigias.
1010 Mira que, para tus ojos,
Te triago el pez de Tobías;

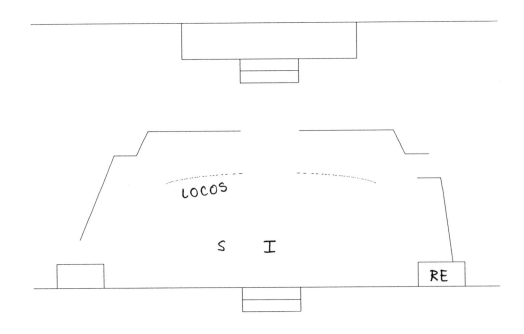

(INSPIRATION.)

Soul become repentant;

[See how I come from Heaven
To stir up the pond,
In order that, in throwing you in its water,
You may reach its banks in health.
Against the filthy spirit,
Just as to Saul, incites you.
Hear the harp of my tongue
And fly from these Stygian [44] *waters.*
See how I bring you
The fish of Tobias [45] *for your eyes;]* [46]

1005

1010

I [John the Baptist] baptise you with waters for repentance... —MATTHEW

Those who threw the stones had laid their garments at the feet of a man named Saul [Paul], who is consenting to Stephen's death... Saul himself began ravaging the church, and entering house after house, he dragged off men and women and committed them to prison. —ACTS

[44] Stygian refers to the river Styx of hell. In ancient times Jupiter obliged the Gods who had purgered themselves to drink of the waters of the Styx, which lulled them for one year into a senseless stupidity; for the nine following years they were deprived of the ambrosia nectar of the Gods.

[45] The father of Tobias had become blind. The angel Raphael, under the guise of a kinsmen to Tobias, named Azarias, accompanied Tobias, journeying to Medea. On the banks of the Tigres River a fish leaped out. Tobias was directed to remove the heart, the liver and the gall of the fish. With the heart and the liver, Tobias was able to defeat his enemy Asmodeus; then upon his return the gall of the eyes of the fish restored sight to his fathers eyes.

[The Book of Tobit was once of the cononical books of the Old Testement. Here was to be found the story of Tobias and the angel Raphael. (M'Clintock, J. and Strong, J. ENCYCLOPEDIA OF BIBILICAL, THEOLOGICAL AND ECCLESIASTICAL LITERATURE. Volume X-SU-Z. Grand Rapids, Michigan: Baker Book House, 1970)]

[46] These lines were not used in the English-language production of the play.

(INSPIRACION.)

Para tu asquerosa lepra,
Del Jordan las aguas limpias;
Del diluvio, en que te anegas,
1015   El arco en las nubes mira,
Y á la paloma de Gracia,
Que te trae de paz la oliva;
Y pues estás, Alma, enferma,
De la culebra mordida,
1020   Vuelve á ver la de metal,
Que da salud con la vista.

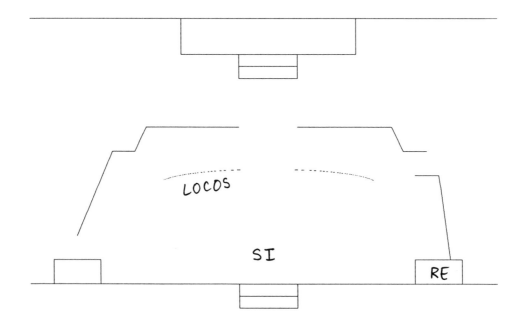

(INSPIRATION.)
[For your loathsome leprosy.
See how I bring you clean water of Jordan
Out of the flood, in which you drowned,] [47]

1015   Look to the arc in the clouds,
       Look to the dove of Grace
       Which brings to you a piece of the olive branch;
       Soul, since you are sick,
       From the bite of the snake,
1020   See again the trumpet of glory,
       Which gives life by looking on it.

So Naanan went down and dipped himself seven times in the Jordan, and his flesh was restored [from leprosy] *like the flesh of a little child.* —2 KINGS

...and again he [Noah] *sent forth the dove out of the Ark; and the dove came to him in the evening and, lo, in her mouth was an olive leaf; so Noah knew that the waters were abated from the earth.* —GENESIS

---

[47] These lines were not used in the English-language production of the play.

(*INSPIRACION.*)
¡Animo, esposa de Dios!
Que él á buscare me envia,
Y él mismo vendrá á buscarte,
1025   Como á la veja perdida.

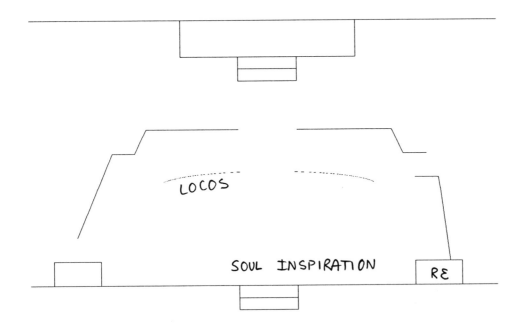

(INSPIRATION.)
Stir yourself, Spirit, bride of God!
For He has sent me to find you,
And He Himself will come to look for you,
1025   As for a lost sheep.

Too drastically cut a long speech does a diservice to Valdivielso's play, and it suggests a lack of full belief in the *auto* as viable theatre, as well as shortchanging the actor, which Narros did not.

In view of the close friendship between Valdivielso and Lope de Vega it may be assumed that he was aware of Lope de Vega's *THE NEW ART OF WRITING COMEDIES* and in sympathy with Lope de Vega's point of view. The long speech of INSPIRATION, as well as other long speeches in *THE HOUSE OF FOOLS* one may equate them with the soliloquy; therefore it is of interest to note what Lope de Vega had to say reguarding the soliloquy.

"...*Manage soliloquies in such a manner that the actor is quite transformed, and in changing himself, changes the listener* [in the audience]."

Los soliloquios pinte de manera
Que se transforme todo el recitante,
Y con mudarse a sí mude al oyente.
    Lope De Vega: *ARTE NUEVO DE HACER COMEDIAS*

If a man has a hundred sheep, and one of them has gone astray, does he not leave the ninety-nine on the mountains and go in search of the one that went astray? And if he finds it, truly, I say to you, he rejoices over it more than over the ninety-nine that never went astray. —MATTHEW

ALMA.

Inspiracion soberana,
Que me consuelas y animas,
Sácame de aquesta reja,
Llévame en tu compañía.
1030 Siento mis yerros y engaños,
Mis pecados y malicias:
Serán fuentes estos ojos,
Para llorar mis desdichas.

INSPIRACION.

Sal, Alma; que poder tengo
1035 Del que tu bien solicita,
Para romper desta reja
Aquestas cadenas frias.
(Rómpense la reja y las cadenas, y sale EL
ALMA.)
Sal, Alma, llégate á mí;
Flaca estás, á mí te arrima;
1040 La Razon te está esperando
Para hacerte compañía.

ALMA.

Vamos, santa Inspiracion,
Llévame á aquesa botica,
Adonde está mi salud
1045 Y el remedio de mi vida.
(Vanse.)

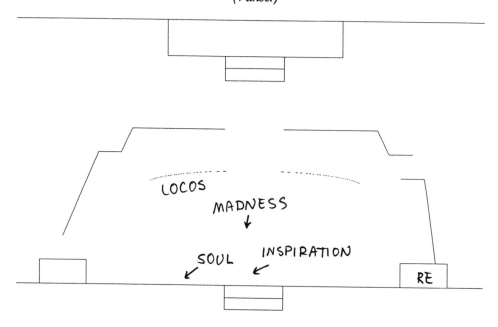

SOUL.
(Reaching for INSPIRATION.)

Soverign Inspiration
Who advises and encourages me,
Take me from this prison,
Take me away with you.
1030   I regret my errors and deceit,
My sins and malice:
These eyes will become fountains
To weep for my misery.

INSPIRATION.
(Helping SOUL up.)

Come out, Soul: seeking your well-being,
1035   I had the power which enables me
To break these bars
To break these cold chains.
(Removing from SOUL the chains.)
Come out, Soul, come close to me;
(They cross right.)
You are weak; lean on me;
1040   Reason is waiting
To accompany you.

SOUL.

Let us go, blessed Inspiration,
Take me to that apothecary
Where is my health
1045   And is the salvation of my life.
(MADNESS awakens.)

INSPIRATION breaks the chains binding SOUL and she arises. SOUL, notwithstanding all of her human weaknesses gains our sympathy and understanding. In all innocence she has been curious, likeable and human in her frailty.

ESCENA XIX

Sale LA LOCURA á lo alto, y LA CULPA en el teatro.—Duespues TODOS LOS
LOCOS.

LOCURA.
Culpa, ¡que el Alma se va!
¡Que la prision ha rompido!

CULPA.
(Saliendo.)
¡Triste yo! ¿qué es lo que he oido?
La Locura voces da.

LOCURA.
1050   ¡Corre, Culpa! ¡corre, corre!

CULPA.
Portero, ¿de qué te quejas?

LOCURA.
El Alma rompió las rejas,
Porque el cielo la socorre.

CULPA.
¿Qué dices?

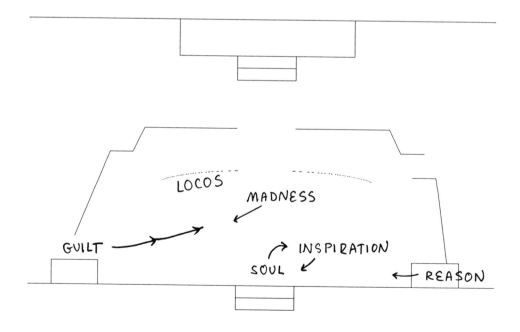

216

SCENE XIX

MADNESS, GUILT, SOUL, INSPIRATION, REASON

MADNESS.

Guilt, Soul is going!
She has broken the prison!

GUILT.
(Entering from down right.)

I am befuddled! What is that I hear?
Madness is shouting.

(REASON goes to her knees.)

MADNESS.

1050   Run Guilt! Run, run!

GUILT.
(Crossing to MADNESS.)

Keeper of the Gate, what are you complaining about?

MADNESS.

Soul has broken through the bars,
For Heaven is helping her.

GUILT.

What do you say?

GUILT enters, looking for SOUL; she is as one drugged, but then she
hears MADNESS shouting.

This is the obligatory scene *(scène-à-faire)* and the action must be wound
up tautly and with intensity, but never at the expense of being unintelligible to
the audience.

LOCURA.

Aquesto pasa.

1055 ¡Corro, porque huendo va!
¡Corre, aguija, que áun está
A las puertas de tu casa!

CULPA.

¡Que el cielo me haga este mal,
Sabiendo que es verdad clara
1060 Que es mi esclava, y que en su cara
Lleva mi hierro y señal;
Y que, aunque se mire en ella,
Miéntras no se arrepintiere
Y sus pecados gimiere.
1065 No pueden echarme della!—
¡Llama á Luzbel, llama el Mundo,
Al Engaño...á la Mentira,
A la traicion, á la Ira,
A las Furias del profundo!
1070 Venid y húndase la tierra,
Que el Alma se nos escapa.

(Salen los demas que quedaron dentro.)

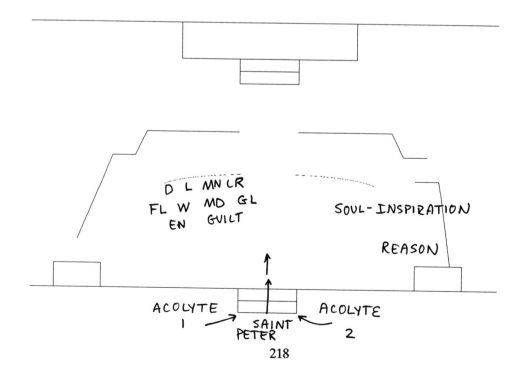

218

MADNESS.
This will pass.
1055 Run because she is fleeing!
Run, make haste, because she is already
At the door of your house!

GUILT.
It is Heaven that brings down this evil on me
Knowing that it is a clear truth
1060 That she is my slave, and that on her face
(Crossing center.)
She wears my brand and seal;
And that, although Heaven looks upon her,
While she may not repent,
And may moan of her sins,
1065 They cannot take her away from me! /
Call Lucifer, call World,
Call Deceit, call Lies,
Call Treason, call Anger,
The Furies of the Deep!
1070 Come and flood the Earth,
So that Soul will not escape us.
(All the locos awaken.)

GUILT awakens to the reality of the situation, and she calls upon all of the *locos* to prevent SOUL's escape.

We see that GUILT is cynical, selfish, and sly.

[Lucifer]
We shall be free; th'Almighty hath not built
Here for his envy, will not drive us hence:
Here we may reign secure, and in my choice
To reign is worth ambition though in Hell:
Better to reign in Hell, than serve in Heav'n.
Milton: *PARADISE LOST*

219

TODOS.
¡A la trápala, trapa, la trapa!
¡Guerra al cielo, guerra, guerra,
Que el Alma se nos escapa!

1075 *¡A la trápala, trapa, lu trapa!*
(Vanse.)

———-

Pórtico de un santuario, cerrado con cortinas.

ESCENA XX

Sale SAN PEDRO, con tunicela y ropa.

SAN PEDRO.
¿Cómo, enfermos, no llegais
Aquesta insigne botica,
Donde el cielo comunica
La salud que deseais?

1080 Llegad, si quereis salud;
Llegad, si quereis consuelo;
Llegad, si quereis el cielo,
Que da el cielo su virtud.

220

LOCOS
(All sing.)

A la trapla, trapala, la trapa!
War in Heaven, War, War,
Soul is escaping us!
1075   *A la trapala, trapala, la trapa!*

SCENE XX

ST. PETER, ACOLYTES, SOUL, REASON
[LOCOS]

(Enter ST. PETER, with Tunicla and robe.)
(The force of ST. PETER's entrance throws the locos back, cowering down stage of their cells..)

ST. PETER.
How is it sick ones, that you do not come
To this renowed pharmacy,
Where Heaven conveys
The health that you seek?
(To locos.)
1080   Come if you wish help!
(To SOUL.)
Come if you wish comfort!
Come if you wish Heaven!
(Crossing to left center.)
For heaven gives its virtue.

ST. PETER's entrance is weighted with gravity and forcefullness.

In a speech of heightened and lyric language, the actor must guard against taking it too solemnly — as unfortunate as throwing it away.

(*SAN PEDRO.*)
Debajo de aquestas llaves,

1085   Que son del eterno coro.
Tengo el divino tesoro
De sus medicinas graves.
Estas llaves os darán
De Dios cuerpo, sangre y vida,

1090   Dándose en Pan por comida,
Sirviendo de velo el pan.
Mas ¿qué gente es la que viene?

ESCENA XXI

SAN PEDRO.—*Sale EL ALMA, y LA INSPIRACION con ella.*

INSPIRACION.
¡Oh, vice-Dios en la tierra!

SAN PEDRO.
¡Oh señora, en quien se encierra

1095   El bien que al Alma conviene!

(*ST. PETER.*)
Under these keys,
1085   Which sound the eternal chorus,
I have the divine treasure
Of these prudent medicines.
These keys will give you
The body, blood, and life of God,
1090   Giving as food the blessed bread,
Serving the Bread covered.
But, who are these peole who come?

SCENE XXI

SOUL, INSPIRATION, GUILT
[LOCOS]

INSPIRATION.
Oh, vice-regent of God on Earth!

ST. PETER.
Oh, good lady, in whom is confined
1095   The good which will benefit Soul!

The voice and the emotions of the actor must hold the attention of the audience.

And he took bread, and when he had given thanks he broke it and gave it to them. "This is my body," he said, "which is given for you. Do this in rememberance of me." ... Likewise he took the cup... saying, "This cup which is poured out for you is the new covenant in my blood." —LUKE

INSPIRACION.

Viene, padre santo, aquí
El Alma enferma y herida.

ALMA.

Vengo en busca de mi vida,
Que, como loca, perdí.
1100   La Inspiracion me encamina
A que diga que pequé.

SAN PEDRO.

La cortina correré
Desta botica divinia.

ESCENA XXII

Dichos.—*LA LOCURA, los locos, LA CULPA, vestida de demonio.*

CULPA.

(*Quiere agarrar al Alma, y ella se ase de san Pedro.*)
Piensas, porque huyendo vas,
1105   Que estás libre de mis lazos?

ALMA.

¡Ay padre, dame tus brazos!

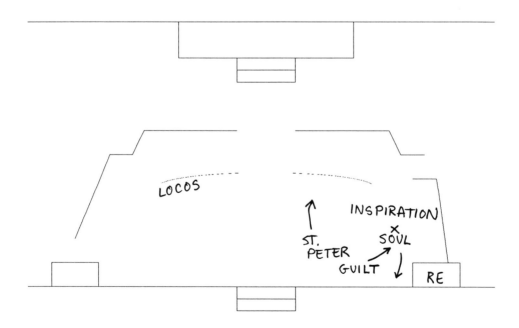

INSPIRATION.
Come, Sainted Father, here is
Soul sick and wounded.

SOUL.
I come in search of my life,
Which, as a mad woman, I lost.
1100 Inspiration accompanies me,
So I may tell that I have sinned.

ST. PETER.
(Turning up stage.)
I will open the curtain
Of this divine apothecary.
(GUILT is stealing toward SOUL.)

SCENE XXII

GUILT.
(Trying to grab SOUL.)
Do you think, because you are fleeing
1105 That you are free of my bonds?

SOUL.
*(GUILT is thrown back by revalation of
CHRIST upstage.)*
Oh, Father, give me your arms!
(SOUL falls into posture of ordination.)

GUILT has been tring to grab SOUL in order to seperate her from ST. PETER. However SOUL clings to ST. PETER.

SOUL is now prepared for the laying on of hands and of being received back into the church.

SAN PEDRO.
Alma, en los de Dios estás.

ESCENA XXIII

Dichos.—*Tocan chirimías y córrese una cortina, y aparece CRISTO, NUESTRO SEÑOR, y del pecho le salen siete cintas encarnadas, que dan en siete cajas como de botica.*

CRISTO.
Esposa del alma mia,
En mi casa estás, no temas; [48]

1110	Pues te has venido á sagrado,

Bien es te valga la Iglesia.
Llega á aqueste pecho roto,
Herido por tu defensa;
Entra en este corazon,

1115	Y verá cuánto me cuestas.

A esta ventana te asoma,
Y podrás mirar por ella
Cómo tengo las entrañas,
Para tu remdio, abiertas.

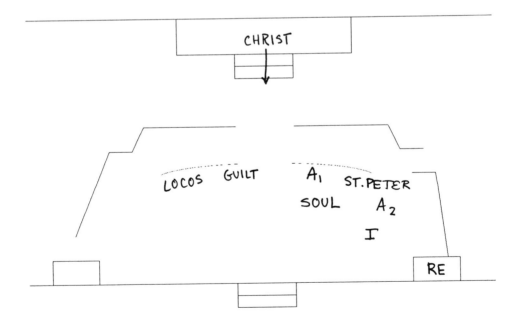

48 En casa estás, no temas.

ST. PETER.
(Crossing between GUILT and SOUL.)
Soul, you are in the arms of God!

SCENE XXIII

ST. PETER, CHRIST
[SOUL, INSPIRATION, REASON, LOCOS]

CHRIST.
(Remaining up stage center.)

Bride of my soul,
You are in my house. Do not be afraid;
1110   Though you have come to the asylum,
The Church will protect you well.
Come to this torn breast,
Wounded in your defense;
Enter into this heart,
(SOUL begins to rise slowly.)
1115   And you will see how much you cost Me.
Look out of this window,
You can see through it
How I have opened my heart
For your salvation.

The actor playing CHRIST, coming on without any plot preparation, must be deeply within the situation into which he enters. He must find the language and make the audience feel the words are coming out for the very first time. If the actor does so, the listeners will feel that the scene of the play is traveling on, getting somewhere. The audience will stay with the actor. The spectator loses interest, his attention wanders, if the performer does not hold him. When that happens the actor is much to blame.

CHRIST gives SOUL the power to resist GUILT.

... A soldier pierced his side with a spear, and at once there came out blood and water. —JOHN

He is the source of your life in Christ Jesus... — I CORINTHEIANS

...him to reconcile to himself all things, ...for in him all the fulness of God was pleased to dwell, and through him to reconcile to himnself all things ...making peace by the blood of his cross. —COLOSSIANS

... You who once were far off have been brought near in the blood of Christ. —EPHESIANS

(*CRISTO*.)

1120	Abrí la bolsa del pecho,
	Por pagar todas tus deudas,
	Y como dí cuanto tuvo,
	Dejéme la bolsa abierta.
	Entra en lugar de mi sangre
1125	Vertida por tus ofensas,
	Pues ella sale por tí,
	Bien puedes entrar por ella.
	Vertí para tu rescate
	El tesoro de mis venas;
1130	Sangre dí, lágrimas pido,
	Lágrimas tus ojos viertan:

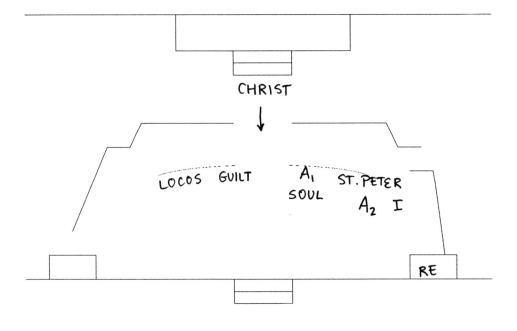

(CHRIST.)

1120   I open the purse of my breast,
To pay all your debts,
And as I gave all I had,
I left the purse open.
Enter the place of my blood
1125   Spilled by your offenses,
Because it flows for you,
You can enter easily by way of it.
For your redemption I spilled
The treasure of my veins;
1130   I gave blood, I asked for tears,
Tears that your eyes may spill:

To make the audience listen and to move the audience in a set speech of great length, the actor always needs to go for the argument if he is to take his audience with him. The goal for the actor is to make the audience follow the set speech clearly. To achieve this the actor needs variety, because monotony or sticking to one tempo in a set speech is fatal. Next, by contrast, the actor must not be too quick or too slow, but, what is the key to all of this, is that the actor must think quickly. When that happens he will have found the natural tempo for a set speech.

CHRIST/CRISTO

NOTA

EL TRAJE DEVE SER
UNA TUNICA SUELTA
A PARTIR DE BAJO DEL
PECHO. LA FALDA CORTADA
AL VIES. ESTE TRAJE
DEVE SER FACIL DE
QUITAR EN EL MOMENTO
DE LA LOCURA DEL ALMA
EN UN PRINCIPIO EL ALMA
STARA ENCERRADA EN UNA
ESFERA DE PLASTICO
TRANSPARENTE COMO UNA
CRISALIDA ASTA EL
MOMENTO QUE LA VIERA
EL DELEITE.
MAQUILLAJE MUY PALIDO

CORONA
FLORES LIGERAMENTE
ROSADAS

PELUCA
DEL MISMO COLOR
DEL TRAJE

GASA
TRANSPARENTE COLOR
HUESO

PIES DESNUDAS

EL ALMA

SOUL/ALMA

(*CRISTO.*)

          Tu amor del cielo me trujo,
          Tu amor me dejó en la tierra,
          Tu amor me hirió en el madero,
1135   Que heridas de amor son éstas.
          Llega á estos brazos abiertos;
          Hazte de aquesta olmo hiedra,
          Para que subas al cielo,
          Que hasta allá su altura llega.
1140   Allega, paloma amada,
          Haz el nido en esta piedra,
          Que vierte arroyos de sangre,
          Para sanar tu dolencia.
          No haya más, dame la mano;
1145   Yo perdono tus ofensas,
          Que me da gusto tu llanto;
          Llora, que en llorar me alegras.
          Esta botica que ves
          Por tu bien dejé en la tierra;
1150   Pide, para tu salud,
          Sus drogas y sus riquezas.
          Lo que á tu dolencia importa
          Es la amada penitencia,
          Que abre las puertas del cielo,
1155   Y entra, sin llamar, por ellas.

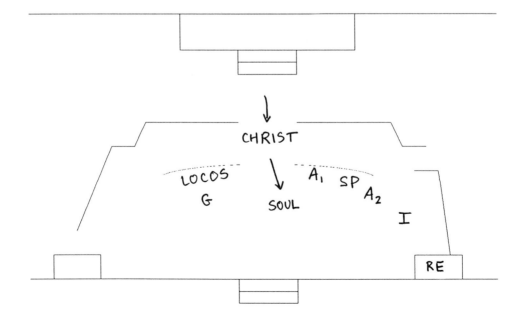

(CHRIST.)
For love of you brought me down from Heaven
For love of you I stayed on Earth
For love of you I was wounded on the cross,
1135   For these are wounds of love.
Come to these open arms;
Make this elm tree into ivy,
So that you may climb up to Heaven,
For its height reaches up to there.
(Crossing down center toward SOUL.)
1140   Come near, beloved dove,
Build your nest in this stone,
Which spills streams of blood,
In order to heal your sickness.
It is finished, give Me your hand;
(Taking SOUL's hand SOUL weeps.)
1145   I forgive your offenses,
Your weeping pleases me;
Cry, for in crying you make Me happy.
This apothecary which you see
I left on Earth for your good;
1150   For your health,
Ask for its medicines and its riches.
What is important for your sickness
Is sweet penance.
That opens the doors of Heaven,
1155   And enter through them without knowing.

What the actor must do to make the audience listen to a long discriptive speech, covering several pages is to make them attend. For a long speech both actor and audience have to work harder. The audience can be made to think the long story is worth listening to, to feel the story as it moves forward as long as the actor is deeply inside the situation. He must 'coin' the language symbolically, as it were, as if the lines were coming out for the first time.

(*CRISTO.*)
Para tranformarte en mí,
Siendo yo tu vida mesma,
Quiero, Alma, que seas por gracia
Lo que yo soy por esencia:
1160   Yo soy Dios, y Dios serás,
Con aquesta diferencias.—
Vosotros, fieros ministros,
Id á vuestra cárcel fiera.
Que de la confesion santa
1165   Quedará más que el sol bella.

SAN PEDRO.
Cese tu justa fatiga.
Pues que Dios salud te da.

INSPIRACION.
Su absolucion tienes ya.

SAN PEDRO.
San Pedro te la bendiga.—

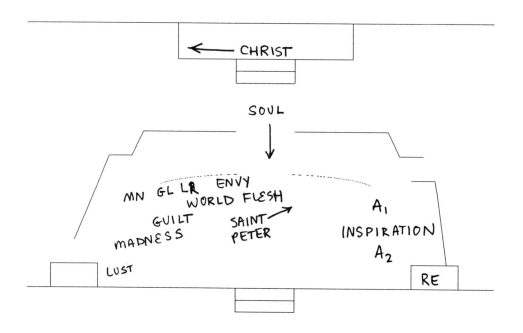

(CHRIST.)
For you to become at one with me,
Since I am your very life,
I wish you to be My Grace
What I am in essence:
1160   I am God, and like God you will become,
With this difference.
Fierce ministers go you
(To locos.)
To your wild prisons,
For by the Holy Confession
1165   Soul has been purified.
(Exiting right.)

ST. PETER.
(SOUL kneels center before him.)
And your pious fatigues,
For God will give you salvation.

INSPIRATION.
Now you have His absolution.

ST. PETER.
St. Peter blesses it for you.
(Communion is performed.)

CHRIST's speech is written formally, rehtorically, all of which can make it seem unreal. It is important to avoid the tone and solemnity of a sermon. Try and get the sweep of the verse, find each image, human details. Fresh 'coin' each phrase, using the words to express the emotions.

Valdivialso's method is simple and concentrated. Inside the actors must be very rich, but outside it's not difficult, only to bring everything inside, with an internalization, minimum of voice, minimum of gesture.

The author of 17th century Spain is talking through his characters in such a way that he wishes his audience to participate in what he is thinking. This needn't sunder the aesthetic distance between actor and spectator.

St. Peter

S. Pedro
y
Sta Iglesia

ST. PETER/SAN PEDRO

COMMUNION MASS

(ST. PETER goes to ACOLYTE and gets bread; elevates host, gives to SOUL.)

> *"Corpus Domini nostri Jesu*
> *Christi / / custodiat animam tuum*
> *In vitam aeternam / / Amen."*
>> *(Second ACOLYTE crosses right of ST. PE-*
>> *TER, with cup of wine. ST. PETER elevates*
>> *wine. ST. PETER gives wine to SOUL.)*
>
> "Sanguis Domini nostri Jesu
> Christi / / custodiat aninam meam
> In vitam aeternam / / Amen."

ST. PETER goes to the first ACOLYTE and gets the wafer; he elevates the host and then crosses to SOUL to give her the host.

Following this ACOLYTE 2 crosses right to ST. PETER with the wine giving it to him center stage. ST. PETER elevates the wine and then crosses to SOUL giving her to drink of the wine from the chalice.

An edict of a bishop of the period reveals that it was customary that there be included in the *auto* the mass at some point appropriate to the unfolding of the dramatic story. ;e.g. The edict made clear that only the devout *autos* would be performed and no other thing "that may divert the people from the devotion and the adoration of the holy sacrament or for the reverence which is due to the presence of so great a Lord [the Host], or which may incite the people to laughter, shouts, or any other unseemly which are repugnent to representations of this kind." [49]

... It was the custom to place the holy sacrament in the middle... and the town council and cathaderal chapter having occupied the `stage or platform *(tabalado)*, placed between the two choirs, the representation of the *auto* took place, after which the divine service was held. The mass and sermon being concluded, the dances were presented in the same place. [50]

---

[49] Rennert, H. A. The Spanish Stage During the Time of Lope de Vega. New York: Dover Publications, Inc., 1963.

[50] Ibid.

LOCURA.

1170   Culpa fiera, ¿qué esperamos?
     Que no hay ver aquellos ojos.

CULPA.

     A nuestro hospital de enojos,
     Desesperados, volvamos.
        (Vanse.)

ALMA.

     Llego, como cierva herida.
1175   A aquestas fuentes de amor,
     Y al hombro del Buen Pastor,
     Como la oveja perdida;
     Como el pródigo arrojado,
     Al anillo y á la estola,
1180   Y de entre una y otra ola,
     Llego al puerto deseado.
     Llego, como indigna esclava,
     A segunda redencion.

SAN PEDRO.

     Y aquí comience el perdon,
1185   Adonde el acto se acaba.
        (Vanse todos.)

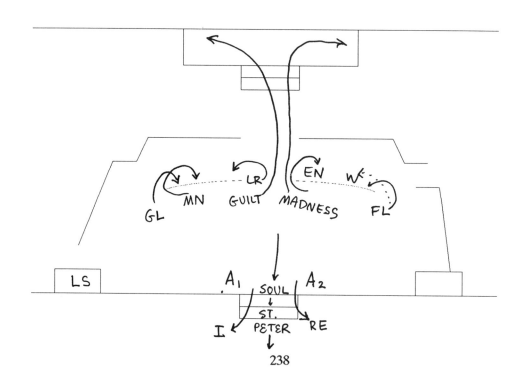

238

MADNESS.

1170 Fierce Guilt, what are we waiting for?
Those eyes are not to be seen here.

GUILT.

Let us return to our asylum
Of angry, raving madmen.
(The locos return to their cells.)

SOUL.

I come, like a wounded deer,
1175 To these springs of love,
And to the shoulder of the Good Shepherd,
Like the lost sheep;
Like the cast out prodigal,
To the ring and the stole,
1180 And between one wave and another,
I arrive at the desired port.
I arrive like an unworthy slave,
I arrive at a second redemption.

ST. PETER.

And here the pardon begins,
1185 And here is where the play ends.
(All down stage exit up and out the center aisle.)

THE END

MADNESS and GUILT are on stage the whole time witnessing SOUL's being saved. With their saying that they must return to their aslyum of angry raving *locos*, they admit defeat. All the *locos* return to their cells, pent up as madmen. The church has triumphed in saving SOUL. This is the Spanish message of the Jesuit Priest and playwright, master Valdivielso.

Locos crawl to original womb positions up stage of their cells at close of the play.

"What man of you, having a hundred sheep, if he has lost one of them, does not leave the ninty nine in the wilderness, and go after the one which is lost, until he finds it. And when he has found it... rejoicing, and... saying, 'rejoice with me, for I have found my sheep which was lost.'..." —LUKE

COMPARATIVE CHRONOLOGY

to

JOSÉ DE VALDIVIELSO [1]

and

THE SPANISH GOLDEN AGE OF THEATRE

[1] *Although José de Valdivielso's exact birth date is unknown, it is generally assumed that he was born somewhere between 1560 and 1565.*

DATE	SPANISH HISTORY	THEATRE AND LETTERS	MUSIC AND OPERA	GRAPHIC AND PLASTIC ARTS
1560-1660	The Golden Age of Spain			
1560	Turkish galleys rout Spanish fleet under the Duke of Medina off Tripoli Madrid becomes capital of Spain	Hsu Wei: "Ching P'Ing Mei," first classic Chinese novel	Orlando di Lasso made Court Kapellmeister in Munich	Tintoretto: "Susannah and the Elders" Baccio Bandinelli, Italian sculptor, died (born 1493) Annibale Carracci, Italian painter, born (died 1609) The Uffizi at Florence founded
1561	Madrid declared capital of Spain by Philip II (see 1560) Mary, Queen of Scots, denied passage through England on returning from France; she lands at Leith, Scotland Baltic states of the Order of the Teutonic Knights secularized	Luis de Góngora y Argote, Spanish baroque poet, born (died 1627)	Jacopo Peri, Italian composer, born (died 1633)	Alonso Berruguete, Spanish painter and sculptor, pupil of Michelangelo, died (born 1480) Michelangelo: St. Maria degli Angeli, Rome Palladio: Convent of the Carità, Venice

WORLD EVENTS	MUNDANE EVENTS	CHURCH AND THOUGHT	KNOWLEDGE AND INVENTIONS
Huguenot conspiracy at Amboise; liberty of worship promised in France King Francis II of France died; succeeded by Charles IX with Catherine de'-Medici, his mother, as regent	Madrid becomes capital of Spain Tobacco plant imported to Western Europe by Jean Nicot Visiting cards used for the first time by German students in Italy	Church of Scotland founded Francesco Patrizi: "Della historia," on the philosophy of history Beginnings of Puritanism in England (-1660)	First scientific society founded at Naples by Giambattista della Porta
Edict of Orleans suspends persecution of Huguenots	Ruy López develops in Spain the modern technique of chess playing Merchant Taylors' School, London, founded St. Paul's Cathedral, London, badly damaged by fire Tulips from the near East first come to Western Europe	Francis Bacon, English philosopher and statesman, born (died 1626) First Calvinist refugees from Flanders settle in England Scottish Church ministers draw up the Confessions of Faith, mainly the work of John Knox	Gabriele Fallopius: "Observationes anatomicae"

DATE	SPANISH HISTORY	THEATRE AND LETTERS	MUSIC AND OPERA	GRAPHIC AND PLASTIC ARTS
1562		Lope Félix de Vega Carpio, Spanish dramatist, born (died 1635) Torquato Tasso: "Rinaldo," epic poem	Gasparo Bertolotti da Salò moves to become first great Italian violin maker Jan Sweelinck, Dutch organist and composer, born (died 1621) Adrian Willaert, Fl. composer, died (born 1490)	Paolo Veronese: "The Marriage at Cana" Tintoretto: "Christ at the Sea of Galilee"
1563	Peace of Amboise ends first War of Religion in France; the Huguenots are granted limited toleration	Blossoming of Spanish mystic poetry: Teresa de Jesús (1515-1582); Luis de Granada (1515-1588); Juan de la Cruz (1542-1563); Luis de León (1527-1591)	William Byrd made organist at Lincoln Cathedral	Juan de Herrera begins to build the Escorial for Philip II of Spain (- 1586) Diego de Siloe, Spanish Gothic architect, died (born 1500) Giovanni da Bologna: Neptune fountain, Bologna (- 1567)
1564	Spaniards occupy Philippines and build Manila Ferdinand I, Holy Roman Emperor since 1556, died (born 1503); succeeded by his son Maximilian II (-1576) Peace of Troyes ends war between England and France	William Shakespeare born April 23 (died 1616) Christopher Marlowe born (died 1593)	One of Andrea Amati's first violins made Lodovico Grossi Viadana, Italian composer, born (died 1627)	Jacopo Tintoretto: paintings for the Scuola di San Rocco (- 1587) Philibert Delorme (1510-1560) begins work on the Tuileries, Paris Michelangelo died (born 1475)

WORLD EVENTS	MUNDANE EVENTS	CHURCH AND THOUGHT	KNOWLEDGE AND INVENTIONS
Shane O'Neill rebels in Ireland

Emperor Ferdinand I signs eight-year truce with Suleiman I of Turkey

Maximilian, son of Ferdinand I, becomes King of Bohemia

English troops occupy Le Havre

French army regains Le Havre | Plague in Paris

French attempt to colonize Florida

John Hawkins makes his first journey to the New World: begins slave trade between Guinea and West Indies

Milled coins introduced in England | Third session of Council of Trent convenes (-1563)

1,200 French Huguenots slain at Massacre of Vassy; first War of Religion begins

English Articles of Religion of 1552 reduced to the Thirty-Nine Articles | Famous French surgeon Pierre Franco died; he performed bladder and cataract operations |
| Charles IX of France (at 13) is declared of age

Maximilian II elected King of Hungary | General outbreak of plague in Europe kills over 20,000 people in London | Council of Trent ends (begun 1545)

John Foxe's "Book of Martyrs," first English edition

Counter Reformation begins in Bavaria

Term "Puritan" first used in England | Gerardus Mercator draws the first accurate map of Lorraine

Ambroise Pare (1509-1590): "Cinq livres de chirurgie" |
| English Merchant Adventurers company granted new royal charter

Catherine de'Medici presents her son Charles IX to his subjects on a three-month tour through France

Ivan IV of Russia, in his struggle for power against the boyars, forced to withdraw from Moscow | John Hawkins leaves on his second voyage to the New World

Horse-drawn coach introduced in England from Holland | Index librorum prohibitorum published after receiving papal approval

John Calvin died (born 1509)

Council of Trent's "Professio Fidei" confirmed by Pope Pius IV

Counter Reformation begins in Poland

Philip Neri founds the Congregation of the Oratory in Rome | Bartolommeo Eustachio: "Opuscula anatomica"

Galileo Galilei, great scientist, born February 15th (died 1642)

Andreas Vesalius, founder of modern anatomy, died (born 1514) |

DATE	SPANISH HISTORY	THEATRE AND LETTERS	MUSIC AND OPERA	GRAPHIC AND PLASTIC ARTS
1565	Knights of St. John, under Jean de La Valette, defend Malta from the Turks; with the arrival of Spanish troops the Turks are obliged to abandon the siege Mary, Queen of Scots, marries Henry, Lord Darnley, her cousin	Torquato Tasso, court poet at Ferrara Arthur Golding's translation of first four books of Ovid's "Metamorphoses"	Cyprien de Rore, Dutch composer died (born 1516) Palestrina: "Missa Papae Marcelli"	Tintoretto: "Flight into Egypt" Giovanni da Bologna: "Samson" Palladio: S. Giorgio Maggiore, Venice
1566	David Rizzio, confidential secretary of Mary, Queen of Scots, murdered in Holyrood House, Edinburgh The future James VI of Scotland born (died 1625), son of Mary and Darnley Calvinist riots in the Netherlands; Regent Margaret of Palma abolishes Inquisition	Earliest English prose comedy: George Gascoigne's "The Supposes," based on Ariosto's "Gli Suppositi" Louise Labé ("La Belle Cordière"), French Renaissance poetess, died William Painter's "Palace of Pleasure Beautified," translation of a collection of Italian novellas	Antonio de Cabezón, Spanish composer, died (born 1500)	Pieter Brueghel: "St. John the Baptist"
1567	Duke of Alba in the Netherlands and begins reign of terror; Margaret of Parma resigns Queen Mary forced to abdicate; makes her stepbrother, the Earl of Moray, regent Lord Darnley murdered, possibly on Earl of Bothwell's orders; Mary, Queen of Scots, marries Bothwell	Richard Burbage, English actor, first player of many Shakespeare heroes, born (died 1619) Elizabeth I recognizes eisteddfod Bardic competitions held in Wales since 12th century Thomas Nashe, English poet and dramatist, born (died 1601)	Waclaw of Szamotuli, Polish composer, died (born 1533)	Pieter Brueghel: "Adoration of the Magi" Giovanni da Bologna: "Mercury," sculpture Titian: "Jacopo de Strada"

246

WORLD EVENTS	MUNDANE EVENTS	CHURCH AND THOUGHT	KNOWLEDGE AND INVENTIONS
	Sir John Hawkins introduces sweet potatoes and tobacco into England	Pope Pius IV died (born 1499) Jacobus Anconcio: "Stratagemata Satanae," advocating religious toleration Pierre de la Place: "Histoire de nostre temps"	Bernardino Telesio (1508-1588): "De rerum natura," foreshadowing empirical methods of science Royal college of Physicians, London, empowered to carry out human dissections Konrad von Gesner, Swiss naturalist and zoologist, died (born 1516)
Suleiman I died; succeeded by Selim II as Sultan of Turkey (-1574) Turko-Hungarian war renewed in spite of truce of 1562	"Notizie Scritte," one of first newspapers, appears in Venice	Cardinal Michaele Ghislieri becomes Pope Pius V (-1572)	Nostradamus, French astrologer, died (born 1503)
Irish rebel Shane O'-Neill assassinated Earl of Morton discovers Queen Mary's so-called Casket Letters In Japan Nobunaga deposes shogunate and centralizes government	Two million Indians die in South America of typhoid fever Rio de Janeiro founded	Francesco Guicciardini: "Storia d'Italia" (posthumously) Maximilian II establishes monastery council to superintend clergy	Alvaro Medana de Neyra (1541-1595) discovers Solomon Islands in Pacific Ocean Hawkins' third journey to West Indies, accompanied by Francis Drake

DATE	SPANISH HISTORY	THEATRE AND LETTERS	MUSIC AND OPERA	GRAPHIC AND PLASTIC ARTS
1568	Don Carlos, son of Philip II of Spain, died (born 1545) Mary, Queen of Scots, defeated at Langside by Moray; takes refuge in England York Conference into Queen Mary's conduct opens; reopens later at Westminster	First public theatre presentation in Madrid First modern eisteddfod for Welsh music and literature held at Caerwys	William Whytbroke, English cleric and composer, died (born 1495)	Juan Fernandez de Navarrete made court painter to Philip II of Spain Robert Smythson works on Longleat House, Wiltshire (-1574) Giacomoda Vignola (1507-1573) begins building the Gesù Church in Rome
1569	Don John of Austria suppresses Morisco rebellion in Granada 40,000 inhabitants of Lisbon die in carbuncular fever epidemic	Alfonso de Ercilla y Zuñiga: "La Araucana," Spanish epic on the conquest of Chile Mikolaj Rej, "Father of Polish literature," died (born 1505)	Thomas Caustun, English composer, died	Pieter Brueghel ("Peasant Brueghel"), died (born 1520) Hans Eworth (Fl. painter): "Queen Elizabeth Confounding Juno"

WORLD EVENTS	MUNDANE EVENTS	CHURCH AND THOUGHT	KNOWLEDGE AND INVENTIONS
Peace between Selim II and Maximilian II Treaty of Longjumeau ends second War of Religion in France Swedes declared Eric XIV unfit to reign and proclaim John III king (-1592)	Alexander Nowell, Dean of St. Paul's, London, invents bottled beer	Jesuit missionaries welcomed in Japan Maffeo Barberini, future Pope Urban VIII, born (died 1644) First translation of the Bible into Czech Tommaso Campanella, Italian philosopher, born (died 1639) Pope Pius V issues revised Brevarium Romanun	Geradus Mercator devises cylindrical projection for charts Costanzo Varolio studies the anatomy of the human brain
Sigismund II of Poland unites Poland with Lithuania: Union of Lublin Rebellion in northern England: sacking of Durham Cathedral Pope Pius V makes Cosimo de'Medici Grand Duke of Tuscany	Public lottery held in London to finance repairs to the port	Richard Tottel translates Henry de Bracton's "On the Laws and Customs of England"	Tycho Brahe begins at Augsburg construction of a 19-foot quadrant and a celestial globe, five feet in diameter Mercator: "Cosmographia," and map of the world for navigational use

DATE	SPANISH HISTORY	THEATRE AND LETTERS	MUSIC AND OPERA	GRAPHIC AND PLASTIC ARTS
1570	Philip II marries as his fourth wife Anne of Austria, another daughter of Maximilian II Earl of Moray assassinated; succeeded as Regent of Scotland by Earl of Lennox Margaret of Valois betrothed to Henry of Navarre	Lodovico Castelvetro (1505-1571) demands introduction of Aristotelian principles to contemporary drama Jean Antoine de Baïf founds Académie de Poésie et de Musique, Paris Robert Henryson: "The Moral Fables of Aesop"	Earliest known music festival to honor St. Cecilia, in Normandy Culminating point of vocal polyphonic a capella style (Palestrina, Orlando de Lasso)	Tintoretto: "Moses Striking the Rock" Nicholas Hilliard: "Queen Elizabeth I," portrait Palladio: "I quattro libri dell' architettura"
1571	Spanish capture Manila, transforming into their island empire of the Philippines Pope Pius V signs alliance with Spain and Venice to fight Turks Don John of Austria defeats Turks, fleet off Lepanto	Tirso de Molina, Spanish dramatist, born (died 1648)	Andrea Gabrieli: "Canzoni alla francese" Michael Praetorius, German composer and author, born (died 1621)	Benvenuto Cellini, Italian goldsmith and sculptor, died (born 1500) Palladio: Loggia del Capitanio, Vicenza Titan: "Christ Crowned with Thorns" Giorgio Vasari, Italian painter and art historian, died (born 1512)

WORLD EVENTS	MUNDANE EVENTS	CHURCH AND THOUGHT	KNOWLEDGE AND INVENTIONS
Peace of St. Germain-en-Laye ends third civil war in France; Huguenots gain amnesty Peace of Stettin: Denmark recognizes independence of Sweden Charles IX of France marries Elizabeth, a daughter of Maximilian II Japan opens port of Nagasaki to overseas trade	Guy Fawkes, English conspirator (Gunpowder Plot), born (executed 1605) Nuremberg postal services begin	Roger Ascham: "The Scholemaster," manual on education Consensus of Sendomir: Calvinists, Lutherans, and Moravian Brothers of Poland ally against Jesuits Pope Pius V issues bull, "Regnans in Excelsis," excommunicating Elizabeth I	Bell foundry of Whitechapel, London, founded Abraham Ortelius (Antwerp): "Theatrum orbis terrarum," first modern atlas, with 53 maps
Sigismund II of Poland died; end of Jagellon dynasty Turks take Famagusta, Cyprus, and massacre its inhabitants Earl of Lennox, Regent of Scotland, killed; succeeded by Earl of Mar Reconciliation between Charles IX of France and Huguenots Negotiations for marriage between Elizabeth I and Henry, Duke of Anjou (abandoned a year later)	Incorporation of Blacksmiths' and of Joiners' Companies, London	Francesco Patrizi: "Discussiones peripateicae," anti-Aristotelian arguments Harrow School founded by John Lyon Jesus College, Oxford, founded by Hugh Price	Johann Kepler, German astronomer, born (died 1630)

DATE	SPANISH HISTORY	THEATRE AND LETTERS	MUSIC AND OPERA	GRAPHIC AND PLASTIC ARTS
1572	Francis Drake attacks Spanish harbors in America English Parliament demands execution of Mary, Queen of Scots Fourth War of Religion begins in France Dutch War of Independence begins Massacre on St. Bartholomew's Day in Paris: 2,000 Hugenots murdered there, among them Gaspard de Coligny	Luis Vaz de Camöens: "Os Lusíados," Portuguese epic poem on voyages of Vasco da Gama Guillaume de Salluste, Seigneur du Bartas (1544-1590): "Judith" John Donne, English poet, born (died 1631) Ben Jonson, English dramatist, born (died 1637)	William Byrd and Thomas Tallis organists at the Chapel Royal	Galeazzo Alessi, Italian architect, died (born 1512) Francois Clouet, French painter, died (born 1522)
1573	Spanish capture Haarlem after seven-month siege Duke of Alba leaves Brussels for Spain	Torquato Tasso: "Aminta," Italian pastoral (published 1580)	Orlando de Lasso: "Patrocinium musices"	Work begun on Mexico City Cathedral (finished 1813) Michelangelo da Caravaggio, Italian painter, born (died 1610) Inigo Jones, English architect, born (died 1652) Paolo Veronese called before Inquisition tribunal in Rome

WORLD EVENTS	MUNDANE EVENTS	CHURCH AND THOUGHT	KNOWLEDGE AND INVENTIONS
Duke of Norfolk tried for treason and executed Estates of Poland declare the monarchy elective Henry of Navarre marries Margaret of Valois, sister of Charles IX of France Earl of Northumberland executed for treason Earl of Mar, Regent of Scotland, died; succeeded by Earl of Morton	Pigeons carrying letters used by Dutch during Spanish siege of Haarlem	Annibale Caro: "Lettere Familiari," history of Tuscan literary language in Italy John Knox died (born 1505) Isaak Luria, Jewish mystic (cabalist), died (born 1533) Pope Pius V died (born 1504); Cardinal Ugo Buoncompagni (born 1502) elected Pope Gregory XIII (-1585)	"Artis auriferae quam chemium vocant," one of earliest books on alchemy, published in Basel Tycho Brahe discovers the "New Star" in the Milkey Way Daniel Sennert, German scientist and physicist, born (died 1637) Society of Antiquaries founded in London
Peace of Constantinople ends war between Turks and Venice Henry, Duke of Anjou, elected King of Poland; returns to France to succeed his brother Charles IX (1574) Fourth French War of Religion ends; Huguenots granted an amnesty Wan-Li (1563-1620) begins reign as 13th emperor of the Ming dynasty in China	First German cane-sugar refinery at Augsburg	Collegium Germanicum established in Rome Francois Hofman: "Francogallia," a treatise on election and deposition of kings	Francis Drake sees Pacific Ocean for first time

DATE	SPANISH HISTORY	THEATRE AND LETTERS	MUSIC AND OPERA	GRAPHIC AND PLASTIC ARTS
1574	Portuguese colonize Angola and found Sao Paulo Spain loses Tunis to Turks	Richard Burbage receives license to open theatre in London	Domenico Maria Ferrabosco, Italian singer and composer, died (born 1513)	Longleat House, Wiltshire, finished (begun 1568) Tintoretto: "Paradiso," Doge's Palace, Venice
1575	Philip II refuses to grant concessions to Dutch rebels at conference in Breda State bankruptcy in Spain	Diego Hurtado da Mendoza, Spanish poet and statesman, died (born 1503) Tasso: "Gerusalemme liberata," epic poems about the Crusades Giovanni Battista Basile, Italian poet, born (died 1632)	William Byrd and Thomas Tallis: "Cationes sacrae," 34 motets Marco da Gagliano, Italian composer, born (died 1642)	Cornelis Floris, Dutch architect, died (born 1514) Guido Reni, Italian painter, born (died 1642) Veronese: "Moses Saved from the Waters"
1576	Philip II makes his half brother, Don John of Austria, Governor of the Netherlands Pacification of the Netherlands discussed at the Congress of Ghent Antwerp sacked by Spanish	Hans Sachs, German poet and dramatist, died (born 1494) Académie du Palais founded in Paris by Henry III, associated with Baïf's Académie of 1570	Tomas Luis de Victoria: "Liber primus," masses and canticles	Palladio: Il Redentore, church in Venice (- 1577) Titian died (born 1477)

WORLD EVENTS	MUNDANE EVENTS	CHURCH AND THOUGHT	KNOWLEDGE AND INVENTIONS
Charles IX of France died; succeeded by his brother Henry III, King of Poland Selim II, Sultan of Turkey, died; succeeded by Murad III Fifth French War of Religion (-1576)		First auto-da-fé in Mexico Jean Bodin: "Discours sur les causes de l'extrême cherte en France," on luxury Hubert Languet: "Vindiciae contra tyrannos," political theories of the Huguenots	Ulissi Aldovrandi: "Antidotarri Bonoiensis epitome," a treatise on drugs Conrad Dasypodius builds the famous Strasbourg clock. Bartolommeo Eustachio, Italian anatomist, died (born 1524)
King Henry III of France crowned at Rheims Stephen Bathory of Transylvania becomes King of Poland (-1586) Mogul Emperor Akbar conquers Bengal Edmund Grindal becomes Archbishop of Canterbury (died 1583)	Outbreak of plague in Sicily, spreading through Italy up to Milan Population figures: Paris census 300,000; London census 180,000; Cologne census 35,000	Archbishop Matthew Parker (1505-1575) leaves his collection of historical documents to Corpus Christi College, Cambridge University of Leiden founded by William of Orange	Tycho Brahe constructs an observatory at uraniborg for Frederick II of Denmark George Tuberville: "Book of Falconrie"
Act of Federation between Holland and Zeeland signed in Delft Edict of Beaulieu tolerating Reformed religion in France Emperor Maximilian II died; succeeded by his brother Rudolf II (1552-1612)		Jean Bodin: "La république," advocating constitutional monarchy League of Torgau, supporting opinions of the Lutherans, draws up Articles of Faith University of Warsaw, Poland, founded	Clusius publishes his treatise on flowers of Spain and Portugal; beginning of modern botany Robert Norman, English hydrographer, discovers magnetic "dip," or inclination Francois Viète introduces decimal fractions

DATE	SPANISH HISTORY	THEATRE AND LETTERS	MUSIC AND OPERA	GRAPHIC AND PLASTIC ARTS
1577	Don John of Austria issues Perpetual Edict to settle civil war in the Nether-lands; it is rejected by William of Orange	"Chronicles of England, Scotland, and Ireland," a history in 2 volumes published by Raphael Holinshed (died circa 1580), (Holinshed Chronicles) Robert Burton, English prose writer, born (died 1525) Remy Belleau, French poet, died (born 1527) George Gascoigne, English author, died (born (1525)	Mattheus Le Maistre, Walloon composer, died (born 1505)	El Greco: "Assumption of the Virgin," altarpiece in San Domingo el Antiguo, Toledo Peter Paul Rubens, Fl. painter, born (died 1640) Tintoretto: "The Doge Alvise Mocenigo"
1578	King of Portugal, Sebastian, killed at Alcazar during the invasion of Morocco	Pierre de Ronsard: "Sonnets pour Hélène," to Hélène de Surgères Guillaume de Salluste, Seigneur du Bartas: "La Semaine," religious epic on the Creation John Lyly: "Euphues, the Anatomy of Wit," complete edition 1617		Adam Elsheimer, German landscape painter, born (died 1610)

WORLD EVENTS	MUNDANE EVENTS	CHURCH AND THOUGHT	KNOWLEDGE AND INVENTIONS
Henry of Navarre recognized head of Huguenot party	Beatrice Cenci, Italian tragic heroine, born (died 1599)	William Allot: "Thesaurus Bibliorum"	William Harrison: "Description of England"
Sixth French War of Religion breaks out		Richard Eden: "History of Travel in East and West Indies"	Johann Baptista van Helmont, Flemish physician and scientist, born (died 1644)
Peace of Bergerac ends sixth War of Religion		Milan Cathedral consecrated by Cardinal Carlo Borromeo	
Francis Drake embarks (November) on voyage around the world via Cape Horn			

James VI takes over government of Scotland after Earl of Morton resigns regency	Levant Trading Company founded in London for trade with Turkey	Jacques Cujas: "Commentaries on Roman Law"	Catacombs of Rome discovered
Don John died (born 1545); Alessandro Farnese, Duke of Parma, succeeds as Governor of the Netherlands	Work begun on Pont Neuf, oldest bridge over Seine River, Paris		
John III of Sweden secretly converted to Catholicism			
Mohammed Khudabanda becomes Shah of Persia (-1587)			
Oatomo Yoshishige, one of the chief rulers of Japan, converted to Christianity			

DATE	SPANISH HISTORY	THEATRE AND LETTERS	MUSIC AND OPERA	GRAPHIC AND PLASTIC ARTS
1579	Portugese merchants set up trading station in Bengal	Samuel Coster, Dutch dramatist, born (died 1665) Edmund Spenser: "The Shepherd's Calendar", 12 ecologues John Fletcher, English dramatist, born (died 1625)		El Greco: "L'Espoiio" Palladio: Teatro Olimpico, Vincenza Frans Snyder, Dutch pinter, born (died 1657)
1580	King Philip II falls heir to throne of Portugal Spanish invade Portugal under the Duke of Alba	Cervantes freed by ransom in Algeria having been captured earlier by Barbary pirates; Camoes of Portugal, creator of the national epic Os Lusiadas, died Luis Vaz de Camöens, Portuguese poet, died (born 1524) John Webster, English dramatist, born (died 1625)	English folk tune "Greensleeves" mentioned for first time Jan Sweelinck made organist at Dude Kerk, Amsterdam	Frans Hals, Dutch painter, born (died 1666) Andrea Palladio, Italian architect,died (born 1508) Robert Smythyson: Wollaton Hall, near Nottingham (- 1610)
1581	Philip II enters Lisbon, Portugal, as Philip I of Portugal Portuguese Cortes submits to Philip II of Spain	George Peele: "The Arraignment of Paris," pastoral play	Coroso: "Il Ballerino," treatise on dance technique "Ballet comique de la Reyne" by Balthazar de Beaujoyeux Vincenzo Galilei: "Dialogo della musica antica e moderna" "Geuzenlied Boek," an anthology of Dutch songs, including national anthem "Wilhelmus van Nassauwe"	Caravaggio: "Martyrdom of St. Maurice: Domenichino (Domenico Zampieri), Italian painter, born (died 1641) Bernardo Strozzi, Italian baroque painter, born (died 1644)

WORLD EVENTS	MUNDANE EVENTS	CHURCH AND THOUGHT	KNOWLEDGE AND INVENTIONS
English-Dutch military alliance signed Signing of Union of Utrecht marks foundation of Dutch Repeblic Francis Drake proclaims sovereignity over New Albion, California	English Eastland Company founded for trading with Scadanavia	English College of Douai removed from Rheims to Rome Sir Thomas North translates Plutarch's "Lives" St. John of the Cross: "Dark Night of the Soul"	
Seventh French War of Religion breaks out Ivan IV, The Terrible, kills his son and heir with his own hands Francis Drake returns to England from voyage of circumnavigation	Venice imports coffee from Turkey to Italy Earthquake in London Italian cooking predominant in Europe New buildings banned in London to restrict growth of city	Jean Brodin: "Démonomainie des sorciers," against witchcraft Jesuits Edmund Campion and Robert Parsons land in England, begin Jesuit mission Francois de la Noue: "24 Discours politiques et militaires," Huguenot point of view on French Wars of Religion	King Frederic II of Denmark builds an astronomical observatory on the island of Ven, between Denmark and Sweden. Prospero Alpini (born Venice, Italy, 1553) becomes the first scientist to learn that plants, like animals, have two sexes
Earl of Morton executed for complicity in Lord Darnley's murder (1567) Akbar conquers Afghanistan Russian conquest of Siberia (-1598) Elizabeth I knights Francis Drake at Deptford	English translation by George Pettie of Stafano Guazzo's "Civil conversations," on courtesy and good behavior Sedan chairs in general use in England	Edmund Campion, English Jesuit, tried for treason and executed Pope Gregory XIII attempts to reconcile Roman Catholic and Russian Orthodox Churches James VI of Scotland sings Second Confession of Faith	William Borough: "A Discourse on the Variation of the Compass or Magneticall Needle" Galileo studies the hanging lamps at the Cathedral of Pisa, directing attention to pendulums which eventually results in accurate clocks Galileo Galilei discovers isochronous property of the pendulum

DATE	SPANISH HISTORY	THEATRE AND LETTERS	MUSIC AND OPERA	GRAPHIC AND PLASTIC ARTS
1582	Completion of church of San Lorenzo In October, the Papal States of Spain and Portugal adopt the Gregorian Calendar; in December it is adopted by France, The Netherlands, and Scandinavia; by England in 1752	Phineas Fletcher, English poet, born (died 1650)	Gregorio Allegri, Italian tenor singer and composer born (died 1652)	David Teniers the Elder, Dutch painter, born (died 1649)
1583	The Duke of Anjou sacks Antwerp and retires from the Netherlands A plot by Francis Throgmorton for the Spanish invasion of England is discovered; Throgmorton is arrested and executed	Queen's Company of Players formed in London by Sir Edmund Tilney Baptista Honwaerd: "Pegasides Pleyn Amorosity," Dutch didactic poem Robert Ganier (1545-1590): "Les Juives," early French tragicomedy	Girolamo Frescobaldi, Italian organist and composer, born (died 1625)	General Toyotomi Hideyoshi (1536-1598) lays foundation of Osaka Castle

WORLD EVENTS	MUNDANE EVENTS	CHURCH AND THOUGHT	KNOWLEDGE AND INVENTIONS
Peace of Jam-Zapolski: Russia loses access to Baltic and abandons Livonia and Estonia to Poland Attempt on life of William of Orange Raid of Ruthven: James VI kidnaped by Protestant nobles Nobunaga, ruler of Japan, assassinated First English colony in Newfoundland founded	Royal Navy gets graduated pay according to rank London's first waterworks founded; water wheels installed on London Bridge	George Buchanan: "Rerum Scoticarum historiae"	Pope Gregory XIII reforms the calendar; it becomes the new Gregorian calendar; as a result, 1582 has 354 days, making it the shortest year on record Richard Hakluyt (1552-1616): "Divers Voyages Toughing the Discovery of America" Urbain Hémand investigates the anatomy of the teeth
Albrecht von Wallenstein, military leader in Thirty Years' War, born (died 1634) Sommerville plot to assassinate Elizabeth I discovered; John Sommerville executed James VI of Scotland escapes from hands of Ruthven raiders after 10 months William of Orange accepts sovereignty of the northern Netherlands	First known life insurance in England, on life of William Gibbons	Edmund Grindal, Archbishop of Canterbury, died (born 1519); succeeded by John Whitgift Hugo Grotius, Dutch statesman and jurist, born (died 1645) Francesco Sansovino: "Del Governo et ammistrazione di diversi regni et republiche"	University of Edinburgh is founded in Scotland as a secular institution Italian philosopher Giordand Bruno outlines his metaphysical ideas Andrea Cesalpino gives a classification scheme for plants based on roots and fruits Joseph Justus Scaliger devises the Julian day count still in use English expeditions to Mesopotamia, India, and Persian Gulf led by merchants Ralph Fitch and John Eldred (-1591)

DATE	SPANISH HISTORY	THEATRE AND LETTERS	MUSIC AND OPERA	GRAPHIC AND PLASTIC ARTS
1584	Last stone laid at Escorial At the instigation of Philip II, William of Orange is assassinated by Balthazar Gérard	Jan Kochanowski, Polish poet, died (born 1530) Francis Beaumont, English dramatist, born (died 1616) John Lyly: "Alexander and Campaspe" produced at Blackfriars Theatre, London	Pietro Vinci, Italian composer, died (born 1535)	
1585	Queen Elizabeth I of England sends aid to Holland against Spain Henry III of France and Elizabeth I of England decline sovereignty of the Netherlands; but Elizabeth takes the Netherlands under her protection On the orders of Elizabeth, Sir Francis Drake attacks Vigo and Santo Domingo	Cervantes: "Galatéa," pastoral romance Teatro Olimpico, in Vicenza, opened Shakespeare leaves Stratford - on - Avon for London Battista Guarini: "Il Pastor fido," pastoral play, given at Turin	Heinrich Schütz, German composer, born (died 1672) Thomas Tallis, English composer, died (born 1505)	Jean Lemercier, French architect, born (died 1654) Veronese: "Apotheosis of Venice," Sala de Gran Consiglio, Venice
1586	Mary, Queen of Scots, recognizes Philip II of Spain as her heir Pope Sixtus V promises financial aid to send the Spanish Armada against England Mary, Queen of Scots, tried for treason (See WORLD EVENTS)	Beginning of Kabuki theatre, Japan John Ford, English dramatist, born (died 1640) Sir Philip Sidney, English poet and soldier, died (born 1551)	Johann Hermann Schein, German composer, born (died 1630)	El Greco: "Burial of count Orgaz" Luis de Morales, Spanish painter, died (born 1510) Rebuilding of St. John Lateran, Rome

WORLD EVENTS	MUNDANE EVENTS	CHURCH AND THOUGHT	KNOWLEDGE AND INVENTIONS
Ivan IV, The Terrible, died (born 1540); succeeded as Czar of Russia by his Fyodor, who relinquishes most of his powers to his brother-in law Boris Godunov William of Orange is assassinated Francis, Duke of Anjou, died (born 1554) Sir Walter Raleigh discovers and annexes Virginia	Branco de Rialto founded in Venice Oldest extant wave-swept lighthouse erected at Cordouan, at the mouth of the Gironde River	Foundation of Accademia dei Scienze, Lettere ed Arti in Lucca Cardinal Carlo Borromeo, Archbishop of Milan, died (born 1538) Reginald Scot: "The Discoverie of Witchcraft," attacking superstition Lucilio Vanini, Italian philosopher, born (died 1619)	Giordano Bruno gives the opinion that the universe in infinite Ju Zai Yu invents equal temperament in music Dutch trading post founded at Archangel, Russia
Hideyoshi sets up dictatorship in Japan	Antwerp loses its importance as international port to Rotterdam and Amsterdam	Pope Gregory XIII died; Cardinal Felice Peretti becomes Pope Sixtus V (-1590) Jesuit University founded in Graz, Austria	Flemish mathematician, Simon Stevinus, gives a systematic account of how to use decimal fractions Fiovanni Battista Benedetti criticizes Aristotle's views on motion John Davis discovers Davis Strait between Canada and Greenland
Sir Francis Walsingham unravels plot to murder Elizabeth I, proving involvement of Mary Queen of Scots in the plan Anthony Babington and fellow conspirators tried and executed for plot Stephen Bathory, King of Poland, died (born 1533)	Corn severely short in England Walter Raleigh imports the habit of smoking tobacco into England from Virginia	Caesar Baronius: "Annales ecclesiastici," history of the Roman Catholic Church Pope Sixtus V fixes number of cardinals at 70; issues bull, "Detestabilis," forbidding usury	Simon Stevinus performs experiment for gravity, by dropping two different weights at the same time and noting that they strike the ground at the same time A 327-ton Egyptian obelisk that the Romans had brought from Egypt in ancient times is raised to a vertical position

DATE	SPANISH HISTORY	THEATRE AND LETTERS	MUSIC AND OPERA	GRAPHIC AND PLASTIC ARTS
1587	Despite protestation of Philip II, Elizabeth I of England has Mary Queen of Scots beheaded Hideyoshi banishes Portuguese missionaries from Japan Pope Sixtus V proclaims Catholic crusade for invasion of England	First company of English players in Germany "Volksbuch von Dr. Faust, " first printed at Frankfurt; English translation 1588 Marlowe: "Tamburlaine," blank verse drama	Monteverdi: first book of madrigals Samuel Scheidt, German organist and composer, born (died 1654) Zeminoth Israel publishes early collection of Jewish songs	Cobham Hall, Kent, begun by Inigo Jones and completed by Adam brothers Osaka Castle, Japan, finished
1588	Defeat of the Spanish Armada Duke of Medina Sidonia sails from Lisbon in command of "invincible" Spanish Armada; defeated by the English under Charles Howard War with France	Robert Greene: "Pandosto, or Dorastus and Fawnia," romance Marlowe: "Doctor Faustus," tragedy Montaigne: "Essais," Volume III Robert Greene: "Menaphon," romance	William Byrd: "Psalms, Sonets and Songs of Sadness and Pietie" Nicholas Yonge: "Musica Transalpina," 57 madrigals published in London	Annibale Carracci: frescoes in Magnani Palace, Bologna Domenico Fontana (1543-1607) works on completion of dome of St. Peter's, Rome (1585-1590) Paolo Veronese, Italian painter, died (born 1528)
1589	Herrera publishes his treatise on Escorial With 150 ships and 1800 men, Sir Francis Drake fails to take Lisbon	George Puttenham: "The Arte of English Poesie" Thomas Nashe (1567-1601): "Antomie of Absurdities," criticism of contemporary literature	Thoinot Arbeau (1519-1595): "Orchésographie," early treatise on dancing, with several dance tunes William Byrd: "Songs of Sundrie Natures"	Caravaggio: "Bacchus" Bernard Palissy, French Huguenot writer on art and pottery, died (born 1510)

WORLD EVENTS	MUNDANE EVENTS	CHURCH AND THOUGHT	KNOWLEDGE AND INVENTIONS
Mary, Queen of Scots, executed at Fotheringay (born 1542) Sir Christopher Hatton (1540-1591) becomes Lord Chancellor A son of King John of Sweden succeeds Stephen Bathory as Sigismund III of Poland (-1632) John Winthrop born (died 1649), first governor of Massachusetts Bay colony	Construction of Rialto Bridge, Venice, by Antonio da Ponte (- 1591)	Antonio Agustino: "Dialogo ..." on numismatics John Knox: "Hystory of the Reformation in Scotland" "Rederijckkunst," Dutch manual on rhetoric Issac Casaubon edits works of Strabo	Richard Hakluyt (1552-1616): "Notable History, Containing Four Voyages made by Certain French Captains Into Florida"
Frederick II of Denmark died; succeeded by Christian IV (-1648) Henry, Duke of Guise, and his brother Louis, Cardinal of Guise, assassinated by order of Henry III; another brother, the Duke of Mayenne, becomes leader of Catholic League	Timothy Bright: "An Arte of Shorte, Swifte, and Secrete Writing by Character," manual of shorthand English Guinea Company founded	Jan Blahoslav's Czech translation of New Testament incorporated in Kralice Bible Thomas Hobbes, French philosopher, born (died 1679) Thomas Stapleton: "Tres Thomae," controversial Roman Catholic tract	Joachim Camerarius: "Hortus medicus"
Catherine de'Medici, Queen Mother of France, died Henry III, King of France, last of the house of Valois, assassinated; on his deathbed he recognizes Henry, King of Navarre, as his successor, who, as Henry IV, is the first Bourbon to become King of France	Forks used for first time at French court The Reverend William Lee (Cambridge) invents the stocking frame, first knitting machine.	Vatican Library opened in Rome Amador Arrais: "Dialogues...," moral and religious themes in Portugese Boris Godunov asserts Moscow's religious independence of Constantinople Kiev Academy founded	The first complete edition of Paracelsus's works published in Basel, Switzerland Gianbattista della Porta's book is the first in the West to mention kites and kite flying Galileo Galilei becomes professor of mathematics at University of Pisa

DATE	SPANISH HISTORY	THEATRE AND LETTERS	MUSIC AND OPERA	GRAPHIC AND PLASTIC ARTS
1590		Shakespeare: "Henry VI,", Parts 2 and 3 Battista Guarini: "Il Pastor fido," pastoral play, published Robert Wilson: "Three Lords and Three Ladies of London," morality play Italian Commedia dell'arte company "I Accesi," begins activities Marlowe: "The Jew of Malta," tragedy	Emilio de' Cavalieri: "Il Satiro," pastoral fable	El Greco: "St. Jerome" Alonso Sanchez Coello, Spanish painter, died (born 1515) Giovanni da Bologna: "Mercury" Leone Leoni, Italian goldsmith and sculptor, died (born 1509)
1591		Luis de León, Spanish poet, died (born 1527) Shakespeare: "Henry VI," Part 1 (-1592) Robert Herrick, English poet, born (died 1674) John Lyly: "Endymion, the Man in The Moon," allegorical comedy	Vincenzo Galilei, Italian lutanist and composer, father of Galileo Galilei, died (born 1520)	Jusepe de Ribera (Los Spagnoletto), Spanish painter, born (died 1652) Guercino (Giovanni Francesco Barbieri), Italian painter, born (died 1666)
1592	Portuguese settle at Mombasa	Historiae de Rebus Hispaniae written by historian Juan de Mariana Philip Henslowe, London theatrical manager, writes his " Diary" (-1603) Thomas Kyd: "The Spanish Tragedy," play Shakespeare: "Richard III," "Comedy of Errors"	Monteverdi: third book of madrigals Lodovico Zacconi: "Prattica di musica," original edition	Jacques Callot, French painter, born (died 1635) Tintoretto: "The Last Supper"

WORLD EVENTS	MUNDANE EVENTS	CHURCH AND THOUGHT	KNOWLEDGE AND INVENTIONS
Catholic League proclaims Cardinal Charles X Henry IV lays siege to Paris, causing famine Shah Abbas I of Persia makes peace with Turkey Akbar of India conquers Orissa The Emperor of Morocco annexes Timbuctoo	Coal mining begins in the Ruhr First English paper mill at Dartford	Pope Sixtus V died; Pope Urban VII succeeds and dies 12 days later Cardinal Sfondrato becomes Pope Gregory XIV	Zacherias Janssen invents the compound microscope Giacomo della Porta and Domenico Fontana complete the dome on St. Peters in Rome José de Acosta: "Historia natural y moral de las Indias" Drake, Hawkins, and Frobisher return from unsuccessful expedition to Spanish coast
Henry IV of France excommunicated by Pope Son of Ivan the Terrible assassinated on instigation of Boris Godunov Christian I of Saxony died	Skittle alleys, in use since end of 12th century, become popular in Germany	Giordano Bruno: "De immenso et innumerabalis seu de universo et mundis" Pope Gregory XIV died; Cardinal Facchinetti becomes Innocent IX Trinity College, Dublin, founded	James Lancaster leaves Plymouth on first voyage to East Indies Francois Viète (1540-1603): "in Artem analyticam isagoge," on using letters for algebraic quantities
John III of Sweden died; succeeded by Sigismund III of Poland Akbar, Mogul Emperor, takes Sind Korea refuses passage of Hideyoshi of Japan's troops to invade China Emperor Rudolf II makes peace with Poland	Plague kills 15,000 people in London Windmills used in Holland to drive mechanical saws	Cardinal Aldobrandini elected Pope Clement VIII Johann Amos Comenius, Moravian educational reformer, born (died 1670) Thomas Sanchez: "De sacramento matrimonii," on aspects of marriage	Korean astronomers observe a nova in the constellation Cetus Galileo develops a theremoscope, a primitive form of thermometer Galileo: "Della scienza mechanica," problems of raising weights Ruined Roman city of Pompeii discovered

DATE	SPANISH HISTORY	THEATRE AND LETTERS	MUSIC AND OPERA	GRAPHIC AND PLASTIC ARTS
1593	Henry IV becomes a Roman Catholic; "Paris is well worth a mass"	Shakespeare: "Titus Andronicus," "The Taming of the Shrew" Christopher Marlowe, English dramatist, killed in tavern brawl (born 1564) Robert Henryson: "Testament of Cresseid," poem (posthumous) London theatres closed because of plague	Paolo Agostini, Italian composer, born (died 1629)	El Greco: "The Crucifixion," "The Resurrection" Guiseppe Archimboldo, Italian painter, died (born 1530) Jacob Jordaëns, Dutch painter, born (died 1678) Nicolas Poussin, French painter, born (died 1565)
1594	Henry IV, crowned King of France at Chartres, enters Paris	London theatres open again Diego Bernades: "Varias rimas ao Bom Jesus," Portuguese religious poems Christopher Marlowe: "Edward the Second," tragedy (posthumous) Shakespeare: "Two Gentlemen of Verona," "Love's Labour's Lost," "Romeo and Juliet" George Peele: "The Battle of Alcazar," play	Elizabeth I sends a Thomas Dallam organ to Sultan of Turkey Orlando di Lasso, Fl. composer, died (born 1532) Giovanni Pierluigi da Palestrina, Italian composer, died (born 1525) "Dafne," by Jacopo Peri (1561-1633), first opera	Caravaggio: The Musical Party" Jean Cousin, French painter, died (born 1522) Giovanni da Bologna: statues of Cosimo I de'-Medici and Fernando de'Medici Tintoretto, Italian painter, died (born 1518)

WORLD EVENTS	MUNDANE EVENTS	CHURCH AND THOUGHT	KNOWLEDGE AND INVENTIONS
Rudolf II renews war against Turkey	Purana Pul bridge built across Musi River, Hyderabad	Pierre Charron: "Les Trois Vérités," French theological treatise	The first description of a modern Chinese abacus appears in China
	Sant' Ambrogio Bank founded in Milan		First French botanical gardens established by University of Montpellier
			Giambattista della Porta: "De refractione, optices parte," with an account of binocular vision
			Anthony van Diemen, Dutch navigator, born (died 1645)
Gustavus Adolphus, future King Gustavus II of Sweden, born (died 1632)	English navigator James Lancaster breaks Portugese trade monopoly in India	Giordano Bruno seized by the Vatican for supporting Copernican theory	Galileo's Golden Rule
			Gerardus Mercator, Flemish geographer, dies in Duisburg, Germany
Akbar takes Kandahar		Richard Hooker: "Of the Laws of Ecclesiastical Polity," volumes 1-4	Galileo's Golden Rule
Edict of St. Germain-en-Laye grants Huguenots freedom of worship			
		Piere Matthieu: "Histoire des deniers troubles de France"	English traveler Ralph Fitch returns from overland journey to India and Ceylon
Turks conquer Raab at Austro-Hungarian border			

DATE	SPANISH HISTORY	THEATRE AND LETTERS	MUSIC AND OPERA	GRAPHIC AND PLASTIC ARTS
1595	Basilica consecrated Henry IV declares war on Spain Spanish land in Cornwall, burning Penzance and Mousehole	George Peele: "The Old Wives' Tale," comedy Shakespeare: "Richard II," "A Midsummer Night's Dream" Torquato Tasso, Italian poet, died (born 1544) Thomas Kyd, English dramatist, died (born 1557) Robert Southwell, English Jesuit poet, hanged at Tyburn (born 1544)	John Wilson, English singer and composer born (died 1674)	Annibale Carracci: "Venus and Adonis"
1596	Spain repudiates its debts English sack Cadiz; Spanish take Calais	Shakespeare: "King John," "The Merchant of Venice" Sir John Harrington: "The Metamorphosis of Ajax," satire Sir John Davies: "Orchestra," poem Blackfriars Theatre, London, opens Edmund Spenser: "The Faerie Queene," Books 4-6	Nicola Amati, the most eminent of all the Amati, born (died 1684) Lodovico Zacconi: "Prattica di musica," reprinted from original edition, Venice, 1592	Caravaggio: "Basket of Fruit" Jan van Goyen, Dutch painter, born (died 1656)

WORLD EVENTS	MUNDANE EVENTS	CHURCH AND THOUGHT	KNOWLEDGE AND INVENTIONS
Sigmund Bathory defeats Turks at Giurgevo	English army finally abandons bow as weapon of war	Pope Clement VIII absolves Henry IV, recognizing him as King of France	Mercator's atlas published posthumously, containing a collection of detailed maps of Europe
Dutch begin to colonize East Indies	First appearance of heels on shoes	Andrew Maunsell: "The Catalogue of English Printed Books"	Sir Francis Drake and Sir John Hawkins leave Plymouth on last voyage to Spanish Main
Sultan Murad III of Turkey died	Warsaw, capital of Poland	Philip Neri, Italian mystic, died (born 1515)	Sir Walter Raleigh explores 300 miles up Orinoco river
Peasant revolt in Upper Austria			

Decrees of Folembray end war of Catholic League in France	Tomatoes introduced in England	Caesar Baronius: "Martyrologium Romanum"	Willem Barents discovers Spitzbergen and Barents Sea
Pacification of Ireland	First water closets, designed by Sir John Harington, courtier and author (1561-1612), installed at the Queen's Palace, Richmond	Jean Bodin, French philosopher, died (born 1530)	Sir Francis Drake died (born 1546)
Peace between Japan and China after Japanese fail to invade Korea		René Descartes, French philosopher, born (died 1650)	Li Shi Zhen's book of more than 1,000 plants and 1,000 animals
Turks defeat Imperial army at Keresztes, northern Hungary			Li Shi Zhen's "The Great Pharmacopoeia:" to distill wine into spirits; known to the Chinese since the seventh century
			Admiral Visunsin of Korea develops the first iron-clad warship.

DATE	SPANISH HISTORY	THEATRE AND LETTERS	MUSIC AND OPERA	GRAPHIC AND PLASTIC ARTS
1597	Second Spanish Armada leaves for England; scattered by storms Philip II opens peace talks with Henry IV	Hernando de Herrera, Spanish poet, died (born 1534) Thomas Nashe: "The Isle of Dogs," satirical comedy Shakespeare: "Henry IV," Parts 1 and 2 (-1598) Aldine Press, Venice, founded 1494, ceases after publication of 908 works	John Dowland: "First Booke of Songes" Thomas Morley" a Plaine and Easie Introduction to Practicall Musick" Orazio Vecchi (1551-1605): "L'Amfiparnasso," Modena	El Greco: "St. Martin and the Beggar" Juan de Herrera, Spanish architect, died (born 1530)
1598	Death of Philip II in royal apartments; Philip III ascends throne Peace of Vervins: Philip II resigns claim to French crown; country united under Henry IV as single sovereign King Philip II of Spain died (born 1527); succeeded by Philip III (-1621)	Lope de Vega: "La Dragontea," fanciful account of Drake's adventures, in verse form Shakespeare: "Much Ado about Nothing," "Henry V" (-1599) George Peele, English dramatist, died (born 1558) Ben Johnson: "Every Man in His Humour"	Johann Crüger, German composer, born (died 1662)	El Greco: "Fernando Niño de Guevara" Giovanni Lorenzo Bernini, Italian sculptor, born (died 1680) Jan Brueghel: "Adoration of the Kings" Francois Mansart, French architect, born (died 1666)

WORLD EVENTS	MUNDANE EVENTS	CHURCH AND THOUGHT	KNOWLEDGE AND INVENTIONS
Sigmund Bathory cedes Transylvania to Emperor Rudolf II Hideyoshi of Japan resumes Korean campaign Re-Catholicization of Upper Austria effected by force William V, Duke of Bavaria, abdicates Dutch found Batavia, Java	English Act of Parliament prescribes sentences of transportation to colonies for convicted criminals English merchants expelled from Holy Roman Empire in retaliation for treatment of the Hanseatic League in London First field hospitals and field dispensaries	Peter Canisius, German Jesuit Counter Reformationist, died Jean de Serres: "Inventaire général de l'histoire de France" James VI of Scotland: "Demonologie," on witchcraft	Corresponding with Kepler, Galileo admits that he has accepted the Copernican scheme of the solar system "Alchemy" by Andreas Libavius, Germany, important text book in chemistry Willem Barents, Dutch navigator, died (born 1547)
Boris Godunov seizes throne; elected Czar of Russia Pope Clement VIII seizes duchy of Ferrara Dutch take Mauritius Ieyasu Tokugawa restores shogunate, which endures until 1867-68		Juan de Mariana: "De rege et regis institutione," on kingship Edict of Nantes grants French Huguenots freedom of worship Francis Meres: "Palladis Tamia," anthology of quotations from 125 English writers Sir Thomas Bodley (1545-1613) begins rebuilding of library at Oxford	Francesco Cavalieri, Italian, scientist, born (died 1647) Carlo Ruini's manual of veterinary science Korean Admiral Visunsin invents ironclad warship

DATE	SPANISH HISTORY	THEATRE AND LETTERS	MUSIC AND OPERA	GRAPHIC AND PLASTIC ARTS
1599	The Spanish Armada under the Duke of Lerma sets sail against England, but is defeated by wind	Mateo Aleman publishes Vita del Picaro Grizman de Alforache Mateo Aleman: "Guzman de Alfarache," picaresque novel Shakespeare: "Julius Caesar," "As You Like It," "Twelfth Night" (- 1600) Building of the Globe Theatre, Southwark, London, where Shakespeare's plays are performed	Luca Marencio,Italian composer, died (born 1553)	Velazquez, Spanish artist, born (died 1660) Anthony Van Dyck, born (died 1641)
1600		Pedro Caldéron de la Barca, Spanish dramatist, born (died 1681) Shakespeare: "Hamlet," "The Merry Wives of Windsor" (-1601) Thomas Dekker: "The Shoemaker's Holiday" Fortune Theatre, London, opened	Andrea Amati, Italian violin maker, died (born 1530) Harps used in orchestras Jacopo Peri: "Euridice," opera Recorder (flute-à-bec) becomes popular in England	Caravaggio: "Doubting Thomas" Building of Royal Palace, Naples, begun Rubens in Italy (- 1608)

WORLD EVENTS	MUNDANE EVENTS	CHURCH AND THOUGHT	KNOWLEDGE AND INVENTIONS
Earl of Essex, Lord Lieutenant of Ireland, arrested on his return to England	In Marseilles first chamber of commerce founded	Fabio Chigi, future Pope Alexander VII, born (died 1667)	Aldrovandi, Italian naturalist, publishes studies on ornithology
Oliver Cromwell, English general and statesman, born (died 1658)	First postal rates fixed in Germany Outbreak of plague in Spain	James VI of Scotland: "Basilikon doron," on divine right of kings	
Duke of Sully, French superintendent of finances, reforms taxation, economic policy, overseas trade, and agriculture			
Henry IV of France divorces Margaret of Valois			
Swedish Diet proclaims Charles of Södermanland Charles IX			

Henry IV marries Maria de'Medici	Amsterdam Bank founded	Persecution of Catholics in Sweden under Charles IX	Giordano Bruno, Italian philosopher, accused of heresy because of his adherence to the theory that Earth revolves around the sun; he is burned at the stake in Rome
Future King Charles I of England born (died 1649)	Population figures (approximately, in millions): France 16, Germany 14.5, Poland 11, Spain 8, Hapsburg dominions 5.5, England and Ireland 5.5, Holland 3	Scottish College founded in Rome	
Ieyasu, as unquestioned ruler in Japan, moves capital to Yedo (Tokyo)			German Athanasius Kircher (1570-1629) invents magic lantern
William Adams, first Englishman to visit Japan, advises on shipbuilding	Wigs and dress trains become fashionable		Dutch opticians invent the telescope
English East India Company founded			

DATE	SPANISH HISTORY	THEATRE AND LETTERS	MUSIC AND OPERA	GRAPHIC AND PLASTIC ARTS
1601	An armada sent by Spain under the Duke of Lerma was once again defeated by strong winds	Historia de Espana by Juan de Mariana Bento Teixeira Pinto" "Prosopopeya," first Brazilian epic Shakespeare: "Troilus and Cressida" (-1602) Thomas Nashe, English dramatist, died (born 1567)	Caccini's new vocal style: "Nuove musiche" Carlo Gesualdo, Prince of Venosa (1560-1613): "Madrigals," to lyrics by Torquato Tasso Thomas Morley: "Triumphs of Oriana"	Alonso Cano, Spanish painter and architect, born (died 1667) Caravaggio: "Conversion of St. Paul" Simon de Vlieger, Dutch painter, born (died 1653)
1602	Spanish traders admitted to eastern Japan Spanish army, after landing in Ireland (Sept. 1601), surrenders to English at Kinsala (Jan.) Spain and England's King James I sign the Peace of London	Lope de Vega: "La hermosura de angélica," epic poem Shakespeare: "All's Well That Ends Well" (-1603) Thomas Dekker: "Satiromastix," satirical comedy Ben Jonson: "The Poetaster," comedy	Francesco Cavalli, Italian opera composer born (died 1676) Hans Leo Hassler (1564-1612): "Lustgarten," collection of German lieder	Agostino Carracci, Italian painter, died (born 1557) Philippe de Champaigne, French portrait painter, born (died 1674)

WORLD EVENTS	MUNDANE EVENTS	CHURCH AND THOUGHT	KNOWLEDGE AND INVENTIONS
Earl of Essex tried for treason and executed Michael, Prince of Moldavia, assassinated by Hungarians Future Louis XIII, son of Henry IV and Maria de'Medici born Abolition of monopolies in England Akbar annexes Khandest "False Dmitri" claiming to be a son of Czar Ivan IV, plots an invasion of Russia	Postal agreement between Germany and France Gobelin family of dyers lend their factory in the Faubourg St. Marcel, Paris, to King Henry IV, who sets up 200 workmen from Flanders to make tapestries Many German "Badestuben" (type of brothel) closed by authorities owing to spread of venereal disease	Pierre Charron: "De la sagesse," a system of Stoic philosophy University of Parma founded	Julius Casserius provides a work illustrating the larynx and the ear Kepler becomes astronomer and astrologer to Emperor Rudolf II Jesuit missionary Matteo Ricci admitted to Peking
Jules Mazarin, future French statesman and cardinal, born in Italy (died 1661) War between Persia and Turkey (-1627) Dutch East India Company founded with capital of 540,000 in Batavia, first modern public company	Paris Charité founded	Emperor Rudolf II, continuing persecution of Protestants in Hapsburg lands, suppresses meetings of Moravian Brethren Ambrosian Library, Milan, founded (opened 1609) Bodleian Library, Oxford, opened	Thomas Blondeville: "Theoriques of the Planets" Tycho Brahe: "Astronomis Instauratae progymanasmata" gives plans of 777 fixed stars Galileo investigates laws of gravitation and oscillation (-1604)

DATE	SPANISH HISTORY	THEATRE AND LETTERS	MUSIC AND OPERA	GRAPHIC AND PLASTIC ARTS
1603		Francisco Gómez de Quevedo: "La vida de buscón," picaresque novel	Jean-Baptiste Besard: "Thesaurus harmonicus," collection of lute music	Carlo Maderna builds the facade at St. Peter's, Rome (- 1612)
		Philip Henslowe, London theatrical manager, ends his "Diary" (begun 1592)	Monteverdi: "Fourth Book of Madrigals"	Palazzo Rospigliosi, Rome, erected by Flaminio Ponzio
			Thomas Robinson: "School of Musicke"	Aert van der Neer, Dutch painter, born (died 1677)
		"The Standard Grammar" by Nudozersky leads to development of modern Czech language		
		Samuel Daniel: "A Defence of Rhyme," in reply to Campion's "Art of English Poesie" (1602)		
1604	Spain and England's King James I sign the Peace of London	Lope de Vega: "Comedias," 25 volumes published (-1647)	Heinrich Albert, German composer, born (died 1651)	Caravaggio: "The Deposition," Vatican
	Peace between England and Spain	Cervantes writes Don Quixote	Company of Musicians incorporated in London	Karel van Mander (1548-1606): "Het Schilderboek," history of art
	Spanish capture Ostend from Dutch after siege of three and a half years	Shakespeare: "Measure for Measure" (-1605)	Orlando di Lasso: "Magnum opus musicum," 516 motets (posthumously)	
		Friedrich von Logau, German author, born (died 1655)	Negri: "Inventioni di balli," on dance technique	
		John Marston: "The Malcontent," tragicomedy		

WORLD EVENTS	MUNDANE EVENTS	CHURCH AND THOUGHT	KNOWLEDGE AND INVENTIONS
Queen Elizabeth I of England died (born 1533); succeeded by her cousin James VI of Scotland as James I of England and Ireland (-1625)	Heavy outbreak of plague in England	Jan Gruter: "Inscriptiones antiquae totius orbis Romanorum"	Founding of Accademia dei Lincei, Rome
		Richard Knolles: "General Historie of the Turkes"	Hugh Platt discovers coke, a charcoal-like substance produced by heating coal
Sir Walter Raleigh tried for high treason and sentenced to imprisonment		Roger Williams, religious controversialist in America, born (died 1683)	Fabricio de Acquapendente discovers the valves in veins
Henry IV recalls Jesuits to France			Benedito de Goes, a lay Jesuit, sets out for India in search of Cathay
Mohammed III, Sultan of Turkey, died; succeeded by Ahmad I (-1617)			
Tokugawa family obtains shogunate in Japan			
"False Dmitri," claimant to Russia throne, defeated by Czar Boris Godunov	Tomsk founded by Russian Cossacks	Richard Bancroft, Bishop of London, elected Archbishop of Canterbury	Johannes Kepler describes how the eye focuses light
First Parliament of James I meets		Robert Cawdrey: "A Table Alphabetical"	Voyages of English East India company to Java, the Moluccas, and Agra
Sigismund III of Sweden finally deposed, his uncle Charles IX assuming title of king		Universities of Oxford and Cambridge granted privilege of Parliamentary representation (withdrawn 1948)	King James I: "Counterblast to Tobacco"
Shah Abbas of Persia takes Tabriz from Turks			
England and France sign commercial treaty			

DATE	SPANISH HISTORY	THEATRE AND LETTERS	MUSIC AND OPERA	GRAPHIC AND PLASTIC ARTS
1605	Cervantes publishes Don Quixote	Cervantes: "Don Quixote," Part 1, published (Part 2, 1615)	Giacomo Carissimi, Italian composer, born (died 1674)	Annibale Carracci: frescoes in the Palazzo Farnese, Rome
		George Chapman: "All Fooles," comedy	Tomas Luis de Victoria: "Officium Defunctorum"	
		Samuel Daniel: "Philotas," tragedy		
			John Dowland: "Lachrymae, or Seaven Teares in Seaven Passionate Pavans"	
		First permanent German theater in Cassel		
		Ben Jonson: "Sejanus," tragedy	Monteverdi: Fifth Book of Madrigals"	
		Shakespeare: "King Lear," "Macbeth" (-1606)		
1606		Shakespeare: "Antony and Cleopatra" (-1607)	First open-air opera in Rome	Adriaen Brouwer, Dutch painter, born (died 1638)
		Thomas Dekker: "The Seven Deadly Sinnes of London," pamphlet		Jan Davids de Heem, Dutch painter, born (died 1683)
		Pierre Corneille, French dramatist, born (died 1684)		Rembrandt van Rijn, Dutch painter, born (died 1669)
		Ben Jonson: "Volpone"		
		Madeleine de Scudéry, French novelist, born (died 1701)		

WORLD EVENTS	MUNDANE EVENTS	CHURCH AND THOUGHT	KNOWLEDGE AND INVENTIONS
Czar Boris Godunov died; son Fyodor assassinated; "False Dmitri" crowned Czar of Russia	Incorporation of Butchers' and shipwrights' Companies in London	Sir Francis Bacon: "The Advancement of Learning"	Gaspard Bauhin (1560-1624): "Theatrum anatomicum," modern anatomy
Jan Zamoyski, Polish patriot, died (born 1541)	English government farms all customs revenue to a London consortium of merchants for an annual rent (-1671)	Pope Clement VIII died (born 1535); Alessandro de' Medici elected Pope Leo XI (April)	Ulissi Aldrovandi, Italian naturalist, died (born 1535)
Akbar, Mogul Emperor of India, died; succeeded by his son Jahangir (-1627)		Pope Leo XI died (born 1535); Camillo Borghese elected Pope Paul V (-1621)	Francis Bacon argues against magic and encourages the development of scientific methods
Guy Fawkes arrested trying to blow up House of Lords	Newspaper Nieuwe Tijdenghen issued in Antwerp		
Barbados, West Indies, claimed as English colony	Biblioteca Anglica, first public library in Rome, founded by Angelo Rosca		
Son Hidetada succeeds Ieyasu as ruler of Japan (-1623)			
Santa Fé, New Mexico, founded			
Guy Fawkes and fellow conspirators sentenced to death	Extensive program of road building begun in France	Johann Arndt: "Wahres Christentum"	Kepler describes the nova first observed in 1604, including its astrological significance
King James I's proclamation for a national flag	Founding of Society of Apothecaries and Grocers, and of Fruiterers' Company, in London	Joseph Justus Scaliger: "Thesaurus temporum," chronology of ancient times	Galileo Galilei invents proportional compass
"False Dmitri" assassinated; boyar Vasili-Shuisky is elected czar			
Peace treaty between Turks and Austrians signed at Zsitva-Torok			
Virginia Company of London sends 120 colonists to Virginia			

DATE	SPANISH HISTORY	THEATRE AND LETTERS	MUSIC AND OPERA	GRAPHIC AND PLASTIC ARTS
1607	Once again, Spain repudiates its debts	Shakespeare: "Coriolanus," "Timon of Athens" (-1608) George Chapman: "Bussy d'Amboise," tragedy Cyril Tourneur: "The Revenger's Tragedy" Thomas Heywood: "A Woman Killed with Kindness," tragedy	William Byrd: "Gradualia" Claudio Monteverdi: "Orfeo," opera	Domenico Fontana, Italian architect, died (born 1543) Hatfield House, Hertfordshire, England, built (- 1611) by John Thorpe for Robert Cecil, Earl of Salisbury
1608	Jesuit State of Paraguay established	Joseph Hall: "Characters of Virtues and Vices" The King's Men, a London actors' company, a play at Blackfriars Theatre Thomas Middleton: "A Mad World, My Masters," satirical comedy John Milton, English poet, born (died 1674) Shakespeare: "Pericles" (-1609)	Girolamo Frescobaldi (1583-1643) made organist at St. Peter's, Rome Monteverdi: "Lamento d'Adriana"	El Greco: "Golgotha," "Cardinal Taverna" Giovanni da Bologna, Italian sculptor, died (born 1524) Sir Walter Cope builds Holland House, Kensington, London (- 1610)
1609	Spain expels the Moors (Moriscos); Spain signs a 12-year truce with the United Provinces (the Netherlands) Twelve years' truce between Spain and Holland	Beaumont and Fletcher: "The Knight of the Burning Pestle" Thomas Dekker: "The Guls Hornbooke," satire of contemporary London life Ben Jonson: "Epicoene, or The Silent Women," comedy Shakespeare: "Cymbeline" (-1610)	Orlando Gibbons: "Fantazies of Three Parts," first example of engraved music in England Thomas Ravenscroft: "Pammelia," collection of rounds and catches	El Greco: "Brother Paravicino" Blue Mosque, Constantinople, built (- 1616) Annibale Caracci, Italian painter, died (born 1560) Rubens: Self-portrait with his Wife, Isabella Brant

WORLD EVENTS	MUNDANE EVENTS	CHURCH AND THOUGHT	KNOWLEDGE AND INVENTIONS
Charles IX crowned King of Sweden "Flight of the Earls" from Ireland to Spain, fearing arrest for attempted insurrection Union of England and Scotland rejected by English Parliament Founding of Jamestown, Virginia, first English settlement on American mainland	Bank of Genoa fails after announcement of national bankruptcy in Spain	Joseph Calasanza organizes in Rome the Brotherhood of Piarist (canonized, 1767) John Cowell: "The Interpreter," a law dictionary (see 1610)	John Norden, English topographer (1548-1625): "The Surveyors' Dialogue," manual of surveying
O'Dogherty rebellion in Ireland collapses Protestant States of Rhineland form Protestant Union The future Emperor Ferdinand III born (died 1657) Second "False Dmitri" defeats Czar Vasili Shuisky, and advances toward Moscow Samuel de Champlain founds a French settlement at Quebec	First checks - "cash letters" - in use in Netherlands Royal Blackheath Golf Club, London, founded; still in existence	St. Francis de Sales (1567-1622): "Introduction à la vie dévote" Alberico Gentili, Italian jurist and philosopher, died (born 1552) William Perkins: "A Discourse of the Damned Art of Witchecraft" posthumously	Cornelius Drebbel, born in Holland, anticipates the production of oxygen by heating salt peter Dutch scientist, Johans Lippershey, invents the telescope Galileo constructs astronomical telescope
John William, last Duke of Jülich-Cleves, died; quarrel about succession between Brandenberg and Neuburg	Founding of Bank of Amsterdam Founding of Charterhouse public school Regular newspapers at Strasbourg and Wolfenbüttel, Germany Tea from China shipped for first time to Europe by Dutch East India Company	Congregation of Female Jesuits founded (dissolved by Pope Urban VIII) Catholic League of German princes formed at Munich against Protestant Union of May 1608 The Emperor Rudolf II permits freedom of religion in Bohemia	The first attempt is made to harness the tides in the Bay of Fundy as a source of power Charles Butler: "De feminine monarchie, or a Treatise concerning Bees" Henry Hudson explores Delaware Bay and Hudson River

DATE	SPANISH HISTORY	THEATRE AND LETTERS	MUSIC AND OPERA	GRAPHIC AND PLASTIC ARTS
1610		Perez de Hita: "The Civil Wars of Granada,"Spanish novel Academy of Poetry founded at Padua Ben Jonson: "The Alchemist," comedy Paul Scarron, French man of letters, born (died 1660) Shakespeare: "A Winter's Tale" (-1611)	Michael Praetorius (1571-1621): "Musae Sioniae," collection of 1,244 church hymns Lodovico Grossi da Viadana: "Symphonies"	El Greco: "The Opening of the Fifth Seal" Michelangelo Caravaggio, Italian painter, died (born 1579) Adriaen van Ostade, Dutch painter, born (died 1684) Adam Elsheimer, German landscape painter, died (born 1578) Rubens: "Raising of the Cross"
1611		Shakespeare: "The Tempest" (-1612) Cyril Tourneur: "The Atheist's Tragedie" Ben Jonson: "Catiline," tragedy John Donne: "An Anatomy of the World," elegy	Tomas Luis de Victoria, Spanish composer, died (born 1548) William Byrd, John Bull and Orlando Gibbons: "Parthenia," collection of music for virginals Johannes Eccard, German composer, died (born 1553) Thomas Ravenscroft: "Melismata," 21 madrigals and other pieces	Erection of Masjid-i-Shah, the Royal Mosque at Isfahan, Persia Rubens: "Descent from the Cross" John Webb, English architect, born (died 1672)

WORLD EVENTS	MUNDANE EVENTS	CHURCH AND THOUGHT	KNOWLEDGE AND INVENTIONS
Henry IV of France assassinated; succeeded by his son Louis XIII (at 9)(-1643) with Queen Maria de'Medici as Regent (-1617) James I prorogues Parliament; Parliament reassembles Elector Palatine Frederick IV died; succeeded by his son Frederick V Skirmishes between English and Dutch settlers in India	Dutch East India company introduces the term "share" The Stationers' Company begins to send a copy of every book printed in England to Bodleian Library, Oxford	Robert Persons, leader of English Jesuits, died (born 1545) John Cowell's "Interpreter" (see 1607) burnt by the common hangman for enhancing authority of the crown	Galileo, turns his telescope to the night sky, observes Jupiter's satellites, naming them "sideria Mediea", writes a series of new letters, makeing him famous all over Europe Thomas Harriott discovers sunspots Henry Hudson sails through Hudson's Straits and discovers Hudson's Bay
Dissolution of Parliament by James I War of Calmar declared by Denmark on Sweden (-1613) Archduke Matthias crowned King of Bohemia; the Emperor Rudolf II resigns bohemian crown Arabella Stuart escapes from Tower of London; is recaptured Charles IX of Sweden died; Gustavus II elected King; makes Axel Oxenstierna Chancellor	Dutch merchants permitted to trade in Japan James I institutes the baronetage as a means of raising money	George Abbot made Archbishop of Canterbury (-1633) Authorized version of the Holy Bible-"King James Bible"- published John Speed: "A History of Great Britain" University of Rome founded	Marco de Dominis (1566-1624) publishes a scientific explanation of the rainbow Le Tour de Condonan, at the mouth of the Garonne River in France, is the first lighthouse to have a revolving beacon Henry Hudson, English navigator, dies

DATE	SPANISH HISTORY	THEATRE AND LETTERS	MUSIC AND OPERA	GRAPHIC AND PLASTIC ARTS
1612		Shakespeare: "Henry VIII (-1613)" Samuel Butler, English satirist, born (died 1680) John Webster: "The White Devil," tragedy	Giovanni Gabrieli, Italian composer, died (born 1557) Orlando Gibbons: "First Set of Madrigals and Motets" Andreas Hammerschmidt, German composer, born (died 1675)	El Greco: "Baptism of Christ" Frederico Barocci, Italian painter, died (born 1528) Louis le Vau, French architect, born (died 1670)
1613		Cervantes: "Novelas ejemplares" Lope de Vega: "Fuenteovejuna" François de La Rochefoucauld, French author, born (died 1680) Fire destroys Globe Theatre, Southwark, London	Pietro Cerone: "El Malopeo y maestro," musical history and theory Monteverdi made maestro di cappella at St. Mark's, Venice	Rubens: "The Conversion of St. Bavon" Salomon de Brosse builds the Château Coulommiers Guido Reni: "Aurora," frescoes in Rome
1614	Maria, Queen Regent of France, seeks to counteract power of nobility	Ben Jonson: "Bartholomew Fayre," comedy John Webster: "The Duchess of Malfi" Sir Thomas Overbury: "Characters"	Girolamo Frescobaldi: "Toccate di Cembalo" Marco da Gagliano: "Masses and Motets" Sir William Leighton: "Teares and Lamentations of a Sorrowful Soule," 54 psalms	El Greco, Cretan-Spanish painter, died (born 1541) Domenichino (1581-1641): "Last communion of St. Jerome" Salzburg Cathedral built by Santino Salari (- 1680)

WORLD EVENTS	MUNDANE EVENTS	CHURCH AND THOUGHT	KNOWLEDGE AND INVENTIONS
The Emperor Rudolf II died; succeeded by Matthias, King of Bohemia	Earliest colonization of the Bermudas from Virginia	Accademia della Crusca publishes the Italian "Vocabolario"	John Gerard, English botanist, dies in London, England
Henry, Prince of Wales, died (born 1594) Treaty between the Dutch and the King of Kandy in Ceylon	Dutch use Manhattan as fur-trading center for first time Tobacco planted in Virginia	Jakob Bohme: "Aurora, oder Mogenröte im Aufgant," mystical philosophy Last recorded burning of heretics in England Roger Fenton (1565-1616): "Treatie of Usurie"	Antonio Nero: "L'Arte vetraria," manual on glassmaking John Smith: "A Map of Virginia" Basilius Besler provides an important work in plant illustration
Peace of Kanärod ends Danish-Swedish War of Calmar Protestant Union of Germany signs treaty of alliance with Holland English colonists in Virginia prevent French colonization of Maryland Michael Romanov, son of the patriarch of Moscow, elected Czar of Russia (-1645), thus founding the House of Romanov Turks invade Hungary	Amsterdam Exchange built Belfast granted charter of incorporation Thomas Bodley ,English diplomat and scholar, died (born 1545), leaving bulk of his fortune to Bodleian Library, Oxford Copper coins come into use John Dennys: "The Secrets of Angling" Hugh Myddleton constructs "New River" cut, to bring water to London	Francisco Suarez: "Defensio catholicae fidei contra anglicanae sectae errores" Oliver de Serra (1539-1619): "The Causes of Wealth"	Samuel de Champlain explores Ottawa River to Alumette Island
Gustavus II of Sweden captures Novgorod from Russians Virginian colonists prevent French settlements in Maine and Nova Scotia	Danish East India Company founded Bankruptcy of Augsburg banking house of Welser Pocahontas, Indian princess, marries John Rolfe; from their son descend many celebrated persons	Jean de Gondi, Cardinal de Retz, French churchman, born (died 1679) Henry More, English philosopher, born (died 1687) Sir Walter Raleigh: "The History of the World"	Physician, Franciscus Sylvius, Germany, is one of the first physicians to abandon the theory that illness is caused by an imbalance of the Four Humors University of Groningen, Holland, founded

DATE	SPANISH HISTORY	THEATRE AND LETTERS	MUSIC AND OPERA	GRAPHIC AND PLASTIC ARTS
1615	Philip III begins Pantheon of the Kings English fleet defeats Portuguese off coast of Bombay Dutch seize the Moluccas from Portuguese	Cervantes: "Don Quixote," Part 2 Mateo Aleman, Spanish novelist, died (born 1547) Samuel Coster: "Spel van de Rijcke Man," farce	Adriano Banchieri (1567-1634) founds Accademia dei Filomusi in Bologna	Salvator Rosa, Spanish painter, born (died 1673) Bernini's "Amalthea," sculpture, Palazzo Borghese, Rome Inigo Jones (1573-1652) becomes England's chief architect
1616	Richelieu becomes Minister of State for Foreign Affairs and War in France	Miguel de Cervantes died April 23rd (born 1547) Francis Beaumont died (born 1584) Thomas Middleton: "The Witch," tragedy William Shakespeare died (born 1564)	Collegium Musicum founded at Prague Johann Jakob Froberger, German organist and composer, born (died 1667)	Frans Hals: "The Banquet of the Civic Guard of the Archers of St. George" Notre Dame Cathedral, Antwerp, finished (begun 1352) Inigo Jones: "Queen's House," Greenwich, London (- 1618) Rubens: "The Lion Hunt"
1617		James I makes Ben Jonson poet laureate Théophile de Viau (1590-1626): "Pyramus et Thisbe," tragedy in verse Martin Opitz founds the Fruchtbringende Gesellschaft, a literary society, at Weimar	Biagio Marini: "Musical Events," sonata for solo violin J. H. Schein: "Banchetto musicale," first dance suite Heinrich Schütz made Kapellmeister of electoral chapel, Dresden (- 1672)	Bartolomé Estéban Murillo, Spanish painter, born (died 1682) Domenichino: "Diana's Hunt" Gerard Terborch, Dutch painter, born (died 1681) Peter Lely, Dutch-English painter, born (died 1680)

WORLD EVENTS	MUNDANE EVENTS	CHURCH AND THOUGHT	KNOWLEDGE AND INVENTIONS
French States General dismissed with promises of reforms Marguérite de Valois died (born 1553) Peace of Tyrnau: the Emperor Matthias recognizes Bethlen Gabor as Prince of Transylvania	Ninon de Lenclos, French courtesan, born (died 1705) Frankfurter Oberpostamts-Zeitung founded by Egenolph Emmel (appears - 1866) Merchant Adventurers granted monopoly for export of English cloth	Jesuits count 13,112 members in 32 provinces William Camden: "Annales rerum Anglicarum," of the reign of Elizabeth I Theodore Agrippa d'Aubigné's "Histoire Universelle," a Huguenot-inspired survey from 1553 to 1602, officially burnt in Paris	William Baffin, England, penetrates to within 1300 kilometers of the North Pole, the closest anyone will be until the 19th century Giambattista della Porta, Italian scientist, died (born 1538) Galileo Galilei faces the Inquisition for first time
Sir Walter Raleigh released from Tower to lead expedition to Guiana in search of El Dorado Ieyasu of Japan died; succeeded by Hidetada, a militant enemy of Christianity Tartars of Manchu invade China (-1620) War between Venice and Austria	Gustavus Selenus (August von Braunschweig): "Chess, or the Game of Kings"	Catholic oppression intensified in Bohemia Paulus Bolduanus: "Bibliotheca philosophica" St. Francis de Sales: "Traité de l'amour de Dieu"	Galileo is prohibited by Catholic Church from further scientific work William Harvey, England, lectures about the circulation of blood to the Royal College of Physicians, England Galileo, hoping to win a prize and pension from Philip III of Spain for finding the longitude at sea, suggests using the satellites of Jupiter; although ignored by Philip, Galileo's method will be used to find longitudes on land
Peace of Stolbovo ends war between Russia and Sweden James I revisits Scotland; meets Scotish Parliament Dutch buy Goree Island, off Cap Verde, from the natives Sir Walter Raleigh, on expedition in Guiana, reaches mouth of Orinoco River	Pocahontas, North American Indian princess, died (born 1595) "Stuart collars" become a fashion for men and women	Francisco Suarez, Spanish philosopher, died (born 1548) John Calvin's collected works published in Geneva (posthumously) Philosopher Elias Ashmole, founder of the Ashmolean Museum in Oxford, England, is born	Willebrord Snellius establishes technique of trigonometrical triangulation for cartography

289

DATE	SPANISH HISTORY	THEATRE AND LETTERS	MUSIC AND OPERA	GRAPHIC AND PLASTIC ARTS
1618	Thirty Years' War (1618 - 1648)

Philip III dismisses Lerma as Chief Minister, appointing his son, Duke of Euceda; the Duke of Lerma is made a cardinal

Peace of Madrid ratified, ending war between Venice and Austria | Teatro Farnese opened at Parma

Gerbrand Adriensz Bredero, Dutch dramatist, died (born 1585)

Richard Lovelace, English poet, born (died 1658) | Guilio Caccini, Italian composer and singer, died ("bel canto") | Building of Aston Hall, Birmingham (- 1635)

Bernini: "Aeneas, Anchises, and Acanius," sculpture

Jacob Jordaens: "Adoration of the Shepherds"

Van Dyck becomes member of the Antwerp guild of painters |
| 1619 | | John Fletcher: "The Humorous Lieutenant," comedy

Marquise de Rambouillet (1588-1665) starts her literary salon in Paris

Beaumont and Fletcher: "A King and No King," "The Maid's Tragedy"

Richard Burbage, English actor, died (born 1567)

Savinien Cyrano de Bergerac, French poet, born (died 1655)

Philipp von Zesen, German poet, born (died 1689) | "Fitzwilliam Virginal Book" compiled by Francis Tregian; a treasury of early English keyboard music

Marco da Gagliano: "Medoro," Italian opera

Heinrich Schütz: "Psalms"

Jan Pieterszoon Sweelinck: "Cantiones sacrae" | Velazquez: "Adoration of the Kings:

Lodovico Carracci, Italian painter, died (born 1555)

Inigo Jones: Banqueting House, Whitehall (- 1622)

Philips Wouwerman, Dutch painter, born (died 1688) |

WORLD EVENTS	MUNDANE EVENTS	CHURCH AND THOUGHT	KNOWLEDGE AND INVENTIONS
In Prague, actions of rebels start Thirty Years' War	James I: "Book of Sports," the Puritans object to playing of popular sports	Robert Balfour: "Commentarii in organum logicum Aristotelis"	Francesco Maria Grimaldi, Italy, provides convincing evidence that light is a wave phenomenon
Sir Walter Raleigh returns to England and is executed	Giro-Bank, Hamburg, founded to improve "Desolate state of currency"	John Stow and E. Howes: A "Summarie of Englyshe Chronicles"	Founding of Dutch - West African Company
Aurangzeb, later Mogul Emperor of Hindustan, born (died 1707)			Kepler: "Harmonius mundi," stating the third law of planetary motion
Richelieu ordered into exile at Avignon			
Louis XIII recalls Richelieu from Avignon and defeats mother Maria de'Medici's supporters	First Negro slaves in North America arrive in Virginia	Johann Valentin Andreae: "Christianopolis"	Martin Böhme "Ein neu Buch von bewehrten Rosz-Arzteneyuen," veterinary science
Archduke Ferdinand elected Holy Roman Emperor		Jakob Böhme: "On the Principles of Christianity"	Johann Jakob Scheuchzer: "Natural History of the Swiss Landscape"
Bohemian Diet deposes Ferdinand, and elects Frederick V, Elector Palatine		Lucilío Vanini, Italian Catholic philosopher, burned as a heretic (born 1584)	Descartes, France, dreams that he should work out the unity of the sciences on a purely rational basis
First colonial assembly in America held at Jamestown, Virginia			William Harvey announces at St. Bartholomew's Hospital, London, his discovery of the cirulation of the blood
Jan Pieters Coen, Dutch explorer (1587-1630), founds Batavia, Indonesia			

DATE	SPANISH HISTORY	THEATRE AND LETTERS	MUSIC AND OPERA	GRAPHIC AND PLASTIC ARTS
1620	The Council of Castile; Philip III died; Accession of Philip IV; Don Gaspar de Guzman, Count Olivares, becomes chief minister to Philip IV	Miklós Zrinyi, Hungarian poet and national hero, born (died 1664)	Monteverdi: "Seventh Book of Madrigals" Michael Praetorius: "Syntagma musicum," musical encyclopedia	Velazquez: "The Water Seller of Seville" Bernini: "Neptune and Triton," sculpture Aelbert Cuyp, Dutch landscape painter, born (died 1691) Jacob Jordaens: "Passage to Antwerp" Van Dyck: "St. Sebastian"
1621	Philip III of Spain died; succeeded by his son Philip IV (-1665) Twelve years' truce between Holland and Spain ends; war resumed	Fortune Theatre, London, burnt down John Fletcher: "The Wild Goose Chase," comedy John Barclay (1582-1621): "Argenis," allegorical political novel Jean de la Fontaine, French poet, born (died 1695) Drama, painting, sculpture flourished under King Philip IV of Spain (-1625)	Michael Praetorius, German composer and musicologist, died (born 1571) Jan Pieterszoon Sweelinck, Dutch musician, died (born 1562)	Bernini: "Rape of Proserpina," sculpture Van Dyck: "Rest on the Flight into Egypt"

WORLD EVENTS	MUNDANE EVENTS	CHURCH AND THOUGHT	KNOWLEDGE AND INVENTIONS
Revolt of French nobles against Louis XIII; Richelieu makes peace	J. P. Bonet: "The Art to Teach Dumb People to Speak," Spanish manual	Johann Heinrich Alsted: "Encyclopaedia septem tomis distincta"	Francis Bacon's work recommends induction and experimentation as the bases of the scientific method
Massacre of Protestants in the Valtelline	Currency inflation in Germany (-1623)	Francis Bacon: "Instauratio magna: novum organum scientiarum"	Johannesvan Helmont coins the term 'gas' to describe substances that are like air
Agreement of Ulm: German Catholic League and Protestant Union	Density of population in Germany per square mile: 35. At time of Julius Caesar approximately 6; census 1900 approximately 160; 1950 approximately 280		Cornelius Drebbel builds a navigable submarine powered by rowers
"Mayflower" lands at New Plymouth, Massachusetts			
	Oliver Cromwell denounced because he participates in the "disreputable game of cricket"		Uppsala University Library founded by Gustavus Adolphus
War moves from Bohemia to the Palatine	"Corante, or newes from Italy, Germany, Hungarie, Spaine, and France," first periodical published with news issued in London (September 24)	Cardinal Roberto Bellarmine, Jesuit leader of the Counter-Reformation, died (born 1562)	Hieronymus Fabricius's work published posthumously elevates embryology to the level of a science
Francis Bacon imprisoned, then pardoned by the King		Robert Burton (1577-1640): "The Anatomy of Melancholy"	Johann Kepler: "The Epitome of the Copernican Astronomer," banned by the Roman Catholic Church
Huguenot rebellion against Louis XIII	Heidelberg University Library sacked by Count Tilly's troops	Pope Paul V died; Alexander Ludovisi becomes Pope Gregory XV (-1623)	
English attempt to colonize Newfoundland and Nova Scotia	Potatoes planted in Germany for the first time		Thomas Munn (1571-1641): "A Discourse of Trade from England unto the East Indies"
			University of Strasbourg opened

DATE	SPANISH HISTORY	THEATRE AND LETTERS	MUSIC AND OPERA	GRAPHIC AND PLASTIC ARTS
1622	English capture Ormuz from Portuguese Count Olivares (the "count duke") becomes chief minister of Spain (-1643)	Molière (Jean-Baptiste Poquelin), French dramatist, born (died 1673) Alessandro Tassoni: "La Secchia rapita" (The Rape of the Bucket), mock-heroic poem Philip Massinger and Thomas Dekker: "The Virgin Martyr," tragedy Henry Vaughan, English mystic and poet, born (died 1695) Charles Sorel: "Francion," French burlesque novel		Willem Kalf, Dutch painter, born (died 1693) Guido Reni: "Job" Rubens: "The Medici Cycle" - 24 paintings on the life of Maria de'Medici, Luxembourg Palace, Paris
1623	Charles, Prince of Wales, travels to Madrid to secure betrothal to Spanish princess; leaves at breakdown of talks	Antonio Hurtado de Mendoza: "Querer por sólo querer," comedy Maciej Sarbiewski (1595-1640), the "Polish Horace," crowned laureate in Rome by the Pope Tulsi Das, Hindu poet, died (born 1532) Philip Massinger: "The Duke of Milan," tragedy	William Byrd, English composer, died (born 1543) Marc' Antonio Cesti, Italian composer, born (died1669)	Velazquez made court painter to Philip IV Inigo Jones: Queen's Chapel, St. James's Palace, Westminster, built (- 1627) Francois Mansart: St. Marie de la Visitation, Paris Guido Reni: "Baptism of Christ" Van Dyck: "Cardinal Bentivoglio"

WORLD EVENTS	MUNDANE EVENTS	CHURCH AND THOUGHT	KNOWLEDGE AND INVENTIONS
Richelieu recalled by Louis XIII to the Council; created Cardinal Ferdinand II and Bethlen Gabor sign peace treaty Treaty of Montpellier ends rebellion of the Huguenots James I dissolves English Parliament	Camillo Baldo: "Treatise of How to Perceive from a Letter the Nature and Character of the Person Who Wrote It" Bruges-Dunkirk Canal finished Papal chancellery adopts January 1 as beginning of the year-up to then March 25 Weekeley Newes issued in London for first time on May 23	Francis Bacon: "History of the Reign of Henry VII" Saint Francis de Sales died (born 1567) Pope Gregory XV canonizes Philip Neri and grants Piarists a constitution	The first German scientific academy is founded at Rostock Bacon: "Historia naturalis et experimentalis" Benedictine University of Salzburg founded Wilhelm Schickardt builds the first calculating machine based on the idea of Napier
The emperor Ferdinand II grants Maximilian, Duke of Bavaria the Upper Palatinate Papal troops occupy the Valtelline Abbas I, Shah of Persia (1586-1629), conquers Baghdad Commercial treaty between Holland and Persia Dutch massacre English colonists at Amboyna, Molucca Islands	First English settlement in New Hampshire, by David Thomas at little Harbor, near Rye Patents law in England, to protect inventors	William Drummond: "A Cypresse Grove," philosophical thoughts on death Pope Gregory XV died; Maffeo Barberini becomes Pope Urban VIII Blaise Pascal, French philosopher and mathematician, born (died 1662)	Bibliotheca Palatina removed from Heidelberg to Rome New Netherlands in America formally organized as a province

DATE	SPANISH HISTORY	THEATRE AND LETTERS	MUSIC AND OPERA	GRAPHIC AND PLASTIC ARTS
1624	England declares war on Spain Cardinal Richelieu made first minister of France (-1642)	Thomas Middleton: "A Game of Chess," comedy, given at Globe Theatre nine times - first "long run" in theatrical history Saruwaka Kanzaburo opens first Japanese theatre in Yedo Martin Opitz: "Das Buch von der deutschen Poeterey"	Marco da Gagliano (1575-1642): "La Regina Sant' Orsola," opera-oratorio Monteverdi: "Il Combattimento di Tancredi e Clorinda"	Bernini: "Apollo and Daphne," sculpture Guarino Guarini, Italian architect and writer, born (died 1683) Frans Hals: "The Laughing Cavalier" Jacques Lemercier: Extension of the Louvre, Paris Nicolas Poussin: "Rape of the Sabine Women"
1625	Spanish General Ambrogio Aspinola (1569-1630) takes Breda from Dutch after 11-month siege	Philip Massinger: "The Bondman," drama Ben Jonson: "The Staple of News," comedy Joost van den Vondel: "Palamedes," political drama John Webster, English dramatist, died (born 1580) Martin Opitz crowned poet laureate in Vienna Thomas Middleton: "A Game of Chess," published	Orlando Gibbons, English musician, died (born 1583) Famous peal of bells installed in the Gate of Salvation, Kremlin, Moscow Heinrich Schütz: "Cantiones sacrae"	Jan Brueghel the Elder, "Velvet Brueghel," died (born 1658) Inigo Jones: Covent Garden Church, Westminster, London Daniel Mylens made court painter by Charles I Nicolas Poussin: "Parnassus"
1626	Richelieu concentrates all power in France in his own hands Treaty of Monzon between France and Spain confirms independence of the Grisons	Honorat de Bueil: "Les plus beaux vers" First production of Shakespeare's "Hamlet" in Germany at Dresden John Aubrey, English author, born (died 1697)	Professorship of music founded at Oxford University by William Heather (1563-1627) Giovanni Legrenzi, Italian composer, born (died 1690)	Rubens: "Assumption of the Virgin," altarpiece at Antwerp Facade of St. Peter's, Rome, finished, consecrated by Pope Urban VIII Jan Steen, Dutch painter, born (died 1679)

WORLD EVENTS	MUNDANE EVENTS	CHURCH AND THOUGHT	KNOWLEDGE AND INVENTIONS
James I's last Parliament; monopolies declared illegal	Dutch settle in New Amsterdam	Jakob Böhme, German mystic, died (born 1575)	Physician Thomas Sydenham is the first to describe measles and to identify scarlet fever
Jan Sobieski, future King of Poland, born (died 1696)	First English settlement in eastern India	John Donne: "Devotions Upon Emergent Occasions"	Pembroke College, Oxford, founded
Virginia becomes crown colony; Virginia Company dissolved	Johannes Baptista van Helmont, Belgian scientist (1577-1644), coins the name "gas" for compressible fluid	George Fox, founder of the Society of Friends, born (died 1691)	Captain John Smith: "A General Historie of Virginia, New England and the Summer Isles"
Anglo-French treaty for Charles, Prince of Wales, to marry Henrietta Maria, daughter of Henry VI			
James I succeeded by Charles I of England and Scotland	Colonial Office established in London	Francis Bacon: "Of Masques and Triumphs"	Giovanni Domenico Cassini, Italian astronomer, born (died 1712)
Wallenstein created Duke of Friedland	First English settlement on Barbados, under Sir William Courteen	Hugo Grotius: "De jure belli et pacis," on international law	Johann Rudolf Glauber (1604-1668), German discovers Glauber's salt
First Parliament of Charles I adjourned to Oxford, because of Plague in London	First fire engines in England		
Tilly invades Lower Saxony	Hackney coaches appear in streets of London		
French occupy the Antilles and Cayenne	Tobacco tax and tobacco monopoly in England		
	Introduction of full-bottomed wigs in Europe		
Peace of La Rochelle between Huguenots and French crown	A royal edict condemns anyone to death who kills his adversary in a duel in France	Francis Bacon, English philosopher and statesman, died (born 1561)	J. B. van Helmont, Brussels, Belgium, proposes that diseases are caused by alien beings
Christina, future Queen of Sweden, born (died 1689)	First French settlement on the Senegal River	John Donne: "Five Sermons"	Jardin des Plantes established in Paris
Salem, Massachusetts, settled by Roger Conant	Peter Minuit of Dutch West India Company buys Island of Manhattan from native Indian chiefs for merchandise valued at $24	Irish College in Rome founded	Santorio Santorio, Italian physician, measures human temperature with the thermometer for the first time
		William Roper: "The Life of Sir Thomas More" (posthumously)	

DATE	SPANISH HISTORY	THEATRE AND LETTERS	MUSIC AND OPERA	GRAPHIC AND PLASTIC ARTS
1627	Richelieu signs treaty with Spain	Lope de Vega made theological doctor by the Pope Luis de Góngora y Argote, Spanish poet, died (born 1561) Francisco Gómez de Quevedo: "Los Sueños," burlesques of hell, judgment day, and the world Ivan Gundulic (1589-1638): "Osman," Croatian epic	Heinrich Schütz: "Dafne" first German opera, libretto by Martin Opitz, given at Torgau Lodovico Viadana, Italian composer, died (born 1564)	Adriaen de Vries, Dutch sculptor, died (born 1560) Frans Hals: "The Merry Drinker" Claude Lorrain arrives in Rome Rembrandt: "The Money Changer" Rubens: "Mystic Marriage of St. Catherine"
1628		Juan Ruiz de Alarcón: "La verdad sospechosa," Spanish comedy John Bunyan, English author, born (died 1688) François de Malherbe, court poet to Henry IV, died (born 1555) Charles Perrault, French author, born (died 1703)	John Bull, English composer, died (born 1562) Robert Cambert, French composer, born (died 1677) Marco da Gagliano: "Flora," opera Heinrich Schütz becomes Monteverdi's pupil at Venice	Velazquez: "Christ on the Cross" Nicolas Poussin: "Martyrdom of St. Erasmus" Andrea Spezza: Waldstein Palace, Prague Taj Mahal, Agra, built (- 1650) Jacob van Ruisdael, Dutch painter, born (died 1682)

WORLD EVENTS	MUNDANE EVENTS	CHURCH AND THOUGHT	KNOWLEDGE AND INVENTIONS
Huguenots rise again; George Villiers, Duke of Buckingham, sails from Portsmouth with a fleet to aid them in defense of La Rochelle; failing to relieve them, he retires Korea becomes a tributary state of China Shah Jahan (1592-1666) becomes Great Mogul of India Wallenstein conquers Silesia. Tilly Brunswick; imperial forces seize Mecklenburg and Jutland; Christian IV withdraws to Denmark	"Company of New France," Canada, incorporated by Richelieu Swedish South Sea Company founded	Robert Boyle, English philosopher and physicist, born (died 1691) Collegium de Propaganda Fide founded Alessandro Tassoni: "Manifesto" attacks the House of Savoy	Francis Bacon's "New Atlantis", a utopian tale, published posthumously, plans for a national museum of science and art The aurochs, the wild ancestor of domestic cattle becomes extinct
Third Parliament of Charles I meets; Oliver Cromwell enters it as Member for Huntingdon La Rochelle capitulates to French crown Dutch occupy Java and the Moluccas Swedish-Danish treaty for defense of Stralsund; Gustavus Adolphus enters Thirty Years' War		Ignatius Loyola canonized by Pope Gregory XV The Alexandrian Codex (5th century) presented to Charles I by patriarch of Constantinople René Descartes: "Règles pour la direction de l'esprit" William Laud (1573-1645) made bishop of London	William Harvey: "Exercitatio anatomica de motu cordis et sanguinis," describes his discovery of the circulation blood First harbor with sluices being constructed at Le Havre

DATE	SPANISH HISTORY	THEATRE AND LETTERS	MUSIC AND OPERA	GRAPHIC AND PLASTIC ARTS
1629		Pedro Calderón de la Barca: "La dama duende," comedy John Ford: "The Lover's Melancholy," romantic play Philip Massinger: "The Roman Actor," tragedy Pierre Corneille: "Mélite," comedy	Heinrich Schütz "Sinfoniae sacrae"	Velazquez: "The Drunkards" Francisco de Zurbaran: "St. Bonaventura" Bernini takes over uncompleted St. Peter's, Rome Pieter de Hooch, Dutch painter, born (died 1683) Van Dyck: "Rinaldo and Armida"
1630	Treaty of Madrid ends Anglo-French war "Day of Dupes" in France: Richelieu overthrows conspiracy of Maria de'Medici, the Queen Mother	Tirso de Molina: "El burlador de Sevilla y convidado de piedra," first of Don Juan plays Thomas Middleton: "A Chaste Mayde in Cheapside," comedy Philip Massinger: "The Renegado," tragicomedy Andres Christensen Arrabo initiates modern Danish literature with his religious poem "Hexaëmeron"	Girolamo Frescobaldi: "Arie musicale" Johann Hermann Schein, German composer, died (born 1586)	Jusepe Ribera: "Archimedes" Rubens: "Blessings of Peace" Michael Willmann, German painter, born (died 1706) Beginning of the High Baroque period in Italy (- 1680)
1631	German Protestant princes hold a convention at Neu Brandenburg, and decide to form alliance with Gustavus Adolphus Tilly destroys Swedish garrison at Neu Brandenburg, sacks Magdeburg, burns Halle, and invades Saxony	John Donne, English poet, died (born 1572) Michael Drayton, English poet, died (born 1563) John Dryden, English dramatist, born (died 1700) Thomas Heywood: "The Fair Maid of the West," comedy Ben Jonson: "The Devil is an Asse," comedy	Philipp Dulichius, German composer, died (born 1562)	Velazquez: "Infanta Maria, Queen of Hungary" Jacques Lemercier: Château Richelieu Baldassare Longhena begins work on church of S. Maria della Salute, Venice Rembrandt: Portrait of his mother

WORLD EVENTS	MUNDANE EVENTS	CHURCH AND THOUGHT	KNOWLEDGE AND INVENTIONS
Charles I dissolves Parliament (March); it does not meet again till April 1640 Peace of Alais ends Huguenot revolt Truce of Altmark signed between Sweden and Poland Commercial treaty signed between Russia and France	Royal charter granted to Guild of Spectacle Makers, London Shah Jahan, the Great Mongul, orders the making of the Peacock Throne Colony of Massachusetts founded	Lancelot Andrewes: "XCVI Sermons" Thomas Hobbes translates "The Peloponnesian War" by Thucydides	Giovanni Branca describes a steam turbine in which steam is directed at veins on a wheel Christian Huygens, Dutch mathematician and scientist, born (died 1695) John Parkinson (1567-1650): "Paradisi in sole Paradisus terrestris," on flowers
John Winthrop founds Boston The future King Charles II born (died 1685) Gustavus Adolphus of Sweden marches his army into Germany The Emperor Ferdinand II dismisses Wallenstein; Tilly is the new commander	Pirates of all nationalities, called "buccaneers," settle in Tortuga, off northwest coast of Hispaniola English poet Sir John Suckling invents, according to John Aubrey's "Brief Lives," the card game cribbage Beginning of public advertising, in Paris	Congregation of the English Ladies founded in Munich Sir John Hayward: "The Life and Raigne of King Edward VI"	Johannes Kepler, German astronomer, dies in Regensburg, Bavaria, Germany Francis Higginson: "New England's Plantation," on living conditions in America Johann Kepler, German astronomer, dies (born 1571)
Tilly invades Saxony Gustavus Adolphus occupies Würzburg and Mainz Maria de'Medici exiled to Brussels Dutch West India Company founds settlement at the Delaware River	French philanthropist Théophraste Renaudot (1586-1653) founds in Paris the Bureau d'adresse, a labor-exchange charity organization and intelligence office T. Renaudot founds the "Gazette" in Paris; from 1752 on, "Gazette de France" Earthquake in Naples; eruption of Vesuvius	Friedrich Spee von Langenfeld: "Cautio criminalis," against witch-hunting	English mathematician William Oughtred proposes symbol "X" for multiplication London Clockmakers' Company incorporated

DATE	SPANISH HISTORY	THEATRE AND LETTERS	MUSIC AND OPERA	GRAPHIC AND PLASTIC ARTS
1632	Gustavus Adolphus sacks Frankfort-on-Oder, signs treaty of alliance with John George, Elector of Saxony, defeats Tilly at battle of Breitenfeld, and occupies Würzburg and Mainz Wallenstein reappointed Commander-in-Chief Portuguese driven out of Bengal	Second Shakespeare Folio published Giovanni Battista Basile, Italian poet and writer of fairy tales, died (born 1575) Thomas Dekker, English dramatist, died (born 1570) Philip Massinger: "The City Madam," comedy John Ford: "Tis Pity She's a Whore," tragedy Philip Massinger: "A New Way to Pay Old Debts," comedy	Jean Baptiste Lully, French-Italian composer, born (died 1687) Monteverdi takes holy orders	Luca Giordano, Italian painter, born (died 1705) Van Dyck made court painter to Charles I Jan Vermeer, Dutch painter, born (died 1675) Christopher Wren, English architect, born (died 1723)
1633	Queen Christina (born 1626), daughter of Gustavus Adolphus, ascends throne of Sweden; five regents, headed by Chancellor Axel Oxenstierna, govern country (-1644)	Plague in Bavaria leads to passion play in Oberammergau Samuel Pepys, English diarist, born (died 1703)	Jacopo Peri, Italian composer and inventor of the recitative died (born 1561)	Jacques Callot: "Les Grandes Misères de la guerre" Rebuilding Pavilion of Seisuji, Kyoto, Japan Rembrandt: "Saskia" Jacob van Campen and Pieter Post: "Mauritshuis, The Hague Willem van de Velde the Younger, Dutch painter, born (died 1707) Van Dyck: "Charles I"
1634	Emperor Ferdinand II for second time deprives Wallenstein of his command, declaring him a traitor; Matthias Gallas (1584-1647) made Commander-in-Chief; Wallenstein assassinated	Corneille: "La Veuve" and "La Suivante," comedies The Oberammergau Passion Play given for first time	Adam Krieger, German composer, born (died 1666)	Zurbaran: "The Siege of Cadiz" Rembrandt: "Artemisia"

WORLD EVENTS	MUNDANE EVENTS	CHURCH AND THOUGHT	KNOWLEDGE AND INVENTIONS
Charles I crowned King of Scotland in Edinburgh Gustavus Adolphus defeats Wallenstein and is killed in action Charles I issues charter for the colony Maryland under control of Lord Baltimore Queen Christina (born 1626), daughter of Gustavus Adolphus, ascends throne	First coffee shop opens in London English settlers in Antigua and Montserrat Russian fur trade center established in Yakutsk, Siberia	Antonio Bosio: "Roma sotterranes," report on excavation of catacombs in Rome John Locke, English philosopher, born (died 1704) Baruch Spinoza, Dutch philosopher, born (died 1677)	Galileo: "Dialogho sopra i due massimi sistemi del mondo" published; finished 1630: on terrestrial double motion Liden University Observatory founded Antony van Leeuwenhoek, Dutch zoologist, born (died 1723)
The future King James II of England, born (died 1701) Charles I revives forest eyre to raise money by fines Edward Winslow (1595-1655), Governor of Plymouth Colony	Dutch settle in Connecticut Trial of the Lancashire witches Reform of English postal service by Thomas Witherings The Royal Scots, oldest regular regiment in British Army, established Wind sawmill erected near the Strand, London	Galileo forced by the Inquisition to abjure the theories of Copernicus First Baptist church formed at Southwark, London John Cotton becomes a religious leader in Boston	English trading post established in Bengal
Treaty of Polianovska: King Vladislav of Poland renounces claim to Russia	Covent Garden Market, London, opened English settlement at Cochin, Malabar	Anne Hutchinson (1591-1643), religious controversialist, migrates to Massachusetts	Jean Nicolet lands on Green Bay; explores Wisconsin Founding of University of Utrecht

DATE	SPANISH HISTORY	THEATRE AND LETTERS	MUSIC AND OPERA	GRAPHIC AND PLASTIC ARTS
1635	Dutch occupy Formosa, English Virgin Islands, French Martinique	Calderón writes "La Vida es sueño;" becomes head of Royal Theatre, Madrid Corneille: "Medée," tragedy Vitzentsos Kornaros' "The Sacrifice of Abraham," first Greek mystery drama Alessandro Tassoni, Italian poet, died (born 1565) Daniel Caspar von Lohenstein, German poet, born (died 1683)	Frescobaldi: "Fiori musicali di toccate," which influences J. S. Bach	Velazquez: "Surrender of Breda" Zurbaran: "St. Veronica's Kerchief" Jacques Callot, French painter, died (born 1592) Philippe de Champaigne: "Portrait of Richelieu"
1636	Dutch settle Ceylon	Corneille: "Le Cid" Italian Fedeli Company performs commedia dell'arte at the French court Philip Massinger: "The Great Duke of Florence," comedy	French theorist Marin Mersenne (1588-1648) publishes his most important work, "Harmonie Universelle," with full descriptions of all contemporary musical instruments Schütz: "Kleine geistliche Concerten," collection of motets	Velazquez: "Prince Baltasar Carlos as a Hunter" Rembrandt: "Portrait of an 83-year-old Woman" Van Dyck: "Charles I on Horseback"

WORLD EVENTS	MUNDANE EVENTS	CHURCH AND THOUGHT	KNOWLEDGE AND INVENTIONS
Franco-Swedish treaty of alliance signed by Richelieu and Ox-tenstierna Thirty Years' War becomes conflict between France and Sweden against the House of Hapsburg Treaty of Stuhmsdorf: 20-year truce between Sweden and Poland Treaty of St. Germain-en-Laye agrees on regular French subsidies to the army of Bernhard of Saxe-Weimar	Marquise de Main-tenon, consort of Louis XIV, born (died 1703) Speed limit on hackney coaches in London: 3 miles per hour First inland postal service in Britain between London and Edinburgh Sale of tobacco in France restricted to apothecaries, only on doctors' prescriptions	Giulio Alenio, Italian Jesuit, publishes the life of Christ for the first time in Chinese Cornelius Jansen: "Mars gallus," against Richelieu	Académie Francaise founded by Richelieu Budapest University established English High and Latin School, Boston, Massachussetts, oldest secondary school in North America,founded Robert Hooke, English physician born (died 1703)
Battle of Wittstock; Swedish troops defeat Saxons Austrian troops retire from Burgundy The Emperor Ferdinand II has his son, Archduke Ferdinand, elected Ferdinand III, King of the Romans Manchus proclaim the Ch'ing Dynasty at Mukden	Tea appears for first time in Paris	Welsh Puritan Roger Williams (1603-1683)) banished from Massachusetts; establishes Providence, Rhode Island; proclaims complete religious freedom	Harvard College, (so called from 1639 in tribute to John Harvard, who endowed it by a legacy,) founded at Newe Towne, Cambridge, Massachussetts, with Nathaniel Eaton as first president

DATE	SPANISH HISTORY	THEATRE AND LETTERS	MUSIC AND OPERA	GRAPHIC AND PLASTIC ARTS
1637	Dutch under Frederick Henry of Orange recapture Breda	Calderón: "El magico prodigioso," religious drama Ben Jonson, English poet and dramatist, died (born 1572) John Milton: "Lycidas," elegy James Shirley: "A Lady of Pleasure," comedy	Dietrich Buxtehude, Danish composer, born (died 1707) Teatro San Cassiano, first public opera house, opens in Venice, sponsored by the Trón family	Frans Hals: "Hille Bobbe" Rembrandt: "Raphael Leaving Tobias" Ribera: "Pietà" Van Dyck: "Children of Charles I"
1638	The future Louis XIV born (died 1715)	José de Valdivielso, author of "El Hospital de los Locos" and other autos sacramentales, died (born 1560?)	Monteverdi: "Eighth Book of Madrigals"	Pieter Brueghel the Younger, Fl. painter, "Hell Breughel," died (born 1564) Adriaen Brouwer, Dutch painter, died (born 1606)

WORLD EVENTS	MUNDANE EVENTS	CHURCH AND THOUGHT	KNOWLEDGE AND INVENTIONS
Ferdinand II died; succeeded as Holy Roman Emperor by his son Ferdinand III (-1657)	Commercial collapse of Dutch tulip trade	Extermination of Christianity in Japan; prohibition of foreign books; European contacts prohibited	René Descartes: "Géométrie"
			Dutch expel Portuguese from Gold Coast
William Prynne, Puritan parliamentarian (1600-1669) condemned, with Henry Burton and John Bastwick, for seditious writing, to be pilloried and mutilated		Thomas Hobbes: "A Briefe of the Art of Rhetorique," based on Aristotle	English emigration to America restricted by royal proclamation
		Introduction of new liturgy into Scotland causes riots	English traders established in Canton
Destruction of Pequod Fort, Connecticut			Daniel Sennert, German Scientist who formulated the conception "Atom," dies (born 1572)
Bernhard of Saxe-Weimer takes Freiburg, defeats Duke of Lorraine at Sennheim, and conquers Breisach	New Haven, Connecticut, founded	Cornelius Jansen, Dutch theologian, father of "Jansenism," died (born 1585)	Galileo: "Discorsi e Dimonstrazioni Mathematiche"
	Soldier-student becomes a common type in Germany	Scottish Covenant drawn up and signed	Anne Hutchinson, leader of the New England Antinomians, is banished from Boston, Massachussetts, and setts up a community in Rhode Island
Franco-Swedish alliance renewed for three years	Swedes settle on Delaware River (New Sweden)	Charles I abandons liturgy and canons in Scotland	
Murad IV of Turkey recovers Baghdad from Persia	Torture abolished in England		

SELECTED BIBLIOGRAPHY

Arias, Ricardo. "El Hospital de los Locos," de Valdivielso, Interpretacion Dramatica de la Metafora Locura-Pecado. Madrid, Spain: Insula, 1977

Bentley, Eric, editor. The Classic Theater Volume 3: Six Spanish Plays. Garden City, New York: Doubleday & Company, Inc. 1959

Bentley, Gerald Eades. The Professions of Dramatist and Player in Shakespeare's Time, 1590-1642. Princeton, N.J.: Princeton University Press, 1986

Bergin, Thomas G. Dante. New York: Orion Press 1965

Calderón, de la Barca. Four Plays: translated by Edwin Honig. New York: Hill & Wang, cc 1961

Calderón, de la Barca. La Dama Duende, El Gran Teatro del Mundo, El Principe Constante. Madrid: D.A.E.T.A., 1945

Chang, Donald K. & Mitchell, John D. The Fox Cat: Substituted For the Crown Prince. A Peking Opera set in the Song Dynasty. Midland, Michigan: Northwood Institute Press, 1985

Cole, Toby & Chinoy, Helen K. editors. Directors On Directing. New York: Bobbs-Merrill, Inc. 1963

Dante, Alighieri. La Divina Commedia [edited: C. H. Grandgent]. Cambridge, Massachusetts: Harvard University Press, 1972

Dozy, Reinhart. Spanish Islam. London: Chatto & Windus, 1913

Fergusson, Francis. Dante [Masters of World Literature]. New York: Macmillan Company, 1966

Flores, Angel. Edited and with introduction. Spanish Drama. Bantum Books, 1962

Gonzalez Pedroso, Eduardo. Biblioteca de Autores Españoles [*autos sacaramentales*]. Madrid: Real Academia Española, 1952

Gómez Moreno, Manuel. The Golden Age of Spanish Sculpture. Greenwich, Connecticut: New York Graphics Society, 1964

Irving, Washington. The Alhambra, Palace of Mystery and Splendor. New York: Macmillan, 1953

Maugham, W. Somerset. Don Fernando: Or Variations On Some Spanish Themes. Garden City, New York: Doubleday & Company, Inc., 1935

Milton, John. English Minor Poems; Paradise Lost; etc. [Great Books of the Western World]. Chicago: Encyclopedia Brittannica, Inc., 1978

Mitchell, John D. Jean Racine's Phèdre On Stage. Midland, Michigan: Northwood Institute Press, 1985

Mitchell, John D. Macbeth Unjinxed. Midland, Michigan: Northwood Institute Press, 1985

Mitchell, John D. Making a Broadway Musical: Making It Run. Midland, Michigan: Northwood Institute Press, 1989

Mitchell, John D. The Green Bird: A Commedia Dell'Arte Play in Three Acts by Carlo Gozzi. Midland, Michigan: Northwood Institute Press, 1985

Mitchell, John D. Theatre: The Search For Style. Midland, Michigan: Northwood Institute Press, 1982

Muller, Herbert J. The Spirit of Tragedy. New York: Alfred A. Knopf, 1956

Ovid, [IV]. Metamorphoses Volumes I, II [Loeb Classical Library]. Cambridge,

Massachusetts: Harvard University Press, 1984

Prescott, William H. History of the Reign of Ferdinand and Isabella. Carbondale, Illinois: Southern Illinois University Press, 1962

Rennert, Hugo Albert. The Spanish Stage In The Time Of Lope de Vega. New York: Dover Publications, Inc., 1963

Shakespeare, William. Hamlet. Buenos Aires: Espasa-Calpe Argentina, S. A. [Coleccion Austral, 1968]

Stuart, Donald Clive. The Development of Dramatic Art. New York: Dover Publications, 1960

Stewart, Desmond. The Alhambra. New York: Newsweek, 1974

Vega, Lope de. Arte Nuevo de Racher Comedias. Buenos Aires: Espasa-Calpe Argentina, S. A. [Coleccion Austral, 1973]

Vega, Lope de. El Caballero de Olmedo. Madrid: Biblioteca Classica Ebro, Editorial Ebro, S. L., 1979

Vega, Lope de. Five Plays [translated by Jill Booty]. New York: Hill & Wang, cc 1961

Watt, W. Montgomery. A History of Islamic Spain. Edinburgh University Press, 1965

MATERIALS AND BACKGROUND

Calvert, Albert. The Escorial. London, 1907

Campbell, Thomas (C.). The Jesuits. New York, 1921

Davies, Trevor. The Golden Age of Spain. London, 1954

Durant, Will and Ariel. The Story of Civilisation, Vol. 6. New York: Simon and Schuster, 1957

Durant, Will and Ariel. The Story of Civilisation, Vol. 7. New York: Simon and Schuster, 1961

Lea, H. C. (P.). History of the Inquisition in Spain, 4v. New York: AMS Press, Inc., 1906

Prescott, W. H. History of the Reign of Philip II, 3v. London, 1878

Trend, J. B. The Civilisation of Spain. Oxford: Oxford University Press, 1952

MUSIC

(Coleccion de Musica Antigua Española)

I.	Las Cantigas de Santa Maria del Rey Alfonso X el Sabio (S. XII-XIII)
II.	La Musica en Cataluna Hasta el Siglo (XIV)
IV.	Codice Calixtino (Siglos XII-XIII) Antifonario Mozarabe (Siglo IX)
VIII.	Antonio de Cabezon en los Organos de Covarrubias y Daroca
X.	Juan Cavanilles en los Organos de Daroca y Toledo (S. XVII)
XI.	Vihuelistas Españoles (Siglo XVI)
XIV.	Diego Ortiz recercadas del "Tratado den Glosas" (1553)

FILMS

(All films are in 16mm and are available on BETA and VHS cassette.)

THE SPANISH GOLDEN AGE OF THEATRE, PT. I, 38 minutes.
(Scenes from Lopé de Vega's *Knight From Olmedo*)
THE SPANISH GOLDEN AGE OF THEATRE, PT. II, 26 minutes.
(Scenes from Calderón de la Barca's *Phantom Lady*)

FOREIGN LANGUAGE FILM

*THE SPANISH GOLDEN AGE OF THEATRE, 13 minutes.
(Spanish soundtrack)

*Contains archive footage.

AUDIO CASSETTE

THE HOUSE OF FOOLS, the IASTA production (in English).

ORDERS AND INQUIRIES

**The Institute for Advanced Studies in the Theatre Arts
IASTA
12 West End Avenue, #304
New York, NY 10023**

(212) 581-3133

**Toll Free Number
(Outside New York)**

1 (800) 843-8334